New and Revised

Fighting *for* Your Marriage

Positive Steps for Preventing Divorce and Preserving a Lasting Love

Howard J. Markman
Scott M. Stanley
Susan L. Blumberg

JOSSEY-BASS
A Wiley Company
San Francisco

Published by

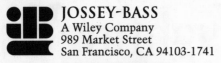

JOSSEY-BASS
A Wiley Company
989 Market Street
San Francisco, CA 94103-1741

www.josseybass.com

Jossey-Bass books and products are available through most bookstores. To contact Jossey-Bass directly, call (888) 378-2537, fax to (800) 605-2665, or visit our website at www.josseybass.com.

Substantial discounts on bulk quantities of Jossey-Bass books are available to corporations, professional associations, and other organizations. For details and discount information, contact the special sales department at Jossey-Bass.

Library of Congress Cataloging-in-Publication Data

Markman, Howard, date.
    Fighting for your marriage : positive steps for preventing divorce and preserving a lasting love / Howard J. Markman, Scott M. Stanley, Susan L. Blumberg.—1st ed., new and rev.
        p. cm.
    Includes bibliographical references and index.
    ISBN 0-7879-5744-5 (pbk. : alk. paper)
    1. Marriage. 2. Interpersonal relations. 3. Interpersonal communication. I. Stanley, Scott, date. II. Blumberg, Susan L., date. III. Title.
HQ734 .M347 2001
306.81—dc21   2001003154

PB Printing   10 9 8 7 6 5   FIRST EDITION

Contents

Acknowledgments

The PREP approach, as presented in this book, is built upon the foundations of researchers of marriage and family relationships from many fields. In particular, the work of the following individuals has been influential in aspects of our work: Don Baucom, Steven Beach, Tom Bradbury, Vernon Call, Andy Christensen, Mari Clements, James Cordova, Steven Duck, Wayne Duncan, Norm Epstein, Frank Fincham, Frank Floyd, Peter Fraenkel, John Gottman, Bernard Guerney, Kurt Hahlweg, Kim Halford, Tim Heaton, Chris Heavey, Amy Holtzwoth-Monroe, Jill Hooley, Ted Huston, Ted Jacob, Neil Jacobson, Matt Johnson, Mike Johnson, Danielle Julian, Ben Karney, Janice Kiecolt-Glaser, Shelle Kraft, Lawrence Kurdek, Doug Leber, Kris Lindahl, Gayla Margolin, Sherrod Miller, Peter Neidig, Pat Noller, Clifford Notarius, Dan O'Leary, Gerald Patterson, Jane Pearson, Lydia Prado, Mari Jo Renick, Caryl Rusbult, Cas Schaap, Ben Silliman, Benard Spilka, Ragnar Storaasli, Kieran Sullivan, Brigit VanWidenfelt, Linda Waite, Robert Weiss, and Ev Worthington. This is only a partial list, for the complete listing would be a chapter unto itself. It is the work of people such as these that has so greatly informed our efforts to help couples.

We also would like to acknowledge those who have worked with us to develop other books for couples based on our approach: David and Claudia Arp, Milt Bryan, Joel Crohn, Pamela Jordan, Janice Levine, Savanna McCain, Daniel Trathen, and Keith Whitfield.

Savanna McCain and Daniel Trathen have been making substantial contributions to this body of work for many years now.

We cannot thank the PREP staff enough for their ongoing support in the effort to reach couples with evidence-based materials. Natalie Jenkins, vice president of PREP, Inc., has brought great drive, energy, and creativity to the task of disseminating this approach to couples around the world. Having solid material that can help couples is one thing; getting it to couples—and those who work to help couples—is quite another, and Natalie leads the staff in making this happen. Many staff members have helped us over the years, and this time we'd like to specifically acknowledge the work of our current staff, including Barb Boonstra, Phyllis Lemons, Mandy Rutt, and Nita Wassenaar—a more talented and kind group you could not find.

Over the years, we've been excited to work with all the branches of our U.S. armed forces. We've had the good fortune to connect over the years with many people who have supported us in meaningful ways as our work has developed, including Bill Coffin and his colleagues in the U.S. Navy: Kathryn Barnard, Michael Cassidy, Lyn Davis, Robert Emde, Scott Halford, Richard Hunt, and Swanee Hunt. All deserve our thanks for their encouragement in expanding our reach to meeting the needs of couples. Bill Coffin, in particular, has been a true visionary in his efforts to support prevention efforts for building strong marriages in both military and civilian communities. He has been an especially potent force in helping bring evidence-based materials to couples throughout the U.S. military services, beginning with the U.S. Navy in the early 1990s. He saw a need and looked for ways to meet it.

Another person who deserves special notice—and who has our deep respect—is Chaplain Glen Bloomstrom of the U.S. Army. Glen has been a tireless leader in bringing PREP training to Army families through the work of the chaplain corps. In the Army, Navy, and Air Force, we've been privileged to get to know and work with hundreds of chaplains who go the extra mile in reaching and supporting the lives of these fine men and women. We've also been delighted to work with Family Advocacy, a group that works hard to help military couples prevent domestic violence in all branches of the service.

These are just a few of the people in our armed forces who have put the military services on the cutting edge of efforts to prevent marital distress and strengthen families. The military does not get nearly the credit it deserves for all these efforts, and we believe they are way ahead of the curve in terms of helping young couples.

We cannot thank our friend, Gary Smalley, enough for his support and encouragement in recent years. It is a rare and humble man who so freely helps others in the same field in which he works. Gary is such a man, and we are inspired by his love and his work. We also thank Diane Sollee for her national efforts to put marriage education on the map. In her development of the Smart Marriages conference, she has provided a place for people from widely divergent backgrounds to join together and share knowledge, expertise, and experiences with the common goal of helping build stronger, happier, and more stable marriages. She is a good friend who shares our passion for prevention.

As we've conducted research on this approach over the years, we have been assisted by bright and energetic research assistants and consultants. The number of these people with whom we've been privileged to work has grown so very large that it's too large to list here, but we deeply thank all these folks who have been so important in our work.

Most of the research reported in this book has been supported over the years by the University of Denver, the National Institute of Mental Health, and the National Science Foundation. We are grateful for the support from these institutions that has enabled us to develop the research basis for the program presented in this book. The emphasis in our book on preventing problems before they develop—in addition to treating them—is one that has been shared by the National Institute of Mental Health, and we express our gratitude for its support of our research program on the possibilities of preventing divorce and marital distress.

We would also like to acknowledge the collaborative spirit and contributions of the National Institute of Mental Health's Family Research Consortium 3, of which Howard was a member. We thank the following bright, talented, and committed researchers, colleagues, and friends for their support, insights, and help in shaping our vision of family research: Mark Appelbaum, Jeannie Brooks-Gunn, Linda Burton, Ana Marie Caucé, Lindsay Chase-Landsdale, Rand Conger, Martha Cox, Marion Forgatch, Della Hand, Stuart Hauser, and Ron Kessler.

The comics presented in the book are the work of our friend and collaborator, Ragnar Storaasli. Not only has Ragnar conducted many of the research analyses of earlier research on PREP, but he has a wonderful knack for humorously capturing many of the key issues that affect relationships. We thank him for all his efforts.

Our editor at Jossey-Bass, Alan Rinzler, has worked with us on many books now. His support and wisdom throughout has been so deeply appreciated by us. He has been a significant force in the quality of what we present to you here. We thank Alan and his staff at Jossey-Bass for their support and expertise during this process.

We would like to acknowledge the role that our clients and seminar participants have played in shaping the ideas and case histories presented in the book. We have disguised their identities in the vignettes through the use of composites and detail changes. Nevertheless, the stories told by many couples over the years are often so strikingly similar that the themes in the case histories we present will speak to a variety of people. We can all learn from each other.

Finally, we want to express our deep sense of appreciation for the couples and families who have shared their lives with us in our various research projects. These couples have opened their hearts and their relationships to our interviewers and video cameras over time. They have shared their struggles and successes, and we hope that the knowledge presented in this book represents some small compensation to these couples, without whom the book could never have been written.

Fighting *for* Your Marriage

To my loving family, for their ongoing support and love
Leah and Mat, Mom and Dad, Barry, Marie, David, and Greg,
I dedicate this book to all of you!
—HM

To Nancy, for your love and kindness through the years entwined
To Kyle and Luke, for the sheer joy you bring
To Mom and Dad, for believing in me, always
—SMS

To my parents, for their love, attention, and support
To Aviva and Natan for the joy they bring me
To Lewis, who makes everything possible
—SLB

Introduction

Things change. Because of that simple fact, we've updated our work in order to bring you what we consider to be an even more practical and potent version of *Fighting* for *Your Marriage*. What you hold in your hand is a major revision of the book we published in 1994. We wrote the original version to help couples build and nurture happy and strong marriages. This book is based on PREP®, which stands for the Prevention and Relationship Enhancement Program. PREP is based on over twenty years of research at the University of Denver as well as on research from universities around the world.

PREP is a program we developed to help couples beat the odds. PREP workshops use specific steps and exercises to teach couples the skills and attitudes associated with good relationships. Because of its roots in solid research and its straightforward approach, PREP has received a great deal of attention from couples across the country, professionals in the field of marital counseling, and the media.

PREP is one of the most extensively researched programs for couples ever developed. The strategies in PREP are based on our study of the key risks couples face as well as the most promising avenues for helping couples lower the risks. Marriage in our culture is risky business, and the costs of marital failure are staggering. The good news is that there are proven strategies that can help you preserve a lasting love. Whether or not you ever take a PREP workshop, this book presents the core of our thinking and strategies for couples.

WHAT'S NEW?

The first edition of the book was very well received among couples and professionals alike. We were pleased to have watched it become a best-seller in the marriage field. Given that, you may ask, "Why change what's working?" Well, a lot has happened in the years since we wrote that first edition—and we're not talking simply about the Internet, Palm Pilots, cell phones, cheaper air travel, and 140 channels on satellite television. We were motivated to make this revision by ongoing changes in three major areas:

1. Societal trends and cultural shifts
2. New discoveries in research on marriage and relationships
3. Improvements in our strategies for success in marriage

Almost as important as the changes we made are the changes we didn't make. If you know our work, you'll recognize that key themes for helping couples have remained rock solid. We wanted this revision to retain the feel the original had: that of a guidebook for a great marriage. We continue to base our work on empirical research. Furthermore, we have retained and even refined the hands-on, action-oriented nature of what we suggest. We are known for taking solid research findings and translating them into usable, specific, and powerful strategies to help couples preserve a lasting love. If you are in a relationship, our goal is to help you with practical, no-nonsense advice. If you are someone who works with couples (such as a counselor or clergy member), our goal is to give you clear and consistent strategies for having a powerful impact with couples.

We will review some of the history of our work and the foundations in our thought and how our thinking has changed in the last eight years. For those of you who are less interested in this background, please just skip ahead to the section in this chapter titled "Improvements in Our Strategies for Success in Marriage," because we'd like you to see what we've changed in this edition. It isn't cru-

cial for you to read this Introduction to understand the rest of what we have to say. You could even go straight to Chapter One and dig in. If that is your plan, we would recommend that you read the two sections here called "How to Get the Most Out of This Book" and "Moving Ahead with Confidence" before moving to Chapter One. But if you are curious, and don't mind the more technical tone we take in this Introduction, reading it will give you a solid overview of the thinking that underlies this revision. In the rest of this book, we'll adopt a far more casual tone.

Societal Trends and Cultural Shifts

Over the past decades, at least six major trends have affected marriage as an institution, couples in their relationships, and the level of concern many have about where all the changes are headed. These trends and changes have continued, if not accelerated, in the last ten years.

Negotiation-Based Marriage

In the six decades since World War II, our society has seen marriages change from relationships in which virtually nothing was negotiable to ones in which virtually everything is negotiable. This trend has been particularly noticeable during the last decade as marriage rates have declined and expectations for love-based, happy marriages have increased. The massive changes in people's expectations for marriage have led to a very different kind of marriage for most couples. Today, marriages require more skill in negotiation between partners than ever before, because there is less that is automatically accepted and more that needs to be decided. This is true for any long-term romantic relationship, whether the partners are married or living together.

What this shift in marriage has meant is that couples are now more greatly affected by their ability to handle conflicts and differences than perhaps ever before. For couples who have wonderful skills in conflict management and problem solving, that's not a big deal. For the vast number of couples who don't know how to work through issues and problems, this shift away from common expectations means more conflict, more unhappiness, and more risk for divorce. So we have expanded our thinking and refined our strategies for helping couples manage the dark and difficult side of their relationships with more skill and confidence.

> *Today, marriages require more skill in negotiation between partners than ever before, because there is less that is automatically accepted and more that needs to be decided.*

Love-Based Marriage

Have you seen a good movie lately? Romantic comedy, action-adventure, or a children's fantasy—whatever the genre, you can't help being affected by all the messages about what people think are most important in having a good relationship: romance, passion, and love. You also can't help but be affected by what is absent from most of those movies: a message that *marriage* is a good place in which to express all that love. (We have nothing at all against romance and passion. In fact, one of the changes in this version of our book is to bring greater emphasis to ways couples can keep those powerful dynamics alive. Further, Howard [coauthor] just edited a volume of essays with Janice Levine on the subject of love and passion. It's called *Why Do Fools Fall in Love?* [2001], also from Jossey-Bass.)

But the movies' perspective on the ultimate importance of romance seems misleading to us. It reflects a shift in many cultures, especially in industrialized nations, toward an expectation of marriage as something that should, above all, bring romance to your life. Further, the implication is that if your marriage does not, you should move on. It's not a marriage worth having. Passionate romance is a lot to expect in a week when the kids are sick, the car is acting up, and you are uncertain about having a job in the months ahead. People marry for love, but when they don't "feel" the love (read: passion), too often they divorce.

Consider a paradox in the statistical trends in marriage and divorce in the United States. Not only has the divorce rate skyrocketed (though it has stabilized at a high rate), but, according to David Popenoe and Barbara Dafoe Whitehead of the National Marriage Project, the number of couples who remain married and who are very happy has been declining. That's a puzzle. You'd think that with more people leaving their unhappy marriages, the bulk of those who stay would be really happy. The best way to explain this is to realize that people are expecting more from their partners and marriages than ever before. If you expect more love and romance but find them hard to achieve, you are going to be less happy. We all measure disappointment in life against what we expect, not against what is necessarily reasonable to get.

Blaine Fowers of the University of Miami has been calling attention to just this dynamic. In his book *Beyond the Myth of Marital Happiness* (2000), he forcefully argues that our focus on marriage as a relationship primarily about happiness has diminished marriage and that we need to reenvision marriage as an opportunity to practice the virtues of friendship, loyalty, and generosity. To simply try to be happier or to be more in love is not the path we suggest you follow. Ironically, that may be the path on which you are least likely to find happiness. Although we want to teach you how to preserve happiness, our focus is on teaching you how to walk the deeper paths of commitment, forgiveness, and friendship. When you walk *these* paths together, you will find happiness and love throughout your journey, because these are the characteristics research tells us predict lifelong happiness and love.

Lower Constraints to Dissolving Marriages

Historian Barbara Dafoe Whitehead wrote the original "Dan Quayle Was Right" piece in the *Atlantic Monthly* and, more recently, the book *The Divorce Culture* (1997). She notes that the great increase in divorce in industrialized nations results from greater affluence, which gives people more options if they want to leave a relationship. Furthermore, she notes that as societies become more consumer oriented, there is an increased emphasis on being satisfied with what we get. "What's in it for me?" becomes a more acceptable way to think. These forces in combination lead people to expect more and to have an easier time leaving if their expectations are not met.

Economic development is wonderful in many ways, but it also means that people have fewer constraints for staying married than in days gone by. That's not all bad. On the positive side, that means people can put more emphasis on their personal choices in the role of building *and keeping* a great marriage. For some, it can make leaving abusive relationships easier. That's surely a good thing. On the negative side, with fewer economic, legal, and moral barriers to divorce, more people choose this option—even when faced with difficulties that many couples could overcome with the right kind of effort. That doesn't mean a couple just survives their problems, but rather that they are learning how to thrive in the relationship.

As with the other changes we've mentioned, these cultural and societal shifts create more pressure on the "right here and right now" than ever before. With people having to work harder to negotiate differences, expecting more in terms of love and passion, and finding it generally easier to leave when unhappy, marriages are less stable than any time in modern history.

Unstable Unions and Fragile Families

Most people desire a happy marriage that lasts a lifetime, but we know that many couples do not achieve one. Although the divorce rate has come down a bit in the United States since its all-time high in 1981, what we see now is a leveling off at what remains a high rate. The current projection is that among young couples marrying for the first time today, about 40 to 50 percent of them will eventually divorce. The trends we just discussed are in large measure responsible for these high divorce rates. Aside from those who divorce, many other couples wind up staying together through many years of unhappiness.

Norval Glenn, a sociologist at the University of Texas, has done a detailed projection wherein he concludes that about 24 percent of couples who marry will remain very happily married until death. Everyone who marries wants to be in that 24 percent who remain together and very happy, but the simple math suggests that most people are not going to walk that path. The odds are not in most couples' favor for having the kind of marriage they long to have. We often say that marriage is the riskiest activity most people ever engage in. Most of this book is about helping you and your partner be in that 24 percent. If enough couples learn the skills and approach we describe in this book, perhaps that percentage can even increase!

In addition to the rising divorce rates, there has also been a vast increase in the number of children born to people who are not married in the first place. This has been one of the greatest changes in family structure in industrialized societies over the past four decades. In the United States, for example, the percentage of children born to mothers out of wedlock has increased from 6 percent in 1960 to 32 percent in 2000.

This is a sweeping, unprecedented change over a relatively short period of time in human history. We can't emphasize strongly enough that there are many single parents doing a wonderful job of raising their children. Nevertheless, the increases in out-of-wedlock births as well as the high divorce rates have led to more children living in fragile families than ever before. That means there are increasing numbers of children at increased risk for economic disadvantage, a lack of father involvement, or both.

Growing Awareness of the Effects of Marital Problems on Adults and Children

The damaging effects of destructive marital conflict and divorce on spouses and children are incalculable. These effects include economic, medical, and mental health problems. Let's focus on children for a moment. There are many studies that now show just how destructive poorly handled marital conflict is for the children living in the homes of fighting parents. When parents regularly argue, especially if in hostile ways, the evidence for the damage done to children is as conclusive as anything gets in our field of research. That children can be harmed by how their parents handle disagreements has led many to conclude that these children would be better off if their parents split up. However, many of these children are hurt by *how* their parents fight, whether or not they stay together. What we mean by that is that these children don't really do that much better if their parents divorce, because their parents still continue to fight—often through the children.

There is also a growing number of studies showing that divorce, in and of itself, has lasting and negative impacts on many children. Judith Wallerstein, who wrote *The Unexpected Legacy of Divorce* (2000), is one researcher who has received a great deal of attention for documenting the long-term effects of divorce on children. She reports that children of divorce are more likely to have a difficult time forming close relationships and to have more difficulty handling conflict, even into adulthood.

Even Andrew Cherlin, a sociologist at Johns Hopkins University who had once been more skeptical about the long-term impacts of divorce, has now concluded that for children of divorce there are long-term, measurable increases in risk of such problems as dropping out of high school, becoming pregnant as a teenager, and having mental health problems. Children of divorce are also at greater risk of living in poverty, because marriage provides families a stronger financial base in life than anything else we know. Cherlin would note that these children are not doomed by any means. In fact, although they are at greater risk, many children of divorce will not fall prey to the problems we've mentioned, for a variety of reasons. Yet there has been a clear trend among researchers and public policy commentators to express greater levels of alarm about the impact of divorce on children.

The most exciting current research relates to the questions of *how* parental conflict and divorce affect children's well-being over time. We are proud to say that several of our former students (and even students of students), now colleagues, are among the major contributors to this area. For example, Mari Clements at Penn State and Jean-Philippe Laurenceau at the University of Miami have been studying how marital conflict and parenting styles affect children's interactions with peers, as well as studying risk factors that predict marital distress and failure. Kristin Lindahl and Neena Malik at the University of Miami have been investigating how marital conflict and parenting styles affect children in both Anglo and Latino families. These researchers are having a great impact on our field.

Although researchers still debate the degree to which destructive parental conflict and divorce are damaging to children, there is wide agreement on the following four points:

1. As highlighted in a seminal report from the National Institute of Mental Health on prevention of emotional problems, marital distress and destructive marital conflict are major generic risk factors for many forms of mental distress and psychopathology.

2. Both destructive parental conflict and parental divorce raise the risk that children will have difficulties later in life; the risks caused by chronic exposure to parental conflict are particularly strong.

3. As noted by Paul Amato at Penn State, couples who have relatively low conflict marriages but who are "no longer in love" actually make up the greatest percentage of divorces. Researchers are increasingly willing to conclude that children of these marriages may well be better off if their parents can work things out.

4. Children do best when they are being raised in stable homes by two parents who love each other, handle conflict well, and provide a base of commitment that brings stability to the lives of those children.

It's this last point that is easiest for us to focus on here, because we want to help couples prevent marital distress and divorce in the first place. Before we go on, we want to emphasize that there are many single parents and divorced parents doing a wonderful job of raising their children. Nothing we have said here should be seen as diminishing that fact. But when you look at the long-term impact of these familial changes on a society, the trends are cause for quite a bit of concern because, on average, fewer and fewer children are being raised in the kind of situation in which they do best.

The negative impacts of marital problems and divorce do not solely occur in the lives of children. Adults suffer greatly as well. For example, marital problems are the number one cause of depression, and depression is the most common mental health problem in our society. Steven Beach at the University of Georgia and a number of colleagues in the field have found that marital dynamics such as emotional connection, support in helping one another cope with the stresses of life, and dependability of the spouse all reduce an individual's likelihood of being depressed. Criticism, blame, and threats of leaving the marriage all put individuals at much greater risk for depression.

Marital distress and divorce cause workers to be distracted and poorly motivated, which leads to great losses in productivity in our society. More recently, research has also documented the powerful effects of marital distress on physical health. As Janice Kiecolt-Glaser of the Ohio State College of Medicine has found in a number of exciting studies, marital distress and conflict not only make you sick at heart but also can literally make you sick in the body.

Little Respect for the Institution of Marriage

There is at least one constant in our ever-changing world: regardless of gender, culture, socioeconomic status, skin color, and language, nearly everyone wants a lifelong, secure, happy, and committed relationship. Despite the near universality of this desire, it appears that in response to the high divorce rate and other bad news, more people are thinking that the pain of divorce can be prevented by avoiding what leads to divorce: marriage. Although it may not seem like a huge change to you, current projections are that about 85 percent of Americans will eventually marry, down from 95 percent in the past. These numbers have moved far more rapidly in the same direction in most European countries. In general, the trend in industrialized nations is for more divorce, less marital happiness, and less marriage in general.

You can avoid marriage, perhaps, but you cannot avoid that ache in your heart for a deeper, lasting relationship. And if the ache is there, the potential for pain and disappointment is there as well. If it aches, it can break. Obviously, some people have been harmed greatly in their marriages and would have been better off if they had never wedded. But simply put, it's not marriage that's the problem.

The greater problem lies inside our relationships, in how we treat one another. Whatever the trends in your country or culture, how *your* relationship fares over time depends more than anything else on how the two of you treat each other. This brings us to a discussion of the kind of research and the approach on which this book is based. In our research, and in our study of the research of others, we focus on learning as much as we can about the secrets of staying happily married and of how unhappy couples unravel. That means

we focus on learning what you, the couple, can do to make a difference in how your marriage does over time.

New Discoveries in Research on Marriage and Relationships

The techniques and strategies in this book are based on solid, up-to-date research in the field of marriage—not on "pop-psych" speculation. Our work is both *empirically informed* and *empirically tested*. By empirically informed, we mean that we take great advantage of a wide range of research findings from many respected scientists in developing our suggestions and in explaining them to you. This will be clear to you as you read on. By empirically tested, we mean that we (and colleagues) have conducted a number of studies looking at the effectiveness of this approach—especially with premarital couples who are starting out happy and wanting to stay that way.

There are exciting advances in our field of marital research, particularly in a new area: that of studying the bigger, deeper meanings to be found in relationships. Historically, the field of marital research has seen two other major themes, or waves. The first area of focus was on marital satisfaction, the second on communication. Let's look briefly at these three waves.

Satisfaction

Thirty or more years ago, if you'd talked to researchers like us, you would've found that what we spent more of our time looking at was happiness—simply put, who's happy in marriage, who's not happy, and who's bouncing around between those extremes. This was important because how happy couples are is closely related to how marriages go over time. If you think about it, however, knowing more about happiness does not lead to very specific strategies for staying happy. If it did, we could stop writing this book now and just conclude with this advice: "Don't worry, be happy." That would not really tell you very much about *how* to make that happiness happen or last (but it would be a really easy read).

Communication

The next big wave in marital research was in the study of communication. This kind of research exploded on the scene in the mid-1970s with the advent of relatively affordable videotape recorders. (At least they were affordable to government-supported research projects.) This technology allowed researchers to do something they hadn't been able to do before: record couples as they talked. That was important because if you can record something, you can watch it over and over. And if you can watch it over and over, you can start to detect key patterns in how couples talk and how couples fight.

It would be hard to overstate how important this wave of research became to the field. Such pioneers as John Gottman, Robert Weiss, Kurt Hahlweg, Howard Markman, and Clifford Notarius began to generate an astounding number of fascinating findings. As you probably realize, this kind of research has played a major role in the development of our approach to helping couples build strong and happy marriages. Many of our core techniques come directly from studies that show how damaging some kinds of negative interaction can be and what is different in the communication of couples who do well over time.

Although the focus on communication is hardly new in the marital field, there are many new studies about how couples communicate that we incorporate in this revision. For example, Andrew Christensen at the University of California-Los Angeles (UCLA) and Christopher Heavey at the University of Nevada at Las Vegas have refined our understanding of the dynamics of pursuit and withdrawal. In other words, there is new information we'd like you to know about to enhance your understanding of why some people tend to pursue discussing issues with their partners and why some people tend to avoid or withdraw from such discussions altogether.

As another example, researchers Frank Fincham at State University of New York at Buffalo and Thomas Bradbury at UCLA, among others, have refined our understanding of the ways in which people's thoughts about their partners affect how they communicate with their partners.

The Bigger Meanings

We are now in an exciting new era for researchers. There is a growing emphasis on the deeper meanings and themes of relationships. The relatively new emphasis on what it all means can be seen in advances in the study of such topics as commitment, acceptance, friendship in marriage, forgiveness, attachment history, and the process of spiritual intimacy in marriage.

As a result of this increasing focus on deeper themes, there are new findings and theories being developed all the time that we think can help couples in their relationships. Research is most meaningful when it is used to create strategies and techniques to help couples move forward in their relationships. We have always followed this path, and this new book is no exception. We'll bring in the newest concepts and show you how to apply them in your own relationship.

Improvements in Our Strategies
for Success in Marriage

We have gotten older, and although it's been questioned by some of our equally older colleagues, we think we've gotten wiser as well. (Our mothers all attest to our growing wisdom.) Over the years, we have worked with thousands of couples, as well as with people who help couples in marriage and family relationships. As a result of this vast experience as well as the new research in the field, we have made three very specific kinds of changes in this revision:

1. We've refined what works well to make it work better.
2. We've added entirely new concepts and strategies that we believe give couples a powerful edge.
3. We've taken the emphasis off anything that seemed less useful or less relevant to couples.

As an example of refinement, we've developed new ways to describe many key themes so that it will be easier for you to remember and use the concepts. For example, we've updated every chapter in this book to reflect new research in the field. We've also added boxes throughout the book that contain special, more in-depth content. These boxes usually describe research that has particularly interesting implications for how you can strengthen your relationship. We've also added an overview of our approach in Chapter One that will give you a great start, up front, on understanding where we're headed and why we say the things we say.

As an example of new strategies, we've added a section in Chapter Eight on self-regulation. Our work has always played up the importance of couples' taking charge of their relationships. For example, we've emphasized, and still emphasize, the importance of mutually agreed-on time-out strategies. These allow you, as a couple, to manage conflicts rather than let conflicts manage you. What we've added to this focus on couple regulation is self-regulation. You stand a better chance as a couple of handling conflicts well if you, as individuals, are learning to handle your own emotions constructively. This is not a book on self-control, but it is a book made better by the addition of thoughts on self-control and personal responsibility.

As an example of changing emphasis, we talked in the first edition about research suggesting that when it came to the experience of physical stress in marital conflict, men had, on average, a more difficult time than women. This now appears not to be the case, and it may even be the other way around. Whatever is going on there, it's a lot more complex than it was looking to researchers ten years ago, and our chapter on gender differences now reflects these complexities.

We'll not bother to detail things we've taken out of this revision of *Fighting* for *Your Marriage* because they are, well, not here anymore.

RESEARCH ON PREP
AND ADVANCEMENTS IN
GETTING THE WORD OUT

We have been busy continuing to conduct research on PREP as well as finding ways to get research-based strategies out of the lab and into the hands of couples and those who work helping couples.

What Research on PREP Reveals

Some of the most important research on the PREP approach has been conducted at the University of Denver. Over the years, our research has been supported by grants from the National Institute of Mental Health, the National Institutes of Health, and the National Science Foundation, and it has resulted in more than fifty scientific and professional publications. Here we will give you a brief example of findings from these studies and those of colleagues with whom we've been privileged to work over the years. Those colleagues include such fine researchers as Kurt Hahlweg at the Technische Universität Braunschweig; Kim Halford at Griffith University in Queensland, Australia; Don Baucom at the University of North Carolina at Chapel Hill; and a long list of talented colleagues at the University of Denver. These are highlights from studies on PREP or variations of it and very similar programs.

As noted earlier, most of the formal research on PREP has been with couples in the transition to marriage. We believe the concepts and principles are just as applicable for happy or unhappy couples, for those who are going to marry or who have been married for fifty years. Our studies (and others) show that marital failure is predictable to a surprising degree, which means that for many couples, the seeds of divorce are present prior to marriage. It does not mean that we researchers are very good at predicting exactly which couples won't make it, but we have gotten pretty good at identifying the factors that greatly increase the odds of divorce.

The factors that predict marital failure range from relatively static dimensions, such as a history of parental divorce, differences in religion, and personality styles, to more dynamic dimensions, such as communication, conflict, and commitment. Because we know what predicts marital failure, there is hope for reducing the risks. To us, the more dynamic factors—how to communicate as a couple, how to handle differences without destructive patterns of conflict, and how to keep the marriage secure—make the most attractive targets for you to work on in your relationship. This is because these dynamic factors are not only highly predictive of divorce but also the most amenable to change. PREP is primarily focused on the dynamic dimensions identified in research as crucial to marital success. Chapter One tells you more about risk factors and why we focus on what we focus on.

Aside from the prediction research, various studies strongly suggest that couples can learn skills, complete exercises, and enhance ways of thinking that increase their odds of success. In our own research on premarital education, we can track the positive effects of preventive interventions for at least five years after the training. Although there is more research to be done, a number of long-term studies have evaluated PREP compared to several different types of control groups, including couples who have received traditional premarital counseling (PMC) and those who have received nothing special for helping their relationship. The following are some of the findings:

• PREP couples have lower rates of premarital breakup and postmarital divorce. In a large-scale study in Denver, PREP couples were one-third as likely to break up as the couples in the control group, up through five years following the program (combining pre- and postmarital breakup). In a recent study in Germany, only 3 percent of the PREP couples had divorced at a five-year follow-up, whereas 16 percent of couples who received traditional PMC (or no PMC) had divorced.

• According to one major long-term study, PREP couples have shown a greater likelihood of maintaining relationship satisfaction for a few years following training.

• According to studies in the United States, Germany, and Australia, PREP couples have lower levels of negative communication and higher levels of positive communication immediately following the program, and they maintain these advantages up to five years later.

• In one study, PREP couples have reported lower levels of physical aggression in the years after taking the program.

• PREP couples enjoy taking the program because of the hands-on, skill-oriented nature of the material; PREP couples often report greater program satisfaction than couples taking other programs.

• Premarital couples taking PREP given by clergy or lay leaders in their religious organization (as well as by university staff) communicate more positively and less negatively following training, compared to couples taking more typical premarital training in their religious organizations.

It is important to note that some of the beneficial effects of a program like PREP appear to be clear as long as four or five years after the training. This does not mean that every couple benefits or that every couple can reduce their risk of divorce. In this field, we need to know far more about which couples get the greatest benefit from which kinds of materials. Also, no matter what the program or material, the beneficial effects probably weaken over time. Therefore, it is important for any couple who benefits from this material to review those things that seem to help their relationship most.

Our research continues in our current project, in which we are testing the effectiveness of PREP delivered within religious organizations. Lydia Prado and Michelle St. Peters at the University of Denver have played ongoing lead roles in this work.

If you would like to read more of the academic descriptions of our work to delve into the mysteries and complexities of such research, you can refer to the Selected Research and References. We know this isn't something most of you will want to do, but for those who would like to read more, the references are there just waiting for you.

Getting the Word Out

We are excited about the opportunities we've had in the past decade to disseminate our work—our concepts, strategies, and research findings—to couples and those who help couples worldwide. This work has been spearheaded by Natalie Jenkins. Natalie is the vice president of PREP, Inc., a company formed by Howard and Scott (coauthors) in 1991 to be the prime vehicle for the dissemination of work based on the PREP approach.

As the lead force in our efforts to get the word out, Natalie has overseen the growth of PREP in many areas, including the following:

• Holding PREP workshops in the United States and in many other countries. We have trained mental health professionals, clergy, health care workers, and lay persons from around the world in this approach. Many of these people use our materials to conduct workshops for couples or in counseling individually with couples.

• The training of hundreds of chaplains and social workers in all the branches of the armed forces of the United States, in order that they can make use of the straightforward strategies of PREP to help the marriages of the active-duty personnel of the services. This work has been particularly gratifying to us, as we've watched how the military services work on the front lines of efforts to help couples prevent marital distress and divorce. The nature of military work involves many stresses on families, and we are proud to help protect and strengthen the marriages of people who serve our country.

• The development and marketing of a wide variety of materials that couples can use to learn the concepts we teach. These include videos and audiotapes for couples and a host of materials for those who present PREP workshops for couples. In collaboration with various experts, we have also developed versions of *Fighting* for *Your Marriage* that are geared to specific groups of couples, such as those in the transition to parenthood, empty nest couples, Jewish couples, African American couples, and couples who prefer a model deeply integrated with the Christian faith. (A list of titles appears in Resources and Training.)

• The development with Chris Saiz of a self-directed course for couples who wish to learn the core communication and conflict management aspects of our work through the use of a coordinated video and workbook.

• The development of a top-notch staff that supports the efforts to market and distribute our materials based on PREP.

This is just a partial list of what we've been doing. Some of the most exciting things are yet to come, and come they will. Natalie Jenkins and William Bailey at the University of Arkansas, along with Scott and Howard, are working on an entire approach to helping couples deal with all of what money means in marriage. The book based on that work will be available from Jossey-Bass in spring 2002. It will rely on some core aspects of the PREP approach, but it will also move more deeply into the complexities of money in marriage.

We're not sitting still. We not only continue to do research on marital success and failure but also are constantly looking for new and better ways to reach more couples with tools that can make a difference.

HOW TO GET THE MOST
OUT OF THIS BOOK

We believe that the recipe for a great relationship includes a cup of love, a cup of commitment, several tablespoons of compatibility of interests, a cup and a half of skill in handling conflicts, and a pinch of magic. We are confinced that you can learn how to build and protect a great relationship if you are motivated to do so. We'll introduce a number of very effective skills for handling conflict and disagreements. We'll also suggest strategies for building and maintaining friendship, commitment, and spiritual intimacy—all that

You can learn how to build and protect a great relationship if you are motivated to do so.

really great stuff that bonds you together. With each skill or principle, we'll also tell you about the underlying theory and research so that you understand why it may work for you. You will find that these techniques are not really difficult to understand, but *they will take some investment to master.* We believe in making things simple, but simple is not always easy. You have to put in the effort to reap the rewards.

One way to invest in your relationship is to discuss the talking points and to complete the exercises at the end of each chapter. The exercises are particularly important since they are carefully designed to help you learn the key concepts and strategies.

MOVING AHEAD WITH CONFIDENCE

Our society has come to a point where most people are divorced, know many people who are divorced, or are surrounded by some pretty unhappy married couples. In fact, those who study the generation following the Xers have found something quite interesting about these folks. They are the most conservative generation in a long time with regard to marriage and family. On average, they value marriage more than the Xers, and they think that being married for life is a worthy goal. Of course, they want to be *happily* married for life. What they lack, however, is confidence that a happy marriage is an achievable goal. In fact, it looks more like an impossible dream to many of them. It might be fine for Don Quixote to dream the impossible dream, but in reality, most people don't get all that excited about dreams that they believe just cannot happen.

On the positive side, you probably know couples who have done well over many years—meaning they have stayed together and stayed happy. They've found a way to preserve their special bond through all the ups and downs of life. Who have your role models been regarding marriage and family relationships? Depending on who you spend time with, you may have either concluded "Yes, it can be done" or "No way, hardly anyone makes this deal work out well."

If you are an optimist about relationships—especially marriage— what we have to offer you in this book can give legs to your optimism. We find it's not enough simply to be optimistic; optimism needs to be paired with specific plans and action, or it's just a good feeling.

Likewise, if you are pessimistic about relationships and marriage, we think you've come to the right place. Our primary goal in writing this book is to teach you the most powerful strategies we know for helping you build confidence in your relationship. In our research, we have found that confidence in marriage is related to such factors as commitment to your partner, friendship with your partner, fewer nasty arguments with your partner, and having fun with your partner. If you take a moment to look at the Contents, you'll find those to be among the core themes of this book.

In short, we want to help the two of you build confidence based on increased competence. Although we make no guarantees, we believe that if you work through the ideas presented here and adapt those that seem to help you the most, you will significantly increase your chances of not only staying together but also experiencing the greater joys of a life together.

Part I

Understanding the Risks on the Road to Lasting Love

1

Four Hallmarks of a Great Relationship: PREP in a Nutshell

Why are you reading this book? Either you have a relationship that you want to improve or you've already developed a great relationship that you want to keep that way for a lifetime. At the deepest level, each of us desires someone to love and someone we can love in return—someone with whom we can share laughter, friendship, work, caring, and support through the good times as well as the hard times in life. People deeply desire this kind of relationship, but we also know that a great many couples don't achieve it. This is a book about helping you restore love that once was there or, if your relationship is great now, helping you stay there and go deeper.

All over the world, people from all walks of life imagine and desire a great relationship. Yet we live in times of great cynicism about relationships in general and marriage in particular. Can partners love each other and stay together for the long term? We think so. We're here to tell you that long-lasting, satisfying love is possible. You could say that we are optimistic about relationships. We know that it's possible for couples to create relationships in which they feel both emotionally secure in the present and confident about the future. All the cynicism of the world cannot smother the fire that burns in each of us for connection at the deepest levels of our heart and soul. Wisely directed, that desire in you becomes the fuel for your efforts to build a lasting love together.

What we provide here are simple, effective ways to develop and protect the love and happiness you seek. By simple, we mean easy to understand. Simple can be powerful, but simple does not mean easy to do. We want to challenge you to put the kind of investment into your relationship that really makes a difference. The principles you'll find here work—if you put the effort into making them work in your relationship.

All the cynicism of the world cannot smother the fire that burns in each of us for connection at the deepest levels of our heart and soul.

This new edition of *Fighting for Your Marriage* is like a travel guide for your journey together. Unlike most travel guides, which talk only about which places to visit, ours spends as much time telling you about key places to avoid (the back alleys where you can get mugged) as it does about the most wonderful places to visit and relax. As you would read a travel guide, you can read this one cover to cover, or you can plan your own journey by reading the chapters that best meet your current needs and goals. In either case, we suggest you finish reading this chapter first, because it highlights the hallmarks of the PREP approach on which this book is based.

PREP IN A NUTSHELL

We use the term *nutshell* because as part of work disseminating PREP in Scandinavia, we took a short but wonderful trip called Norway in a Nutshell. Well, here is PREP in a nutshell. We hope you enjoy this short journey as much as we did ours!

As you know by now, this book is based on our program called PREP, which stands for the Prevention and Relationship Enhancement Program. Over the years, we have used our research and experience working with couples to constantly refine, update, and improve what we have to say. Through all our work over many years, we can identify four major themes—hallmarks if you will—

of our approach. These four hallmarks will help you understand the essence of our advice to you:

1. Be safe at home.

2. Open the doors to intimacy.

3. Do your part and be responsible.

4. Nurture security in your future together.

Be Safe at Home

Everyone wants to be honored and treated nicely—especially by loved ones and especially by a mate. Our good friend Gary Smalley has been advising couples for many years. In the course of all his reading, writing, and counseling, he has come to believe that the most important thing of all is to honor one another. He and his coauthor John Trent have even written a book on honor, called *The Gift of Honor.*

The simple reality is that most of us are the least honoring of those we love the most. We get frustrated, angry, or disappointed, and off we go, talking to this person we love the most in ways that don't seem very loving at all. Instead of sharing honor and respect, too many couples become mired in painful conflicts that tear at the heart of their relationship. Over decades of research in our lab and others, one of the strongest findings is that how couples handle conflict tells a powerful story about how they will do in the future. Couples who handle their differences and conflicts poorly, with put-downs and hostility and harsh views of one another, are the most likely to develop serious problems.

Because conflicts are a common (and expected) part of relationships, many couples think that it's their differences and disagreements that cause the greatest problems in their marriage. To be sure, strong differences in backgrounds and viewpoints do make conflicts more likely. But twenty-five years of research tell us that success in marriage is related not so much to the nature of the differences between two partners as to how the partners handle the differences they have. If you want to have a great relationship, the way you handle differences matters more than what those differences are.

We will spend a good deal of time looking at the ways couples handle conflicts and talking about what can be done to protect your relationship from the patterns that are most destructive. These are the dark alleys we want to help you avoid on your travels. When we say "Be safe at home," we are pointing out that emotional safety is essential to having the kind of deeply connected, loving relationship you seek. In the context of this discussion, we mean safety in terms of how you talk to one another.

If you want to have a great relationship, the way you handle differences matters more than what those differences are.

In Chapter Two, we will describe for you common danger signs, behavior patterns that make it feel very unsafe in relationships. Unsafe to share what you really think. Unsafe to express what you desire. Unsafe to bring up an issue of concern. Unsafe to be yourself with your partner, who is the person with whom, more than anyone else on the planet, you want the greatest safety. So we'll teach you powerful techniques and ways of thinking that can help the two of you handle the issues of your life and protect the best parts of what you have together.

In Chapter Three, we will look at some of the differences (and similarities) in how men and women handle conflicts. Although self-help books often exaggerate differences between men and women in terms of what they want and how they communicate, there are nevertheless key dynamics we want to explore.

One of the most frustrating patterns that many couples fall into occurs when one partner tends to pursue talking about issues and the other frequently withdraws from such talks. This pattern is strongest in couples who are having troubles managing their issues well. And, as you already know too well if you experience this, the pattern tears at the fabric of your relationship.

Although of course there are many exceptions to the stereotype of a female who tries to talk and a male who clams up, it's nevertheless very common for women to complain that men won't talk or listen, and for men to complain that women seem to want to stir up conflict too much of the time. Unfortunately, men can come to believe that women like to criticize, and women can come to believe that men just don't care. We think men's and women's desires are actually much more positive than this. In essence, our observation is that women want to talk more, and men want to fight less. Both those goals are positive and worthy. If a couple knows how to talk safely about whatever they need to talk about, and if they know how to regulate negative emotions, they will be able to talk without fighting. We want to teach you ways to do this if you don't already have ways that work for you.

We'll get to these themes soon enough. For now, relax a bit, resist the temptation to be negative, agree not to fight, and make every effort to treat each other with honor, politeness, and respect.

Open the Doors to Intimacy

Since our first edition, we and many other marital researchers have focused more and more on the positive side of relationships. Have you ever worked with AAA to help you plan a vacation? One of the things they do for members who are about to travel is provide maps that have the best routes already highlighted. That's what these exciting new directions in our field are doing for us—and you. The results of many new studies highlight the best routes you can take to protecting and preserving a lasting love—the tunnels of love and the bridges over troubled waters.

We all know that conflicts are inevitable and need to be handled, but people do not get and stay married to handle conflict together "till death do us part." They want to be married for all the great things relationships offer: deep friendship, companionship, spiritual meaning, fun, passion, parenting, and connection with the core values of life. If you'll take a moment to look over the Contents, you'll see that this is not a book dealing only with communication and conflict management. We focus throughout on the greatest things about lifelong love and commitment, and we have much to say to you about the good stuff. You can enrich and deepen your connection together in many ways, and we want to help you. But there is a very important linkage between what we say about conflict and issues and what we say about fun, friendship, spirituality, and sensual connection.

The positive side of relationships is often mysterious (delightfully so), but there is little mystery to us about the ways in which the forces of attraction (love, fun, passion, friendship) can be destroyed by damaging types of conflict. In a way, these mysterious forces are like alpine flowers that are beautiful and awe inspiring but also vulnerable to being stepped on and crushed through carelessness and thoughtlessness. You must nurture these most wonderful aspects of relating if they are to bloom into their full glory. So as you move forward on your journey, make a commitment to keep fun and friendship alive and thriving.

Do Your Part and Be Responsible

A core theme in our model is teamwork. If you adopt our approach, you are agreeing to work as a team on your relationship. This means you agree to not fight destructively, to commit yourself to keeping fun and friendship in your relationship, and to make the relationship a safe emotional harbor. Most important, marital teams succeed only when each member does his or her part. We're asking you to think about what you contribute to your marriage, to focus on what you put in rather than on what you get out of the relationship.

We place great responsibility on each partner in a marriage to work on his or her end of the relationship to give it the best chance for lasting and committed love. As just one example, this means that when conflict arises, or when you perceive your partner as acting unfairly, you do the most constructive things you can do. Far too often, when people think their partner is being unfair or is behaving inappropriately, they feel relieved of the responsibility to be the best partner they can be. We're here to tell you, and tell you strongly, that you need to hold up your end of the relationship even when you don't think your partner is doing his or her share. The major exception to this guideline is if there is ongoing victimization of one person by another. That may call for strong actions of a different sort than what we focus on here.

Our emphasis on personal responsibility inoculates you against one of the major sources of relationship distress: the tendency we all have to use our *perceptions* of our partner's negative behaviors to justify our own. You are a team. But you are also two individuals, and each of you exercises the most control over your relationship by controlling your own thoughts and actions in it.

What's My Part?

If you are serious about doing everything you can on your end of the relationship to make it all it can be, here are some simple guidelines you might keep in mind:

- Do positive things for your partner and the relationship. Most people know what to do to please their partner. Do you regularly do the things that make a difference?
- Decide to let negative or annoying comments bounce off you. If there are ongoing concerns you need to deal with, deal with them at a time when you are both calm and you can get your partner's attention in a constructive way.
- Be the best person you can be in your relationship. Take responsibility for your own issues, personal growth, awareness, and mental and physical health. Have you ever noticed how much better looking some people become after they go through a divorce? Many people put all kinds of effort into personal improvements when they're "out on the market." Yes, this is a crass way to say it, but it's the truth. We've seen it and you've seen it. Why not give that kind of effort to taking good care of yourself now? If more people did this, fewer people would end up looking for the next relationship.

In the face of problems or pain in relationships, too often people think, "I married the wrong person!" Thinking this way leads to depression and hopelessness. A great marriage is predicted not so much by your finding the right partner as by your being the right partner.

One other point before we move on. Many people think they cannot bring their behavior under better control unless they first understand it. Although it can be beneficial to have insights into why you or your partner do some of the things you do (for good or ill), you don't have to have it all figured out to know some of the most important "right things" to do. If you're waiting for more insight and not doing some things

A great marriage is predicted not so much by your finding the right partner as by your being the right partner.

that you know would help keep your relationship on track, you are not being wise. Do what you can do now, while you figure out more of what you can do later.

Nurture Security in Your Future (Together!)

A husband recently shared in his first session that his one goal for therapy and his relationship was to provide a cocoon of commitment around his family. His voice is echoed by countless other partners, and we are listening. Building something meaningful together and hanging on to it is critical. Couples who do the best over the long term do so partly because they have a sense of just that: the long term.

Commitment is a major theme in our approach and throughout this book. Not only do we devote a chapter to it, but the concept flows through everything we have to share with you. We'll look at commitment in terms of sacrifice, forgiveness, protecting priorities, and developing teamwork. But more than anything else, commitment is knowing that you can count on each other to be there for one another and to support and help one another.

Artis and Pam were in their forties. Both had been married before and divorced. They fell in love at first sight and married quickly, but six months after marrying, they were having trouble. They came in to get some help, saying they were arguing a lot and that they were worried about losing their loving feelings. When they fought, one or both would wonder if they should really be together, and would say so. They began to wonder if they had deceived themselves into thinking they were in love, if maybe they'd only fallen in lust at first sight.

We told them that there was nothing wrong with falling in love quickly. This is one common pathway for couples, and for those couples, it can be a most magical and wonderful experience. (However, it can be very wise to know your partner a good while before marrying.) But even when your love feels like heaven, you still have to learn to live together on earth. And that's where our advice came in. Artis and Pam worked with us to set up some rules for how to handle it when they got angry: no name-calling, no pulling away, no swearing. Further, they would each try to calm down and figure out together what the issue was.

They learned fast. They used the depth of their love as motivation—there was too much at stake not to handle things better. After a while, they were doing much better handling conflicts and disappointments. They were increasingly able to talk safely and openly about their vision for their future together. That was surely different from threatening it, as they had been doing.

Artis and Pam love bike riding. In fact, you could call them hard-core bikers. They started to use biking metaphors to think about their relationship and their goals. For Pam (who above all wanted closeness), the ideal was an image of being on a tandem bike, going to the same place, riding the same path, but each doing his or her own part. For Artis, the image of them riding two separate bikes was more powerful, because he valued a little more autonomy than she did. Nevertheless, they were going on a journey together. They might not be so tightly joined at every moment, nor did they always have to move at the same pace, but they both knew they were traveling together to the same place.

The two of them reached a key turning point, though, when they realized that they really did want their marriage to last forever.

They felt they had something very special that needed to be treasured and protected. We suggested that if preserving their marriage was truly their goal, they needed to say to one another that they were together "no matter what." Partners need this depth of security. The most touching thing was Artis and Pam's coming back in one day, both wearing T-shirts they had made with the letters NMW on them—No Matter What.

Deeply knowing that you can count on your partner brings another very important kind of safety to your relationship. Earlier we talked about safety in terms of being able to be open and not fearing damaging conflicts. Here we're talking about safety that comes from the sense of security and permanence in your relationship. The importance of this second sense of safety is best captured by M. Scott Peck, in *The Road Less Traveled* (1985, p. 141): "Couples can not resolve in any healthy way the universal issues of marriage: dependency and independence, dominance and submission, freedom and fidelity, for example, without the security of knowing that the act of struggling over these issues will not destroy the relationship."

As we move through our approach, we'll give you many suggestions for how to think and act on commitment concerns. We'll encourage you to develop and nurture a vision for your future together. This brings us to a warning we'd like to give those of you who struggle with higher levels of conflict and frustration. In order to give your relationship a better chance, do not do or say things that threaten the stability of your relationship. Try not to act in ways that allow the things that bond the two of you together to slip any further away. In other words, do your part to make things go as smoothly and positively as possible. We'll suggest many more specific strategies, but for now, do what you can to hold the line against further erosion in your relationship. You need a secure base of attachment in your marriage for all the rest of the really good things to happen.

KEY RISKS TO A LASTING LOVE

Behind our focus on the four themes we have described here is an emphasis on knowledge based in research, sound theory, and extensive clinical experience. Most other programs and books for couples are neither empirically informed nor empirically tested. As noted in the Introduction, PREP and this book are both. If you'd like to read more about this subject and you've not already read the Introduction, please refer back to it. Further, there are many references to important research in the Selected Research and References (for the seriously curious).

We now have the benefit of a few decades of research into what factors are most likely to raise the risks of a couple not doing well. The key to preventing marital distress, divorce, and unhappiness is to reduce the risk factors and to increase the protective factors. Our goal in PREP and in this book is to help you do both. We discuss major risk factors in this section. Protective factors are all the good things in relationships—friendship, fun, spiritual and religious involvement, and aspects of commitment—and you've probably noted that we have chapters on all these. Before we look at the major risk factors, we'd like to tell you what we think is the most common path to marital unhappiness and divorce.

How a Marriage Dies

OK, so that's not the cheeriest heading in the book. It is the title of a talk Scott started giving to groups years ago that is based on the work we've done over the years to better understand marital success and failure. (Scott is great at sizzling titles. In one of our videos, he uses some really creative ones: "Four Couples Arguing" and "A Couple Who Has Practiced a Lot." Chokes you up, right?)

What follows is not the kind of humorous talk we'd prefer to give. Instead, the themes are deadly serious. But it does summarize in one swoop the core of our theory of how the average marriage dies. Here it goes:

- You meet. Most couples don't go further if they never meet. (You knew that.)

- You are attracted to one another and start to spend time together.

- You like this person, and it's mutual. Joy. Thrill. Sparks. Warmth. Heat.

- You become a bit anxious about whether or not this person will stay in your life. You start to make commitments to one another because commitment reduces anxiety about staying attached.

- You get married.

- Problems happen. They just do, and they will happen to you. For some couples, they are easy problems, for others, they are very difficult and even gut-wrenching— such as having a seriously ill baby.

Couples whose marriages are in danger will show early signs of poorly managed conflict.

- You have difficulty managing conflicts and problems as they come your way in life. You don't work as a team on problems. Conflicts become more frequent and more intense. The number of times you are together that become painful seems to go steadily up. You don't communicate well together, and you start to get nastier about it all. Danger ahead.

Most couples experience periods of conflict and/or neglect of the positive side of their relationship, even if the marriage is following a healthier path.

- Life gets busier. You have a home to take care of, probably kids that need time and attention; your work begins eating up more time, and money pressures mount.

- You begin to neglect the parts of life that bonded you together. You have fun less often. You go out infrequently. You don't just sit down together or take walks to talk as friends much anymore, and when you do, it often turns into an argument.

- This is the big turning point. One or both partners begin to associate the presence of the other with pain and stress rather than with support or pleasure. Friendship together becomes a distant memory (if it is remembered at all). Danger is not just on the horizon; the bridge is out.

- The future becomes something to threaten in arguments: "Why should I stay with you?" "Maybe we need to get a divorce."

- Now you experience the total erosion of dedication to one another and investment in the relationship. You're forgetting why you went on this journey in the first place.

- In the absence of forces that constrain some couples to stay together (for example, poor alternatives), you divorce. If you have a lot of constraint commitment and you do not redevelop dedication and satisfaction, you stay married and miserable.

Clearly, we're hoping to help couples stay off this very common path. It leads to a destination that no couple seeks when the partners start out together, but many end there just the same. You don't have to be on this path. We're here to tell you how to avoid it. If you are already far along on the trip we've described here, we want to tell you some powerful ways to change your course.

Risk Factors for Marital Problems

Many of these risk factors relate to stable, individual characteristics of each partner. You could think of these factors this way: all other things being equal, the more these factors are present in the lives and backgrounds of the marriage partners, the greater the risk to the well-being of that marriage over time. Here is a list of such factors. The list is not exhaustive, but it covers the biggies.

- Having a personality tendency to react strongly or defensively to problems and disappointments in life

- Having divorced parents

- Living together prior to marriage

- Being previously divorced, yourself or your partner

- Having children from a previous marriage

- Having different religious backgrounds

- Marrying at a very young age (for example, at the age of eighteen or nineteen; the average these days is about twenty-five or twenty-six years of age for first marriages)

- Knowing each other for only a short time before marriage

- Experiencing financial hardship

There is something very important about this list that we'd like you to notice: once a couple is married, they can do nothing to directly lower any of these risks. In our academic publications, we call these factors *static* because they are relatively unchangeable. Reflecting on these factors can be useful in understanding how much risk the two of you may have, but there is little you can do to change any of these—and certainly not quickly.

Racism: A Widely Ignored Stress for Couples of Color

In general, couples of color face more challenges than majority couples because of discrimination in general and racism in particular. In a companion book, *Fighting for Your African American Marriage*, our coauthor Dr. Keith Whitfield writes:

Racism is an important and often underestimated factor in the stress that can occur in relationships among African Americans. The very nature of this form of bigotry ranges from ignorance to unjust treatment to acts of violence against people of color, but this intolerance produces anger, hostility, and frustration in those who are on the receiving end of it. The stress of racism does not always take an obvious or insidious form. It can be much more subtle and, like water over a rock, wear away at your personhood. It can also leave you distrustful of the world and others—or worse, even distrustful of yourself. . . .

All of these subtle or obvious situations build to produce frustration and uncertainty about the world around us. We carry this yoke about our shoulders and then we go home. Home to our spouse and perhaps a family—both requiring time, patience, understanding, and love. But the world has just spit in your face; "I don't think that I can really feel love right now!"

[. . .] We believe that couples of color and interracial couples experience special risks (thanks to factors such as discrimination) but also special protection from factors such as strength of extended family and religious institutions. At the same time, our research with couples of color (and couples from other cultures and nations) to date suggests similar results in terms of other risk and protective factors as well as regarding positive effects of the PREP approach.

As we've discussed, it's critically important for couples to develop a strong sense of being on the same team in life together—and this may be all the more true for couples facing the added burdens of discrimination.

In contrast to the static factors shown in the preceding list, there are risk factors that relate more directly to how you treat one another, how you communicate, and how you think about your relationship. We call these *dynamic* risk factors because, although they do increase the risk that a couple won't do well, they can all be changed with some thought and choice and effort.

- Negative styles of talking and fighting with each other, such as arguments that rapidly become negative, put-downs, and the silent treatment

- Difficulty communicating well, especially when you disagree

- Trouble handling disagreements as a team

- Unrealistic beliefs about marriage

- Different attitudes about important things

- A low level of commitment to one another, reflected in such behavior as failing to protect your relationship from others you are attracted to or failing to view your marriage as a long-term investment

- Not practicing faith together

In general, higher levels of risk (due to either static or dynamic factors) are particularly tied to greater difficulties in handling problems and negative emotions well. For example, studies suggest that people whose parents divorced are more likely to come into marriage as adults with communication problems and also a diminished belief or trust that their relationship can work in the long term. In essence, even the static factors tend to express themselves through the dynamic factors.

All other things being equal, the more static or dynamic risk factors you have, the more likely you are to experience difficulties. But remember, we're relationship optimists. We want to help you face risks head-on and beat the odds. The good news is that research by our colleague Kim Halford at Griffith University in Queensland, Australia, suggests that some high-risk couples can benefit greatly from our approach.

Because you can't do much to change the static risk factors, it is wisest to focus your efforts on what you can change—the dynamic factors—and that's what we do throughout this book. (And if you don't have many risk factors, we think we have much to offer you in terms of ways to stay on that path and experience deep love and connection.) We want to help you change in ways that make a difference. We want to help you go from "I do" to "We can."

MOVING AHEAD ON YOUR JOURNEY

Now that you better understand how we think, you are ready for the next part of your journey through this book. Remember, our travel advice can be summarized by four key instructions:

1. Be safe at home.
2. Open the doors to intimacy.
3. Do your part and be responsible.
4. Nurture security in your future together. Build your cocoon.

Now choose the next stop on your journey. We've organized our themes into four major parts of the book:

1. Understanding the Risks on the Road to Lasting Love
2. Teaming Up to Handle Conflict
3. Enjoying Each Other
4. Staying the Course

Although we have put the material in the order we believe makes the most sense for most couples, there may be a part of the book that the two of you would rather start with because of your particular needs, desires, or concerns. Bon voyage!

2

Destructive Patterns:
Signs of Danger Ahead

In this chapter, we focus on four specific ways couples commonly destroy their relationships. You need to battle against these patterns, instead of against one another—that's the essence of fighting for your marriage. Decades of research by many different researchers have confirmed the destructive power of the dangerous patterns we cover here. We want you to team up to defeat these forces that threaten your happiness.

We cover danger signs so early in the book because we know that if you experience a lot of these negatives in your relationship, you will find it hard to do many of the positive things we recommend in the rest of the book. This stuff is toxic. It's poison in your well. Left unchecked, these four patterns can erode all the positive things that drew the two of you together in the first place. Here they are:

1. Escalation
2. Invalidation
3. Negative interpretations
4. Withdrawal and avoidance

Once you understand these patterns, you can learn to recognize them and then use some simple tools to protect your relationship.

WHAT THE FOLKS IN
WHITE LAB COATS SEE

OK, we don't really wear white lab coats, but we *are* talking about serious research: research involving couples, all volunteers, who are videotaped as they talk about issues in their relationships. These conversations are then studied very carefully by teams of trained research assistants who look at how the couples talk, how emotional they get, and how they handle the situation when things get heated, among other things. Study of these tapes is very important because we've discovered over the years that people are not very good reporters of how they actually behave with their mates. What the researchers see is often different enough from what people report that this kind of data has proven very valuable for more fully understanding how marriages do over time. As the baseball great Yogi Berra once said, "You can observe a lot just by watching."

You might think as you read on that we're moving into some pretty negative topics right off the bat in this book. We have much to say about the positives later, but there is a reason we'll take a long look at the nasty stuff up front. For most of us the negatives in life are more salient than the positives. You understand this in some very basic ways in life. One critical negative comment from a family member or coworker can wipe out many other good things that have happened that day. Such researchers as Cliff Notarius and Howard (coauthor), as well as John Gottman at the University of Washington, have estimated that one negative interaction can wipe out the effect of five—or even as many as twenty—positive exchanges. Acid burns.

WHAT HAPPENS WHEN CONFLICTS
ARISE BETWEEN YOU?

In this section we're going to give you the opportunity to think about the negative patterns you see in your own relationship. As part of a project that relationship expert and best-selling author

Gary Smalley was working on some years ago, we developed a set of survey questions to assess many different aspects of people's relationships. Roughly one thousand people were chosen at random by telephone to answer the questions we assembled.

In part of the survey, we asked questions geared toward the danger signs discussed in this chapter. Because we also asked questions about things like happiness, friendship, fun, sensual connection, and commitment in marriage, we were able to get a good sense of how answers to the questions about the danger signs related to other aspects of people's relationships.

We now invite you each to answer these questions on a separate piece of paper and total up your scores. When you are finished, put your answers aside and keep reading; don't share your answers with your partner at this time. At the end of the chapter, we'll talk more about what your scores might mean. First we'll look in depth at the four danger signs.

RELATIONSHIP DYNAMICS SCALE

Please answer each of the following questions in terms of your relationship with your partner. We recommend that you respond to these statements by yourself (not with your partner). Use the following 3-point scale to rate how often you and your partner experience each situation described: 1 = never or almost never, 2 = once in awhile, 3 = frequently.

1. Little arguments escalate into ugly fights with accusations, criticisms, name-calling, or bringing up past hurts.

2. My partner criticizes or belittles my opinions, feelings, or desires.

3. My partner seems to view my words or actions more negatively than I mean them to be.

4. When we have a problem to solve, it is as though we are on opposite teams.

5. I hold back from telling my partner what I really think and feel.

6. I feel lonely in this relationship.

7. When we argue, one of us withdraws—that is, doesn't want to talk about it anymore or leaves the scene.

ESCALATION: WHAT GOES AROUND COMES AROUND

Escalation occurs when partners respond back and forth negatively to each other, continually upping the ante so that conditions get worse and worse. Negative comments often spiral into increasing anger and frustration. It's not just the increasing emotional intensity that causes the problem; it's the tendency to move from simple anger to hurtful comments to and about each other. As John Gottman points out, almost all couples exchange anger for anger from time to time. It's

when you move from being angry and frustrated to showing contempt for the other that the greatest amount of damage is done.

Couples who are happy now and likely to stay that way are less prone to escalation; if they do start to escalate, they are able to stop the negative process before it erupts into a full-blown, nasty fight.

Ted, a thirty-four-year-old construction worker, and Wendy, thirty-two, who runs a catering business out of their home, were married for eight years when we first saw them. Like many couples, their fights started over small issues:

TED: (*sarcastically*) You'd think you could put the cap back on the toothpaste.
WENDY: (*equally sarcastically*) Oh, like you never forget to put it back.
TED: As a matter of fact, I always put it back.
WENDY: Oh, I forgot just how compulsive you are. You're right, of course!
TED: I don't even know why I stay with you. You are so negative.
WENDY: Maybe you shouldn't stay. No one is barring the door.
TED: I'm not really sure why I do stay anymore.

One of the most damaging things about arguments that are escalating out of control is that people say things that threaten the very lifeblood of their marriage—things not easily taken back. As their frustration mounts, people go from wanting to be heard by the other to wanting to hurt the other. At these times, people often hurl verbal (and sometimes even physical) weapons. You can see this pattern with Ted and Wendy, where the stakes quickly rise to include threats of ending the relationship. Negative comments are hard to take back, and these reckless words do a lot to damage any sense of closeness and intimacy. Forgiveness is possible, as we describe in a later chapter, but it's better to prevent the nasty things from being said in the first place.

Although partners can say the meanest things during escalating arguments, such reckless remarks often don't reflect what each really most often thinks and feels about the other. You may believe that people reveal their "true feelings" in the midst of fierce fights; we do not believe that is usually the case.

In their argument, Wendy mentions Ted's being compulsive because she really wants to hit him below the belt. At a more tender moment between them, he once shared his concerns about being so driven, and told her that growing up he had learned this style to please his father. Wendy's escalating anger led to her use of this past hurt to win the battle. When escalation leads to the use of intimate knowledge as a weapon, the damage to the future likelihood of tender moments is great. Who is going to share deeper things if the information may be used later when conflict is out of control in the relationship? Not you and not your partner.

You may be thinking, "We don't fight like cats and dogs—how does this apply to us?" Escalation actually can be very subtle. Voices don't have to be raised for you to get into the cycle of returning negative for negative. Yet research shows that even subtle patterns of escalation can lead to divorce. Consider the following conversation between Max and Donna, newlyweds in their twenties who are just starting out in an apartment in Denver.

MAX: Did you get the rent paid on time?
DONNA: That was going to be your job.
MAX: You were supposed to do it.
DONNA: No, you were.
MAX: Did it get done?
DONNA: No. And, I'm not going to, either.
MAX: (muttering) Great. Just great.

Being newlyweds, Donna and Max are very happy with their marriage. Imagine, however, years of small arguments like this one taking a toll on their marriage, eroding the positive things they now share. This process only makes things worse over time, as more and more damage is done.

It is very important for the future health of your relationship to learn to counteract whatever tendency you have to escalate as a couple. If you don't escalate very much, great; your goal is to learn to keep things that way. If you do escalate a fair amount, your goal is to recognize it—and stop.

Short-Circuiting Escalation

All couples escalate from time to time, but some couples steer out of the pattern more quickly, and much more positively. Compare Ted and Wendy's argument, earlier, with Maria and Hector's. Maria, a forty-five-year-old sales clerk for a jewelry store, and Hector, a forty-nine-year-old attorney who works for the Justice Department, have been married twenty-three years. Like most couples, many of their arguments are about everyday events.

MARIA: *(annoyed)* You left the butter out again.

HECTOR: *(irritated)* Why are little things so important to you? Just put it back.

MARIA: *(softening her tone)* Things like that are important to me. Is that so bad?

HECTOR: *(calmer)* I guess not. Sorry I was nasty.

Notice the difference. Like Ted and Wendy's, Hector and Maria's argument shows escalation, but the couple quickly steered out of it. When escalation sequences are short-circuited, it is usually because one partner backs off and says something to de-escalate the argument, thus breaking the negative cycle. Often this requires the simple humility of choosing to soften your tone and put down your shield. Although in our culture these days we don't talk a lot about humility, there are few approaches more powerful for making wonderful things happen in relationships.

For her part, Maria softens her tone rather than getting defensive. For his part, Hector makes the decision to back off and acknowledge Maria's point of view. Softening your tone and acknowledging your partner's point of view are potent tools you can employ to diffuse tension and end escalation. Often that's all it takes. As we go on, we will be teaching you a number of other ways to keep escalation in check.

If you have very many negative interactions such as these, you may need to recognize that you have to give up needing to win. When you really want to win—to beat your partner in this argument you are having right now—you end up losing even if you do win. It's in your best interest, and that of your relationship, to soften things when you disagree and try to work together against the problem. The coming chapters give you many strategies to help you do this.

INVALIDATION: PAINFUL PUT-DOWNS

Invalidation is a pattern in which one partner subtly or directly puts down the thoughts, feelings, or character of the other. Let's take a closer look at this pattern, which can take many forms. Here are two other arguments between Ted and Wendy and between Maria and Hector.

WENDY: *(very angrily)* You missed your doctor's appointment again! You are so irresponsible. I can see you dying and leaving me, just like your father.

TED: *(bruised)* Thanks a lot. You know I am nothing like my father.

WENDY: He was a creep and so are you.

TED: *(dripping with sarcasm)* I'm sorry. I forgot my good fortune to be married to such a paragon of responsibility. You can't even keep your purse organized.

WENDY: At least I am not so obsessive about stupid little things.

TED: You are so arrogant.

MARIA: *(with a tear)* You know, I'm really frustrated by the hatchet job Bob did on my evaluation at work.

HECTOR: I don't think he was all that critical. I would be happy to have an evaluation as positive as that from Fred.

MARIA: *(turning away with a sigh)* You don't get it. It upset me.

HECTOR: Yeah, I see that, but I still think you are overreacting.

These examples are quite different, but both show invalidation. The first example is much more caustic, and hence damaging to the relationship, than the second. With Ted and Wendy, you can feel the *contempt* seeping through. The argument has settled into an attack on character. That's the most damaging of all.

Although Maria and Hector do not show the contempt displayed by Ted and Wendy, Hector is nevertheless subtly putting down Maria for the way she is feeling. He may even think that he is being constructive or trying to cheer her up by saying, "It's not so bad." Nevertheless, this kind of communication is also invalidating. Maria feels more hurt now because he has said, in effect, that her feelings of sadness and frustration are inappropriate.

The contemptuous invalidation displayed by Ted and Wendy in the first example is more obviously destructive than the more subtle forms of invalidation. But any kind of invalidation sets up barriers in relationships. Invalidation hurts. It leads naturally to covering up who you are and what you think because it's just too risky to do otherwise.

Preventing Invalidation

In both of these dialogues, the couples would have done better if each partner had shown respect for and acknowledged the viewpoint of the other. Note the difference in how these conversations could have gone.

WENDY: *(very angry)* I am very angry that you missed the doctor appointment again. I worry about you being around for me in the future.

TED: *(bruised)* It really upset you, didn't it?

WENDY: You bet. I want to know that you are going to be there for me, and when you miss an appointment that I'm anxious about, I worry about us.

TED: I understand why it would make you worried when I don't take care of myself.

MARIA: *(with a tear)* You know, I'm really frustrated by the hatchet job Bob did on my evaluation at work.

HECTOR: That must really tick you off.

MARIA: Yeah, it does. And I also get worried about whether I'll be able to keep this job. What would we do?

HECTOR: I didn't know you were so worried about losing your job. Tell me more about how you're feeling.

In these dialogues, we've replayed the issues but with very different outcomes for both couples. (By the way, it's not a bad idea at all for you and your partner to agree to call for a "replay" when you need one. When you've blown it, one of you could say, "Let's do that over. We can do better than that." Or simply, "How about a rewind?") In these positive examples, there is ownership of feelings, respect for each other's character, and an emphasis on validation. By validation, we mean that the one raising the concern is respected and heard. You don't have to agree with your partner to validate his or her feelings. Our research shows that invalidation is one of the very best predictors of future problems and divorce, but the amount of validation doesn't say as much about the health of a relationship as the amount of *invalidation* does. Does this finding mean that validation is not so important? Of course not, but it does mean that stopping invalidation is more crucial. Respectful validation inhibits invalidation. But to be validating takes discipline, especially when you are really frustrated or angry.

NEGATIVE INTERPRETATIONS: WHEN PERCEPTION IS WORSE THAN REALITY

Negative interpretations occur when one partner consistently believes that the motives of the other are more negative than is really the case. This can be a very destructive, negative pattern in a relationship, and it will make any conflict or disagreement harder to deal with constructively.

Margot and David have been married twelve years, and they are generally happy with their relationship. Yet their discussions at times have been plagued by a specific negative interpretation. Every December they have had trouble deciding whether or not to travel to her parents' home for the holidays. Margot believes that David dislikes her parents, but in fact, he is quite fond of them in his own way. She has this mistaken belief because of a few incidents early in the marriage that David had long forgotten. Here's how a typical discussion around their issue of holiday travel plans goes:

MARGOT: We should start looking into getting plane tickets to go visit my parents this holiday season.

DAVID: (*thinking about their budget problem*) I was wondering if we can really afford it this year.

MARGOT: (*in anger*) My parents are very important to me, even if you don't like them. I'm going to go.

DAVID: I would like to go, really I would. I just don't see how we can afford a thousand dollars in plane tickets and pay the bill for Joey's orthodontist too.

MARGOT: You can't be honest and admit you just don't want to go, can you? Just admit it. You don't like my parents.

DAVID: There is nothing to admit. I enjoy visiting your parents. I'm thinking about money here, not your parents.

MARGOT: That's a convenient excuse. (*storms out of the room*)

Given that we know David really does like to go to Margot's parents, can you see how powerful her negative interpretation has become? He cannot penetrate it. What can he say or do to make a difference as long as her belief that he dislikes them is so strong? If a negative interpretation is strong enough, nothing the one on the receiving end of it can do will change it. In this case, David wants to address the decision they must make from the standpoint of the budget, but Margot's interpretation will overpower their ability to communicate effectively and will make it hard to come to a decision that makes both of them happy. Fortunately for them, this problem is relatively isolated and not a consistent pattern in their marriage.

When relationships become more distressed, the negative interpretations mount and help create an environment of hopelessness and demoralization. Alfred and Eileen are a couple who were high school sweethearts; they've been married eighteen years and have three children, but they've been very unhappy in their marriage for more than seven years—in part due to the corrosive effect of strong negative interpretations. Although there are positive things in their marriage, almost nothing each does is recognized positively by the other, as we can see in this conversation about parking their car.

ALFRED: You left the car out again.

EILEEN: Oh. I guess I forgot to put it in when I came back from Madge's.

ALFRED: *(with a bit of a sneer)* I guess you did. You know how much that irritates me.

EILEEN: *(exasperated)* Look, I forgot. Do you think I leave it out just to irritate you?

ALFRED: *(coldly)* Actually, that is exactly what I think. I have told you so many times that I want the car in the garage at night.

EILEEN: Yes, you have. But I don't leave it out just to tick you off. I just forget.

ALFRED: If you cared what I thought about things, you'd remember.

EILEEN: *(anger rising in her voice now)* You know that I put the car in nine times out of ten.

ALFRED: More like half the time, and those are the times I leave the garage door up for you.

EILEEN: *(disgusted, walking away)* Have it your way. It doesn't matter what reality is. You will see it your way.

This may sound like a minor argument, but it's not. It represents a long-standing tendency for Alfred to interpret Eileen's behavior in the most negative light possible. For the sake of argument, assume that Eileen is absolutely correct when she says that she simply forgot to put the car in the garage and that this happens only about one in ten times. Alfred sees it differently, especially in his interpretation that she leaves the car out mostly to upset him.

One of the greatest difficulties with negative interpretations is that they are very hard to detect and counteract. They easily become woven into the fabric of a relationship because we all have a very strong tendency toward *confirmation bias*, which is the tendency to look for evidence that confirms what we already think is true about others or situations. In other words, once formed, negative interpretations do not change easily. Even though we can be wrong in our assumptions, we will tend to see what we expect to see.

In the example here, Alfred has the expectation that "Eileen does not care one bit about anything that is important to me." This assumption colors the good things that do happen. In distressed relationships, there is a tendency for partners to discount the positive things they do see, attributing them to causes such as chance rather than to positive characteristics of the partner. Because of Alfred's negative interpretations, Alfred attributes the times Eileen does put the car in the garage to his own action of leaving the door open and not to her intention to put it there. She can't win this argument, and as long as Alfred maintains his negative mind-set, they will not be able to come to an acceptable resolution.

Frank Fincham of the State University of New York in Buffalo and Tom Bradbury of UCLA have found that one person's holding such negative thoughts about the other makes it more likely that the other will respond with hostility and rejection in return. So, in the example here, Alfred makes a very negative assumption about Eileen's motivations (that she wants to irritate him), and Eileen ends up angry and pulls away from him in return.

Negative interpretations are a good example of mind reading. You are mind reading when you assume you know what your partner is thinking or why he or she did something. When you mind-read positively, it tends not to cause any harm. But when your mind reading includes negative judgments about the thoughts and motives of your partner, you may be heading toward real trouble in your marriage.

So it is very important to be on guard for the tendency to view your spouse harshly. After all, a marriage would be in truly terrible shape if either partner routinely and intentionally did things just to frustrate the other. It's more common that the actions of one partner are interpreted negatively and unfairly by the other, even without intending to do so.

Part of the real problem here is that when you consistently make negative interpretations of your partner, you'll tend to feel more justified about hurting him or her in return. You'll justify taking revenge. Although most people don't like to think of that strong a word in a marital context, it's a perfectly accurate description of what so commonly happens. Thinking you are entitled to hurt your partner back for some perceived hurt of yours will keep your relationship derailed.

For High-Conflict Couples with Children

For those of you who have children, the stakes involved with your managing conflicts well are very high indeed. Research, such as that conducted by Robert Emery and colleagues of the University of Virginia, has conclusively documented strong links between parents' conflict and adjustment problems for children. Mark Cummings and his colleagues at Notre Dame have documented three kinds of conflict parents often have (whether or not about parenting):

1. *Destructive conflict.* There is verbal or even physical aggression. (This type of conflict is essentially similar to the danger signs we are describing here.)

2. *Constructive conflict.* There is not agreement, but there is more respectful and shared discussion of the disagreement.

3. *Constructively handled conflict.* Partners work through the problem to a resolution.

Children become more sad, angry, and fearful when regularly exposed to destructive conflict. Worse, if parents tend regularly to make negative interpretations of each other's motivations and behavior, their children learn to do the same in relation to their peers' behavior. They are learning from their parents.

So what can you do? Disagree, but don't fight nasty. If you have a conflict in your children's presence, let them also see you coming back together—they often can't see how you do that. In terms of how your children will be affected by your conflicts, your coming back to some point of emotional harmony is more important than resolving whatever you are fighting about. So do your kids a favor. Work together to manage your conflicts well and with respect.

Battling Negative Interpretations

We are not advocating some kind of unrealistic "positive thinking" here. That won't cut it when battling negative interpretations. These are like weeds with really long roots, and you have to get a good hold of the roots and yank away to rid your relationship of such perceptions. You may have to dig down within yourself a bit (or a lot). Negative interpretations are something you have to confront within yourself. Only you can control how you interpret your partner's behavior.

First, you have to ask yourself if you might be being overly negative in your interpretation of things your partner does. Second—and this is hard—you must push yourself to look for evidence that is contrary to the negative interpretation you usually make. For example, if you believe that your partner is uncaring, and generally see most of what he does in that light, you need to look for evidence to the contrary. Does he do things for you that you like? Could it be that he does nice things because he is trying to keep the relationship strong? It's up to you to consider your interpretation of behavior that others may see as obviously positive—or, at least, less clearly negative. There are more suggestions at the end of this chapter to help you battle your negative interpretations.

As you work through this book and consider making many positive changes in your relationship, be sure you try to give your partner the benefit of the doubt in wanting to make things better. Don't allow inaccurate interpretations to sabotage the work you are trying to accomplish. Choose to be a relationship optimist by assuming the best, not the worst, about your partner.

WITHDRAWAL AND AVOIDANCE: HIDE AND SEEK

Withdrawal and *avoidance* are different manifestations of a pattern in which one partner shows an unwillingness to get into or stay with important discussions. *Withdrawal* can be as obvious as getting up and leaving the room or as subtle as "turning off" or "shutting down" during an argument. The withdrawer often tends to get quiet during an argument or may agree quickly to some suggestion just to end the conversation, with no real intention of following through.

Avoidance reflects the same reluctance to get into certain discussions, with more emphasis on the attempt to not let the conversation happen in the first place. A person prone to avoidance would prefer that the topic not come up, and if it does, he or she may withdraw.

Let's look at this pattern as played out in a discussion between Paula, a twenty-eight-year-old real estate agent, and Jeff, a thirty-two-year-old loan officer. Married for three years, they have a two-year-old baby girl, Tanya, whom they adore. Paula was concerned that the tension in their relationship was starting to affect their daughter.

PAULA: When are we going to talk about how you are handling your anger?

JEFF: Can't this wait? I have to get these taxes done.

PAULA: I've brought this up at least five times already. No, it can't wait!

JEFF: (*tensing*) What's to talk about, anyway? It's none of your business.

PAULA: (*frustrated and looking right at Jeff*) Tanya is my business. I'm afraid that you may lose your temper and hurt her, and you won't do a damn thing to learn to deal better with your anger.

JEFF: (*turning away, looking out the window*) I love Tanya. There's no problem here. (*leaving the room as he talks*)

PAULA: (*very angry now, following Jeff into the next room*) You have to get some help. You can't just stick your head in the sand.

JEFF: I'm not going to discuss anything with you when you are like this.

PAULA: Like what? It doesn't matter if I am calm or frustrated—you won't talk to me about anything important. Tanya is having problems, and you have to face that.

JEFF: (*quiet, tense, fidgeting*)

PAULA: Well?

JEFF: (*going to closet and grabbing sweater*) I'm going out to have a drink and get some peace and quiet.

PAULA: (*voice raised, angry*) Talk to me, now. I'm tired of you leaving when we are talking about something important.

JEFF: (*looking away from Paula, walking toward the door*) I'm not talking, you are; actually, you're yelling. See you later.

Many couples do this kind of dance when it comes to dealing with difficult issues. One partner *pursues* dealing with issues (Paula) and one *avoids* or *withdraws* from dealing with issues (Jeff). This scenario is very common—and very destructive to the relationship. As is true of the other patterns presented, it does not have to be this dramatic to predict problems to come. Even lower levels of avoidance and withdrawal are among the most powerful predictors of future relationship unhappiness and divorce. We will focus more on these dynamics in the next chapter when we talk about differences between men and women. For now, keep this point in mind: pursuit and withdrawal may be normal in relationships, but normal isn't necessarily good.

Pursuit and withdrawal may be normal in relationships, but normal isn't necessarily good.

Preventing Withdrawal and Avoidance

With regard to withdrawal, you want to be an abnormal couple, and we want to help you be strange (not strangers). If you are seeing this pattern in your relationship, keep in mind that it will likely get worse if you allow it to continue. That is because as pursuers push more, withdrawers withdraw more. And as withdrawers pull back, pursuers push harder. Furthermore, when issues are important, it should be obvious that trying to avoid dealing with them will only lead to damaging consequences. You can't stick your head in the sand and pretend important or bothersome problems are not really there.

In the case of withdrawal and avoidance, the first, best step you can take right now is to realize that you are not independent of one another. Your actions cause reactions, and vice versa. For this reason, you will have much greater success if you are working together to change or prevent the kinds of negative patterns discussed here. Withdrawers are not likely to reduce avoidance unless pursuers pursue less, or at least pursue more constructively. Pursuers are going to find it hard to cut back on pursuing unless withdrawers deal more directly with the issues at hand.

In your marriage, you need to keep the lines of communication open, but do so in such a way that neither feels the urge to withdraw. That means talking without fighting. We will get much more specific on how to combat these patterns in the next few chapters.

HOW YOU START TALKING MAY DETERMINE HOW YOUR TALKING WILL GO

After many years of research, John Gottman has begun emphasizing something that we find very compelling. Some years ago, he determined that 96 percent of the time, how couples begin talks about issues determines the subsequent course of the conversation. This means that if you start out angry when you raise a concern, the resulting talk is likely to be an angry one, and the two of you are not very likely to pull out of it. All the more true if you start with an edge of hostility. If you start out on a more positive note, you are very likely to be able to keep the conversation on that level.

More recently, John has gotten more specific. His research has led him to recommend the importance of raising concerns gently. In fact, he calls this "gentle start-up." What a great point this is. He suggests that the gentle start-up is particularly important for wives when raising concerns with husbands and that it's particularly important for men to respond with attention and concern for what the wife says. Frankly, we'd like to recommend this advice to each of you, male or female. If you raise concerns directly but more gently with your partner, you are far more likely to have a good conversation. If you work to pay serious attention to concerns your partner raises, when he or she raises them, you are going to have better conversations. You could call this *respect in action*.

As we will make clear in the chapters ahead, this advice is not meant to imply that *any* time is the best time to go ahead and talk through an issue. Many times are going to be the wrong time. We want you to have control over the timing of your discussions as a couple. But any time you want to talk to your partner about a concern, remember: how you raise it will determine a lot about how the concern will be received. It's a lot easier to aim the ship in the right direction from the start than to change directions once it has already picked up speed.

Talking Points

1. Destructive patterns of arguing can reflect a great deal about where your marriage is heading in the future.

2. You control the tone of your arguments and how positive your approach is to one another.

3. Above all, show respect to one another.

 # EXERCISES

What Your Quiz Scores Mean

Take out the sheet with your answers from the quiz earlier in the chapter. We want to give you some suggestions related to how you scored. These questions are based on our twenty years of research at the University of Denver on the kinds of communication and conflict management patterns that predict if a relationship is headed for trouble.

The average score was 10 on this scale. Although you should not take a higher score to mean that your relationship is somehow destined to fail, higher scores can mean that your relationship may be in greater danger unless you and your partner make some changes.

These ranges are based only on your individual ratings—not your total as a couple. Therefore, the two of you may come up with scores that land in different ranges. If so, we generally recommend thinking of the higher score as the one that is more likely to reflect how you are doing. That's not to say that the one with the higher score is "right" more than the one with a lower score, but rather that any higher score reflects significant concerns that both partners should take to heart.

7 to 11

If you scored in this range, your relationship is probably in good or even great shape *at this time*, but we emphasize "at this time" because relationships don't stand still. In the next twelve months, you'll either have a stronger, happier relationship, or you could be heading the other direction. To think about it another way, right now you are traveling along and have come to a green light. There is no need to stop, but it is probably a great time to work on making your relationship all it can be.

12 to 16

If you scored in this range, you are coming to a yellow light. You need to be cautious. Although you may be happy now in your relationship, your score reveals warning signs of patterns you don't want to let get worse. You'll want to take action to protect and improve what you have. Spending time to strengthen your relationship now could be the best thing you could do for your future together.

17 to 21

If you scored in this range, think of yourselves as approaching a red light. Stop. Think about where the two of you are headed. Your score indicates the presence of patterns that could put your relationship at significant risk. You may be heading for trouble—or are already there. But there is good news. You can stop and learn ways to improve your relationship now!

Going Deeper

Now we're going to ask you to think about the patterns in a lot more detail. Please take a pad of paper and write your answers to these questions independently from your partner. When you have finished, we suggest you share your perceptions. If doing so raises conflict, however, put off further discussion of your answers until you have learned more in the next few chapters about how to talk safely on tough topics.

Before getting into specific questions about the four negative patterns, consider the following one about your overall impression of how you handle conflict together: When you have a disagreement or argument, what typically happens? In answering this question, think about the patterns described in this chapter.

Escalation

Escalation occurs when you say or do something negative, your partner responds with something negative, and off you go into a real battle. Escalation is the snowball effect, whereby you can get increasingly angry and hostile as the argument continues.

1. How often do you think you escalate as a couple?
2. Do you get hostile with each other during escalation?
3. What or who usually brings an end to the fight?
4. When you are angry, does one or the other of you sometimes threaten to end the relationship?
5. How do you as an individual *feel* when you are escalating as a couple? Do you feel tense, anxious, scared, angry, or something else?

Invalidation

Invalidation occurs when you subtly or directly put down the thoughts, feelings, actions, or worth of your partner. This is different from simply disagreeing with your partner or not liking something he or she has done. Invalidation includes an element of belittling or disregarding what is important to your partner, either out of insensitivity or outright contempt.

1. Do you often feel invalidated in your relationship? When and how does this happen?

2. What is the effect on you?

3. Do you often invalidate your partner? When and how does this happen?

4. What do you think the effect is on him or her? On the relationship? What are you trying to accomplish when you invalidate your partner? Do you achieve your goal?

Negative Interpretations

Negative interpretations occur when you interpret your spouse's behavior much more negatively than he or she intended. It is critical that you open yourself to seeing the possibility that your view of your partner could be unfair in some areas. These questions will help you reflect on this idea.

1. Can you think of some areas in which you consistently see your partner's behavior as negative?

2. Reflect on this awhile. Do you really think that your negative view of his or her behavior is justified?

3. Are there some areas in which you have a negative interpretation but are open to considering that you may be missing evidence to the contrary?

4. List two or more issues for which you are willing to push yourself to look for the possibility that your partner has more positive motivations than you have been thinking he or she has. Next, look for the evidence that is contrary to your negative interpretation.

Withdrawal and Avoidance

As we will be discussing in the next chapter, men and women often deal quite differently with conflict in relationships. Most often, males are more prone to withdraw from discussion of issues in relationships, women more prone to pursue.

1. Is one of you more likely to be in the pursuer role? Is one of you more likely to be in the withdrawer role?

2. How does the withdrawer usually withdraw? How does the pursuer usually pursue? What happens then?

3. When are you most likely to fall into this pattern as a couple? Are there particular issues or situations that bring out this pattern?

4. How are you affected by this pattern?

5. For some couples, both partners tend to pursue or withdraw. Is that true for your relationship? Why do you think this happens?

3

Changing Roles, Changing Rules:
Men and Women in Conflict

People often stress how different men and women are, and how these differences cause so many problems in marriage. We don't have nearly enough space to discuss all the issues surrounding the differences between men and women. Nor can we begin to cover the vast number of studies that have put differences between men and women under the microscope. Instead we'll talk about some of the major differences between men and women, especially about how marriage affects them and how they behave in marriage—differences that research suggests really do matter. More important, we will focus on what the two of you can do to make sure that the gender differences that affect you most in your marriage are the fun kind, not the kind to battle over.

WHAT'S TRUE AND WHAT'S FALSE?

What do you believe are some key differences between men and women when it comes to marriage? We've got a quiz for you. True or false? Go ahead and write down your answers. We'll wait for you.

1. Men are more rational than women.

2. Women are more likely to be depressed if they are married.

3. Men live longer if they are married, whereas women who are married have poorer health.

4. Women tend to report less happiness in marriage than men.

5. Most men hate talking with their wives and therefore avoid it if they can.

6. In dual-earner marriages, men and women do an equal amount of housework.

7. Men are more attracted to women who are somewhat insecure.

8. Women are more committed to their marriages than men are.

9. Men, being more competitive, are more likely than women to have already looked at the correct answers below so that they can get a higher score on this quiz.

10. When conflicts arise, men are more likely than women to shut down or pull away.

What's All the Fuss About?

We want to say something very important here about research on differences between men and women. When researchers talk about differences between any groups or along any dimensions, they are talking about broad average differences between the groups. Translation: they're talking about differences that tend to be true for many people, but there are still likely to be a great number of exceptions. That's why you could add the words *on average* to just about any sentence in the rest of this chapter whenever we talk about differences between men and women.

Whatever aspect of relationships you look at, you will find that there are far more differences between individuals in how they think and act than can be explained solely by the sex of those individuals. There are real differences, on average, between men and women in marriage. You've likely noticed that. But it's also true that the differences between men and women in marriage have been highly inflated. What we mean by that is that men and women are really a lot more similar in what they want out of marriage than they are different. Both want to be loved, close, and connected, and to have a deep friend for life in a mate.

We'd also like to point out that researchers tend to focus on things they can measure rather than on the more elusive, mysterious side of relationships. What does this mean? It means that some of the most magical and important similarities and differences between men and women may never be studied because they cannot be measured. Despite this difficulty, we think we can explain the importance of some of the frustrating differences men and women often experience in relating with one another.

Let's briefly go through the true-false test. First, the answers. Look back to the questions. The correct answers are (1) false, (2) false, (3) false, (4) false, (5) false, (6) false, (7) false, (8) false, (9) did you? and (10) true. We'll briefly tell you what the research says about each statement.

1. *Men are more rational than women.* This is a long-standing myth. Usually people who believe this think it has something to do with not being emotional, as though "rational" and "emotional" traits couldn't exist in the same person. There are plenty of studies that do show that women, on average, express more emotion in their conversations than men. We said "express" because the jury is still out on whether or not they "feel" more emotion, or if men really "feel" less. Deborah Tannen, of Georgetown University, is a

leading researcher and author in the field of emotional communication, and we'll steer you in her direction if you want to explore
this topic further.

2. *Women are more likely to be depressed if they are married.* This is
a myth based on one relatively flawed, poorly designed study many
years ago. The truth is that both men and women are considerably
less likely to be depressed if they are married, as compared to single
women or divorced women. But some research seems to show that
women are more likely than men to be depressed as a result of marital problems. So two things are true that can sound a bit inconsistent: women may be more prone to depression when their marriages
are not doing so well (but many men are too), and both women and
men gain a significant buffer against depression when married—
especially when happily married.

3. *Men live longer if they are married, whereas women who are married have poorer physical and economic health.* OK, this one was a bit
tricky. You could say it's half true. Married men do live significantly
longer than unmarried men. However, the myth is that women are
generally harmed by marriage, not only in terms of health but also
economically. A preeminent researcher who has made a long-term
study of the effects of marriage on men and women is Linda Waite
of the University of Chicago. In a book called *The Case for Marriage*
(2000, p. 163), she and Maggie Gallagher sum up the research this
way: "Both men and women live longer, healthier, and wealthier
lives when married, but husbands typically get greater health benefits from marriage than do wives." They go on: "Both men and
women are safer, more sexually satisfied, and wealthier, if married,
but women benefit more on sexual satisfaction, financial well-being,
and protection from domestic violence, and they benefit about
equally on emotional well-being" (p. 171).

The benefits they discuss are found in comparing married
women with single or cohabiting unmarried women. We all know
many exceptions to these findings. We know women who are miserable in their marriages or, worse, abused in their marriages. How-

ever, it is a myth that only men and not women benefit from marriage. Although it is true that men get a more dramatic health benefit than women, marriage is good for both men and women. Better yet, there is virtually nothing you can do in life that has more power to enhance your life than to build and protect a great and happy marriage. It's also one of the best things you could possibly do to enhance your children's well-being.

4. *Women tend to report less happiness in marriage than men.* A few studies over the years have found this to be true. However, even in large samples, across a wide range of couples, the differences are just too small to measure. Further, women are just as likely as men to report that marriage enhances their overall well-being. Our colleague Mari Clements, at Penn State University, has studied how couples develop and change over time, and finds that women are as happy as men, or happier, when it comes to their relationships.

> *There is virtually nothing you can do in life that has more power to enhance your life than to build and protect a great and happy marriage.*

5. *Most men hate talking with their wives and therefore avoid it if they can.* There are indeed strong silent types. There are weak silent types. There are a lot of quiet people, male and female. Men haven't cornered the market on introversion or shyness. However, even those women who don't feel that their husbands want to talk to them can often recall that their husbands were quite talkative earlier on in their relationships (whether before marriage or early in it). If that sounds like your relationship, stay tuned. Later in this chapter, we'll come back to focus on why and when men talk or don't talk—and what wives (and husbands) can do about it.

6. *In dual-earner marriages, men and women do an equal amount of housework.* Nope. No way. Some of you are not exactly surprised to read that. It sounds like a nice idea, but it just isn't so. Even though more women than ever before work outside the home, they have generally not been able to reduce much of the traditional workload

at home. Our nationwide survey data suggest, though, that men whose wives work outside the home do somewhat more of the housework than men whose wives don't work outside the home. So even though men are doing more housework than ever before, the sharing of work is still just not very close to equal for most couples. For many couples, the subject of housework is an area in which expectations and poor problem-solving skills collide to create a lot of heat. We'll come back to this theme in the chapter on expectations.

7. *Men are more attracted to women who are somewhat insecure.* Over the years, we've heard people suggest that men prefer women to be somewhat dependent and insecure. Perhaps this idea comes from a belief that this makes men feel more powerful. Not so. Both men and women are more attracted to people who act and feel more secure in relationships. In fact, the need to feel secure is one reason commitment (see Chapter Fifteen) is so crucial between the two of you: there is no way to feel secure when the commitment is uncertain, no matter how secure you feel as an individual.

8. *Women are more committed to their marriages than men are.* A number of studies have tested this over the years. One of the most important kinds of commitment is what we call dedication. Dedication to one's partner can be expressed in many ways. In two large studies, we have found almost no differences between the dedication levels of husbands and wives. There are some nuances we will look at later in the book, but by and large, there is every reason to believe that the average man is as dedicated as the average woman in marriage. Of course, we'll encourage you to do far better than average when it comes to showing and acting on your commitment to one another.

Men can be as dedicated as women, but they may demonstrate their commitment differently. In each new study we conduct, we see evidence suggesting that the level of dedication men have and show in marriage may be particularly important for the happiness of women.

9. *Men, being more competitive, are more likely than women to have already looked at the correct answers below so that they can get a higher*

score on this quiz. Did you look? There really does seem to be a difference between men and women when it comes to competition of some kinds. Surely there are many women who love to compete and win, but men seem more often to be the ones who are driven toward the kind of success that comes from competing and winning. As noted by Carol Gilligan, author of *In a Different Voice,* women are more likely than men to put the goal of preserving relationships ahead of winning when in conflict with others. Such matters are complex and vary greatly from relationship to relationship.

10. *When conflicts arise, men are more likely than women to shut down or pull away.* Of all the beliefs widely held about men and women in marriage, this one has the greatest amount of support in sound marital research.

Now that we have your attention (we do, don't we?), we will now spend the rest of this chapter exploring this last quiz item— the only one that expresses something clearly supported by sound research. Men do tend to withdraw more than women when talking with their mate. We will discuss why this occurs, how it affects marriage—and, if you experience it, what you can do about it.

WHEN ONE WANTS TO TALK AND THE OTHER DOESN'T

As we discussed in the chapter on danger signs, a couple in which one partner pursues and one withdraws is at the most risk for marital distress and divorce. Furthermore, the research shows that it's a pattern closely associated with differences between men and women. Let's look deeper.

What Do You Want?

Try this little experiment: get on the Internet, go to an online bookstore, and plug some version of these questions into its search engine: "What do women want?" or "What do men want?"

You will find more than a few related titles. In our casual review, it seemed to us that there were more books about what women want than about what men want. Does that mean that people are more interested in what women want? Or that men can't describe what they want, so no one writes about it? Or worse, that people just take men for granted and assume we all know what men really want? Or are women still so unsure about what they want that they aren't ready to read about what men want, and need to figure out what they want? Dizzying, isn't it?

OK, let's make this simpler and ask yourself two questions that are far more important than those above: What does my partner want? and What do I want?

Our chapter on expectations is focused on helping the two of you figure out what you want and expect, and what you are going to do about those wants and expectations. Here we are looking at what seems to be different about what men and women may want when they are talking about issues or are in conflict.

Sometimes you can tell what people want by looking at what they complain about. Women often voice concerns about withdrawn, avoidant husbands who will not open up and talk. When their husbands act that way, women feel shut out and get pretty unhappy. Often they begin to feel that their husbands don't care about the relationship. This is the most common complaint we hear from women who come in for marital counseling. It's very important to women for their husbands to communicate openly and often. Women do appear to value and seek communication about how the relationship is going more than men do.

Sometimes you can tell what people want by looking at what they complain about.

In contrast, men frequently complain that their wives get upset too much of the time, griping about this or that and picking fights. Dare we use the N word (hint: rhymes with *bag*)? Usually men feel hassled and want peace—at any price. Often at a price way too steep for women. In one way or another, we hear men saying they want some way to stop having fights with their wives. In essence, it seems very important to them to have harmony and calm in their relationships with their wives.

This is all well and good until you put a man and a woman together. Take Mel and Sandy, a couple who had been married ten years when we saw them. Mel was the manager of a restaurant, and Sandy was a schoolteacher who was taking a few years off to be at home with their children while they were young. As is true for many couples, money was tight. Mel worked long hours to make ends meet. Sandy was torn between her desires to be home with the kids and to be back teaching, bringing in some income. Sandy deeply desired to talk with Mel about her conflicted feelings, but he never seemed interested in hearing what was on her mind on this subject. Sandy's frustration grew daily. She felt that he was avoiding talking with her about anything more important than the weather. The following conversation was typical, taking place one Saturday morning while the kids were out playing.

SANDY: (*sitting down by Mel and looking at him*) I sure wish I could relax about money. When I see you worrying so much, it's just . . . I wonder if I'm doing the right thing, you know, being here at home.

MEL: (*not looking up from the paper*) It'll all work out.

SANDY: (*She's thinking, "He doesn't want to hear it. I wish he'd put that damn paper down."*) I don't know. Am I really doing the right thing taking off from teaching? I think about it every day. Some days, I . . . you know, I'm not sure.

MEL: (*He tenses while thinking, "We always end up fighting when we talk about money. Why is she bringing this up now? I thought we'd settled this."*) I really think you're doing the right thing. It's just harder to make the budget work, but we'll get back on track. I don't think we need to hash it out again.

SANDY: (*She's thinking, "Why can't he relax and open up more? I want to talk and know he is listening."*) I can tell you really don't want

to talk about it. It bugs me that you can't talk with me about this.
You always either change the subject or get real quiet.

MEL: *(He takes a deep breath and lets out a loud sigh. He wants to say something to stop the escalation, but no good idea comes to mind. He says nothing. He feels tense.)*

SANDY: *(feeling very frustrated, with anger growing)* That's exactly what I mean. You just close me out, again and again, and I'm tired of it!

MEL: *(He's thinking, "I knew it. We always fight when we talk about money.")* Why do you do this? I'm just sitting here relaxing. It's the only time I have all day to sit still, and you pick a fight. I hate this! *(He throws the paper down, gets up from the table, and walks into the living room.)*

To sum up Sandy's and Mel's concerns bluntly, she wanted him to "open up," and he wanted her to "shut up." At face value, it sounds as though they had very different goals for their relationship, but it's not that simple. She was looking for a way to connect, to be intimate with Mel, and he cut her off. Are men afraid of, or not interested in, intimacy? We don't think so. Yet that is the most common interpretation of the difference between men and women in marriage.

What Is "Intimate" to You?

Many people have concluded that men are less interested in intimacy and seek to avoid it. But maybe intimacy is in the eye of the beholder. There is little doubt that men and women naturally seek out different kinds of intimacy, but that's different from saying that men are not as interested in it.

Whereas women tend to define intimacy more in terms of verbal communication, there is some evidence that men define intimacy more in terms of shared activities. This is a critical point to keep in mind. When a female asks her husband to spend some time talking about feelings, she may be showing her preference for intimacy; but so is a male who asks his wife to take a walk or make love.

These preferences parallel our upbringing: little girls work on verbal intimacy, and little boys "hang out" with others while doing activities—especially activities with rules, such as sports. If you watch little girls and compare them to little boys, you'll see that relationship patterns go way back. Whether it's because of physical differences or the ways we're raised, girls tend to talk more about relationships than boys, and they put more time and energy into maintaining them. Many people would say this is true for adults as well.

Whereas women tend to define intimacy more in terms of verbal communication, there is some evidence that men define intimacy more in terms of shared activities.

Before we leave the topic of intimacy, here's some simple but powerful advice: you should spend more time figuring out what is intimate for your partner rather than assuming too much about what your partner likes and wants based on his or her gender. Further, the happiest couples have usually developed the capacity to connect on several dimensions of intimacy, including verbal communication, shared activity, and sensual partnership, to name a few.

CONFLICT, THE BIG DIFFERENCE

If men and women both want intimacy and are only different in the ways they prefer to attain it, what accounts for the widespread perception that men are just not interested in protecting and nurturing intimacy? Let's look at the possible reasons why someone might withdraw from talking to his or her partner:

1. The withdrawer is not interested in intimacy.

2. The withdrawer simply does not want to change in some way and therefore refuses to talk about the subject.

3. The withdrawer is pulling a power move in which he or she is "showing" the pursuer that the pursuer does not have control.

4. The withdrawer fears arguing with the pursuer and is attempting to stop what looks like a fight coming.

We certainly don't believe that point one has any merit. As just discussed, we think men and women both desire intimacy, though they may well have different preferences for what form it will take. As for point two, surely there are times when a person does not want to change something and avoids talking to his or her partner about the topic. Worse, there are times in some relationships when one shuts the other out, deliberately, as a kind of power move. That's also called being passive-aggressive, and it's very destructive. So point three is valid, and when a partner acts this way, it powerfully undermines the relationship.

Having discussed the possible validity of points one through three, we think those are, most often, negative interpretations of what the withdrawal means. In our interviews with couples, and especially with withdrawers, the reason we most often hear is number four. Withdrawers are not avoiding intimacy; they are avoiding conflict. This is one of the most important differences between men and women in intimate relationships. In the face of conflict, men are more likely to withdraw than women.

Whereas women may actually have more negative physiological reactions to conflict in marriage (see the box "You Make Me Sick"), most men don't seem to handle conflict in marriage as well as most women. They may express too much anger, but very often they tend to clam up and close down. What's sad is that men and women who are doing this dance really want similar changes to make things better. We see this in our counseling practice: we ask couples to list their goals for therapy, and the people who put "to talk more" as their first goal often have "to fight less" as another major goal, and vice versa. We want to help the two of you do both.

Although this dynamic is not motivated by an avoidance of intimacy, it can nevertheless have serious consequences for intimacy. That's because when men go into conflict avoidance mode, their

choices concerning intimacy become more limited. If an argument seems at all likely, the energy that might go into connecting is too often diverted toward preventing the fight. Comfortable talking as friends can rapidly evaporate if storm clouds appear to be looming on the horizon. This explains, in part, why it so often looks to pursuers as though withdrawers are avoiding intimacy. But watch carefully: the withdrawal usually gets rolling when the nature of the talking starts to shift.

Who's Raising the Issues?

Although many researchers have done an admirable job of bringing more light to the pursuer-withdrawer pattern, one whose work stands out is Andrew Christensen at the University of California-Los Angeles. In addition to his excellent research on the topic of acceptance in marriage, he has made a long-term study of what happens between two partners when one pursues and one withdraws. He calls it the demand-withdraw pattern.

One of the fundamental points that Christensen makes is that this pattern is most often triggered when one partner wants some kind of change or wants to discuss some issue that the partner feels he or she needs to talk about. Whether it is the female or the male who desires the discussion, males are more likely to withdraw than females. However, Christensen and colleague Chris Heavey found that the pattern was strongest when the woman was asking the man for changes. Further, there is strong reason to believe that women raise issues more often than men. A number of studies show this clearly. In part this is because women often feel more responsible for how relationships are going and are therefore going to feel that it's their job to bring things up—issues, problems, conflicts.

NEGATIVE INTERPRETATIONS, ROUND TWO

As the "Who's Raising the Issues?" box mentions, women are more likely to feel it is their job to watch out for how the relationship is doing; this explains why some of them get so frustrated or angry with their husbands. From the woman's point of view, she's trying to take care of the relationship or deal with something that needs resolution, but the man will have nothing to do with this type of talk. In many ways, people can be the most vulnerable when they are really motivated in their relationship. They care. They are showing it. When you try to do something you think is good for the relationship and the other does not seem to appreciate it, it can leave you hanging out there and feeling alone.

Think more about Mel and Sandy. His withdrawal was very frustrating to her. She wanted to talk through a significant concern— how the decision they had made for her to stay home with the children for a time was increasing the level of stress on him. Mel wasn't pulling back from talking because he didn't want to change, nor did his withdrawal have anything at all to do with power. His withdrawal was driven by his discomfort in having this kind of talk with Sandy. He'd come to believe that talking about issues like this usually led to fights between the two of them, and he did not want to fight with Sandy. He loves her.

There is irony here, and we think it is a common one. She wanted to express her concern about him and felt he wouldn't let her do that. He wanted to avoid a fight with her at all costs, yet his pulling back, if anything, guaranteed the fight. So, as is true of most couples, when one withdrew, the other tended to up the ante and push harder. This can be motivated by frustration that something is not going to get resolved. On a deeper level, it can be motivated by panic—panic that the partner is detaching from the relationship.

Emotional Attachment

Susan Johnson is a researcher of marriage and marital therapy at the University of Ottawa. She has focused on the dynamics of emotional attachment in marriage. She notes that everyone needs secure attachment with others, and for most of us, we expect the most secure and deepest attachment with our mates. If one partner sees the other's withdrawal as a sign of a weakening attachment, great energy and fury can flow into pursuit. The withdrawer hears more **threat** and pulls away further, and the pursuer turns up the volume. Off the couple goes. For many couples, their very worst fights start in this way.

Johnson has developed a whole system of counseling couples that is based on the theory and research on emotional attachment. One of the most striking things she's found is that a couple is most likely to improve when the woman believes that the man really does care and really is committed. There's no confidence in a future if your mate really doesn't care about you and your concerns. That's very demoralizing, whether or not it's actually true. And it's demoralizing for both of you.

Mel and Sandy were finding pursuit and withdrawal a painful dance. Imagine how much more destructive it could have become if each had started thinking the worst of the other. Sandy could have started to think that Mel's withdrawal meant he didn't love and care for her. That would be really terribly serious, if true. He might have started believing that Sandy just liked to stir up conflict—to control him or nag him. Such thoughts would have gotten them rolling—downhill all the way. These kinds of interpretations are devastating, and they are usually inaccurate. As we said in Chapter Two, once negative interpretations get going, it's very hard to get things back on track. You can do it, but you have to work at it, looking hard for evidence that is contrary to the unfair view of the other.

You think your partner doesn't care, and that that's what's behind his withdrawal? Look, and look hard, for evidence that tells you he does care. You think your partner gets some secret pleasure in hassling you? We really think that's unlikely. If you have concerns about something—work to raise them firmly but gently. The loudest voice can't get the attention of someone who doesn't want to listen.

You Make Me Sick

Janice Kiecolt-Glaser of the Ohio State University College of Medicine has been studying the physical reactions people have to conflict in marriage. In her own and others' work, poorly handled marital conflict has negative effects on the functioning of the cardiovascular, immune, and endocrine systems. Studies also suggest that whereas men tend to show more of these negative effects than women when it comes to general life stress, women tend to be even more negatively affected, physiologically, by marital conflict.

In our first edition, we made the point that from a life stress perspective, men are, in various ways, more physically vulnerable than women. We (along with a number of colleagues) had thought at that time that this might be why men are more likely than women to withdraw from talking. Yet the latest research shows that women take the greater hit when it comes to bodily stress reactions related to conflict in marriage.

We still believe that fear and anxiety over conflict with their wives lead many men to withdraw when conflicts arise; but having heard what so many men have told us, we now think this is related less to physiological stress and more to psychological distress. For women, it looks as though they are so motivated to keep their relationships strong that they're at risk for becoming sick when these goals seem to be blocked. For this and many other reasons, we have come to believe that it is important for women to keep pushing on important concerns in relationships. However, life is so much better when two people are pulling together rather than one having to push the other.

Do you want to live long and prosper? Men: look for ways to show your wife that you are concerned about how your relationships is doing. Actively respond to your wife as a teammate, not an enemy. By doing so, you will be protecting her and your marriage.

Rates of Male Versus Female Withdrawal: A National View

In conjunction with a project of our friend and colleague Gary Smalley, we conducted a nationwide random phone survey in 1995 of people who were either married (most of the sample), engaged, or cohabiting. One of the questions we asked was this: "Who tends to withdraw more when there is an argument?" The answers of both men and women were virtually identical as to who was most likely to pull away.

42 percent said the male.

26 percent said the female.

17 percent said both.

15 percent said neither.

For many couples, who withdraws depends mostly on what the topic is. Regardless, we think the advice we have to offer will apply to any couple who finds one partner or the other withdrawing about some issue.

We did something very simple with this data. We compared the people who said "neither" with those who said either the male or the female tended to withdraw. We compared them on overall happiness, sense of friendship, commitment, sensual satisfaction, fun, and their reports of the danger signs we discussed in Chapter Two. Those who said that neither tended to withdraw were doing better, in each and every way, than those who said that either might withdraw.

As we have already mentioned, withdrawal, like all the other danger signs we stress, is both common *and* a bad sign for your relationship. There are many experts who suggest that men are just this way and women are just that way, and that the key is simply to accept these differences. Acceptance is great—usually. However, when experts suggest that men's (or women's) tendency to withdraw is OK, the message goes too far in light of what's best for most couples. It encourages acceptance of a pattern that is hurtful for the two of you together.

Changing the Dance

Now we know what couples do wrong. What can they do that's right? Let's recap. We believe that the pursuit-withdrawal pattern discussed in this chapter is a major contributor to the death of many marriages. We believe the following:

- The person more likely to withdraw in any talk is the one who feels more anxious about the topic or tone of the talk.

- The person who withdraws is very likely the one who feels less confident that something good for the couple is about to happen.

- Our avoidance and withdrawal in relationships is often similar to our behavior in other areas of life: most of us pull away from things that we're not sure we can handle well.

- In most marriages, pulling back has far more to do with conflict than with a lack of commitment or caring.

- Partners have to work together to stop this dance.

You are not very likely to experience this pursuing and withdrawing dance when you are talking about something you both enjoy talking about. This is one of the ways that friendly talks between mates are so fundamentally different than conflictual talks. When you are talking as friends, there is very little risk of conflict and rejection. In talks about issues and concerns, in contrast, there is a much higher risk of unpleasant conflict erupting. If you regularly experience the danger signs, you may find that all your talking is affected, because you are never sure when things will turn sour.

Bottom line? If you are both committed to staying close, being friends, and being a team in dealing with life, you have to be able to talk safely about the issues that come up and that are more difficult to talk about. You also have to be able to protect the great things that bond the two of you together. You need to protect your relationship from poorly handled conflict. At times, that means dealing with issues head-on, but with mutual respect and a sense of teamwork. At other times, protecting your relationship means keeping issues and conflicts from wrecking or intruding on the great times that bond the two of you together. A great deal of what's ahead in this book is designed to help the two of you protect your relationship from the sense that no time together is emotionally safe.

Reading this chapter, you may have been thinking that even though men are more likely than women to withdraw in marriage, there are other areas in which men are less intimidated by conflict:

sports, the military, business. What do these situations have in common, and how do these settings tend to differ from marriage? Rules! Rules that bring some degree of structure to the conflict. We think that one powerful way to make talks safe is to have agreed-on rules for when and how you will talk about the more difficult matters in life. Our goal in this book is to teach you a set of rules that will help you handle emotional conflict and make it safe to find intimacy in your relationship.

Talking Points

1. Decide when to talk about issues and concerns that could make one or the other of you uncomfortable because of the potential for conflict. If you decide together that it's a good time to deal with something, the two of you are far less likely to do the pursuit-withdrawal dance.

2. When you are talking about issues and concerns, do whatever works for the two of you to make it safe. Safety is the best antidote to withdrawal. When you learn the Speaker-Listener Technique (Chapter Five) and it is working well for you, use it at these times.

3. Look for the best in your mate, not the worst. Although you may be frustrated, your partner may have good intentions behind those negative behaviors.

    EXERCISES

The exercises we suggest here call for reflection. We want you to think about the questions here and plan some time to talk together about your *own* perceptions of how these patterns work for *you*. Most of the exercises in this book will have you focus together on your relationship. Here it's more up to each of you to consider how the pattern works within you.

Thinking About What You Do

You were asked in the preceding chapter to consider who withdraws more and who pursues more. Here we ask you to reflect on why you do what you do, whichever role you identify with more. If you avoid or withdraw, why do you do that? Is it about power or about being afraid of change or about being afraid of conflict? How does physiology or upbringing fit in with your pattern? If you tend to pursue, why? What are you seeking when you pursue? Are you looking for more intimacy or for proof of commitment?

Talking About Your Thinking

After reflecting on your own understanding of what you do in your relationship, plan some time together to discuss your perceptions. You should focus on this being an open, nonconflictual talk. Share with each other your own perceptions of why *you* do what *you* do, not why you think your partner does what he or she does. This is a time to share and feel closer—a start to understanding how to communicate more effectively.

Part II

Teaming Up to Handle Conflict

4

When What You Heard Isn't What I Said: Understanding Filters in Communication

Have you ever noticed that what your partner hears can be very different from what you were trying to say? You may say something you think is harmless, and suddenly your spouse is mad at you. Or you may ask a question, such as "What do you want for dinner?" and your partner starts complaining about your not doing your share of the work.

We have all experienced the frustration of being misunderstood. You think you are being clear, but your partner just doesn't seem to "get it." Or maybe you are just sure you "know" what she said yesterday, and today she says something that seems completely different.

Like the rest of us, Mary and Bob can relate to this common problem. Their jobs leave them exhausted at the end of each day. One Thursday night, Bob was home first and reading the paper while waiting for Mary. He was thinking, "I sure am wiped. I bet she is, too. I'd really like to go out to eat and just relax with her tonight." Good idea, right? Here is what happened (what they are thinking or hearing is in parentheses):

BOB: (*thinking he'd like to go out to dinner with Mary, as she comes in the door*) What should we do for dinner tonight?

MARY: (*hears "When will dinner be ready?"*) Why is it always my job to make dinner? I work as hard as you do.

BOB: *(hears her response as an attack and thinks, "Why is she always so negative?")* It is not *always* your job to make dinner. I made dinner once last week!

MARY: *(The negative cycle continues, because Mary tends to feel she does everything around the house.)* Bringing home hamburgers and fries is *not* making dinner, Bob.

BOB: *(With frustration mounting, he gives up.)* Just forget it. I didn't want to go out with you anyway.

MARY: *(confused, as she can't remember him saying anything about going out)* You never said anything about wanting to go out.

BOB: *(feeling really angry)* Yes I did! I asked you where you wanted to go out to dinner, and you got really nasty.

MARY: I got nasty? You never said anything about going out.

BOB: Did too!

MARY: You're never wrong, are you?

Sound familiar? You can see where things went wrong for them on this evening. Bob had a great idea, a positive idea, yet conflict blew out the evening. Bob was not as clear as he could have been in telling Mary what he was thinking. This left a lot of room for interpretation, and interpret Mary did. She assumed that he was asking—no, telling—her to get dinner on the table as she walked in the door.

This kind of miscommunication is all too common and frequent in relationships. Many of the biggest arguments start with one of you misunderstanding what the other meant, with the misunderstanding itself being what then drives the angry words. What is it that gets in the way of clear communication? Filters.

Filters change what goes through them. A furnace filter takes dust and dirt out of the air. A filter on a camera lens alters the properties of the light passing through it. A coffee filter lets the flavor through and leaves the gunk behind. As with any other filter, what goes through our "communication filters" is different than what comes out. When what you say (or what you intended to say) is not the same as what your partner heard, then a filter is at work.

FIVE KEY FILTERS

We all have many kinds of filters packed into our heads. These affect what we hear, what we say, and how we interpret things. They are based on how we are feeling; what we think; what we have experienced in our life, family, and cultural background; and so on. Let's look at five types of filters that can affect couples as they struggle for clear communication:

1. Distractions

2. Emotional states

3. Beliefs and expectations

4. Differences in style

5. Self-protection

Distractions

A very basic kind of filter has to do with attention. When you say something to your partner, do you have his or her attention, or don't you? Both external and internal factors in your environment can affect your ability to pay attention. External factors are such things as noisy kids, a hearing problem, a bad phone line, or background noise at a party. Internal factors include feeling tired, thinking about something else, or planning what you still have to do this evening. The key is to make sure that you have your partner's attention and that you give your attention when it really counts most. For important talks, find a quiet place if you can, and don't answer the phone or turn on the TV. Make it easier to pay attention to one another, and try not to assume that your partner is ready to listen right now just because you are ready to talk. Ask.

Emotional States

Moods greatly affect communication. For example, a number of studies demonstrate that we tend to give people more benefit of the doubt when we're in a good mood and less when we're in a bad

RAGNAR STORAASLI

mood. If you are in a bad mood, you are more likely to perceive whatever your partner says or does more negatively, no matter how positive he or she is trying to be. Have you noticed that sometimes, when your spouse is in a bad mood, you get jumped on no matter how nicely you say something? (We know that you never do this, so we won't ask if you ever notice how your moods affect your mate.)

The best defense against allowing these kinds of filters to damage your relationship is to acknowledge the filter when you are aware that it's there. Here is an example. Marta had a stressful day at work. She just got home. It's dinnertime, and she's in the kitchen cooking macaroni. Tom just got home, too. He's sitting in his favorite easy chair reading the mail.

Tom: This bill for the phone company got missed again. We better get this paid.

Marta: *(snapping with anger)* I'm not the one who forgot it. Can't you see I have my hands full? Do something helpful.

Tom: I'm sorry. I should have seen you were busy. Rough day?

Marta: Yes. I had a very frustrating day. I don't mean to snap at you, but I've had it up to here. If I'm touchy, it's not really anything you've done.

Tom: Maybe we can talk about it some after dinner.

Marta: Thanks.

Without using the word "filter," Tom and Marta acknowledged one was there. Marta had a bad day and was on edge. They could have let this conversation escalate into an argument, but Tom had the good sense to see he had raised an issue at the wrong time. He decided not to get defensive and chose to become gentle with Marta in her frustration. Marta responded by telling Tom, in essence, that she had a filter going—her bad mood. Knowing this helped him be less defensive in reaction to her mood. Don't use a filter as a reason to treat your partner badly.

Many kinds of emotional filters can exist in any one person. If you are angry, worried, sad, or upset about anything, it can color your interpretation of what your partner says and your response. Tom's response was helpful because it opened the door for Marta to clarify her emotional filter and allowed them to de-escalate and be clear with one another.

Beliefs and Expectations

Many very important filters arise from how you think and what you expect in your relationship. Many studies in the fields of psychology, medicine, and law demonstrate that people tend to see what they expect to see in others and in situations. You are not immune to the tendency to look for or hear in others what you are expecting. If you think you are, that's an arrogance you might want to do without in life. Trust us: you do this, though some people do it far more than others. It takes some humility to accept that you don't always get it right in how you size up others or their motivations.

Studies show that expectations not only affect what we perceive but can influence the actual behavior of those around us. For example, if you believe that someone is an extrovert, she is more likely to sound like an extrovert when talking with you, even if she is normally introverted. We "pull" behavior from others consistent with what we expect. This is why, in part, so many old habits and patterns of communication come back with full force during the holidays when you are around the family you grew up in (if you do not regularly see them). Everyone's got their expectation filters working, and everyone is reacting to the mix.

This next example shows how difficult it can be to get around mental filters. Alex and Helen are a couple who came to one of our workshops. They were having problems deciding what to do for fun when they had free time. But they rarely got their act together to get out and do something, so both were frustrated. This conversation was typical for them. Note how each acted as if they could read the mind of the other:

ALEX: (really wanting to go bowling, but thinking that Helen was not interested in going out and doing anything fun together) We have some free time tonight. I wonder if we should try to do something.

HELEN: (thinking that she would like to get out but hearing the tentativeness in his voice and thinking he really doesn't want to go out) Oh, I don't know. What do you think?

ALEX: Well, we could go bowling, but it could be league night, and we might not get in anyway. Maybe we should just stay in and watch TV.

HELEN: (thinking "Aha, that's what he really wants to do") That's sounds good to me. Why don't we make some popcorn and watch the tube?

ALEX: (He's disappointed, thinking "I knew it. She really doesn't want to make the effort to get out and do something fun.") Yeah, OK.

In this conversation, there was no escalation, invalidation, or with-drawal. Nevertheless, they did not communicate well due to the fil-ters involved. Alex's belief that Helen doesn't like to go out colored the entire conversation so much that the way he asked her to go out led her to think that he wanted to stay in. He "knew" that she really didn't want to go. That's called mind reading. As we discussed in Chapter Two, the kind of mind reading that damages marriages most is the kind that includes a negative assumption about what the other is thinking or feeling. In other words, you think you know why your partner said or did something, and you judge him or her based on your guess. Of course, we are all sometimes right when we mind-read like this. But we are very often wrong. This is a specific form of neg-ative interpretation that can be especially difficult to stop. Try hard.

Alex could see only that they stayed in once again because that is what Helen wanted. His mental filter pulled the conversation in this direction and became a self-fulfilling prophecy. Helen also did a good deal of mind reading. In this conversation, she assumed she knew that Alex really wanted to stay in, and participated in a dis-torted conversation in which neither said what he or she wanted. If they had been able to communicate clearly, without any filters, they would have concluded that both of them wanted to get out and would have probably tried the bowling idea first.

Differences in Style

Everyone has a different style of communicating, and different styles can lead to filtering. Perhaps one of you is much more expressive and one of you more reserved. You may have some trouble under-standing each other because you use such different styles.

Styles are determined by many influences, including culture, gender, and upbringing. Sometimes, style differences rooted in fam-ily backgrounds can cause great misunderstandings, becoming pow-erful filters that distort communication.

Sue and Tod came from very different families. His family has always been very expressive of all manner of emotion. They tend to show great intensity when emotional. It's just their way. Sue's family has always been more reserved. As a result, a slight raising of the voice could mean great anger in her family, whereas it would hardly be noticed in Tod's. In many conversations, therefore, Sue would overestimate the intensity of Tod's feelings, and Tod would underestimate Sue's feelings. For example:

TOD: What did it cost to get the muffler fixed?

SUE: Four hundred and twenty-eight bucks.

TOD: (intense, getting red quickly) What? How could they possibly charge that much! That's outrageous.

SUE: (lashing out) I wish you could stop yelling at me! I've told you over and over that I cannot listen to you when you are yelling!

TOD: I am not yelling at you. I just can't believe it could cost that much.

SUE: Why can't we have a quiet conversation like other people? My sister and brother-in-law never yell at each other.

TOD: They don't talk about anything, either. Look, four hundred and twenty-eight dollars is too much to pay, that's all I'm reacting to.

SUE: Why don't you take the car in next time. I'm tired of being yelled at for things like this.

TOD: Honey, look. I'm not upset at you. I'm upset at them. And you know I can get pretty hot, but I'm not trying to say you did anything wrong.

SUE: (calming down) Well, it seems that way sometimes.

TOD: Well, I'm not upset at you. Let me give that place a call. Where's the number?

Sue and Tod are caught up in a misunderstanding based on differences in style. You'd think that after so many years of marriage they'd understand each other a little better, but even so, they did a great job of not allowing things to escalate. As in preceding examples in which the conversation got back on track, one partner figured out that there was a filter distorting the intended message and took corrective action. Here, Tod forcefully clarifies that he is not mad at Sue.

Being more aware of how your differing styles affect your communication can go a long way toward preventing misunderstandings. We recommend that you give some thought to these differences between the two of you and talk about their effect on your communication.

Self-Protection

This last kind of filter comes right from the fear of rejection with which we all struggle in intimate relationships such as marriage. Fear is the big enemy of secure and warm attachment. This filter is operating when our fear of rejection stops us from saying what we truly want or feel. Even something as simple as, "Wouldn't you like to go see that new movie with me?" can reflect a fear of rejection. Instead of expressing it directly ("I'd like to see that new movie; want to go?"), we often hide our desire because directly speaking of it reveals more of who we are, and that increases the risk of rejection. This may not matter a lot when it comes to movies, but when it comes to feelings, desires, and expectations in marriage, a lot of misunderstanding can result.

Think of this filter as causing you not to know each other as well as you otherwise might. As we discuss in more detail in the next chapter, when this filter is operating, you may not say what you really feel or need in your relationship, for fear of a negative reaction that leads to being hurt.

THE JOYS OF MEMORY MATCHING

Some of the biggest arguments couples have are about what was actually said in the past. How often have you wished that you had a tape recording of a previous conversation? This happens to all of us. These differences in memory occur in great measure because of the variety of filters that operate in all relationships. Any of the filters we've discussed can lead to differences—and arguments—about what was actually said or done in the past.

One great nonmarital example of this happened in major league baseball. A New York Mets player was quoted in the paper as saying something derogatory about a teammate. The teammate confronted him, and the player denied the slam. The offended player then confronted the reporter, who said he had the remarks on tape. A meeting was arranged between the three of them, and the recording clearly indicated that the player had indeed made insulting remarks. Upon hearing the tape, he said, "But that's not what I meant!" Having a tape recording at these frustrating times would not be as useful as you think. (But it could be really fun for others to watch!)

Read again the conversation between Bob and Mary in this chapter. Notice that they ended up arguing about what was actually said at the start of the conversation. He truly thinks he asked her out to dinner, but what he said was vague. She truly thinks he told her to get dinner on the table, which also is not what he said.

Think for a moment. Unless you just met last week, you probably can think of some whopper arguments that the two of you have had over memory disputes. We do not know any couples who are able to argue about whose memory is more defective and then end up sharing moments of romantic bliss. This train does not go to that station. But there is a nice sheer cliff that it runs along; you can get a great view just before you tumble over the side and crash down the mountain.

We recommend two things that can save your relationship from such fruitless arguments about the past. First, don't assume your memory is perfect. Have the humility to accept that it isn't. There's that H word again. It's nice to see that colleagues in our field are finding this word more and more useful in thinking about what couples need more of to stay happy and connected. There are countless studies in the field of psychology that show how fragile human memory is, how susceptible it is to distortion by motivation and beliefs. Yours is not as good as you tend to think it is. Accept that you both have filters and that there is plenty of room for you to say or hear things differently than what was intended.

Second, when you disagree, don't persist in arguments about what was actually said in the past. You will get nowhere. Don't get stuck in the past, even if it was five minutes ago. Shift the topic to what you each think and feel in the present. A lot of times, doing this takes humility, because the fastest path out of arguments about memory is to say something like this: "I'm not sure what I said exactly, but I want to tell you what I meant to say, OK?" Listen carefully and nondefensively when your partner clarifies something in this way. Something very artful is happening, and you don't want to miss it.

Slow down here a bit and think about this. Maybe even meditate on it. In the argument between Bob and Mary, note how a response of *humility* on the part of Bob would have defused the entire argument. That would require moving to a more *gentle* stance and putting away any need to win the argument about what words were just said. What if Bob were to say this: "You know, I'm not sure what I said when you came in the door. Maybe I wasn't clear. What I meant to say is that I wanted to take you out to dinner and just relax. I know you've had a hard week, and I have, too. I'm sorry if I was not clear enough."

> Gentleness and humility are the most powerful forces you have for staying close and keeping love alive.

What is our great need to defend our memories? Instead of clarifying what we wanted to convey, with humility, most of us are prone to risk days of peace and harmony in our marriages to win this point about mental superiority. Is this a kind of insecurity? Is it because we feel invalidated by what our partner assumed? Life's way too short (and so is your memory) to waste this time and squander close connection in this way. We now come to one of the points in this book where we'll say something of such profound importance that if you both really get it, and act on it, you are virtually guaranteed an awesome relationship: gentleness and humility are the most powerful forces you have for staying close and keeping love alive.

LOOK FOR FILTERS AND
USE THIS CONCEPT

We hope you understand how important it is to be aware of filters in your communication with one another. We all have filters. Either we react to them with little awareness, which can cause damage to the relationship, or we learn to look for them when conversations go awry. Get in the habit of "announcing your filter" when you are aware that you have one.

For example, suppose you've had a bad day and are mad at your boss. When you come home, share what happened with your partner and then say, "So if I seem short or distant, it's not you, it's because of what happened at work." Or suppose you've had a recent argument with your spouse about an issue, such as sex, and you are having another meeting to talk about it. You might say, "I know I'm sensitive about sex, so I may not be real clear in what I'm trying to tell you right now, but I'm very clear that I want us to understand each other better here."

The two most important things about filters are that (1) everyone has them, and (2) filters are not intrinsically good or bad. What counts is whether or not you let them distort your communication. We all have differing moods and levels of attention, and differences in beliefs, experiences, and upbringing. These can all result in filters that block clear communication. The goal is to recognize filters before they can do any damage.

Talking Points

1. We all have filters, and they are constantly affecting what we say and hear.

2. Humility is the little-used greatest power for good in your relationship.

3. Recognizing and acknowledging your filters will go a long way toward improving your communication and your relationship.

 EXERCISE

Thinking About Your Filters

Here is the list of filters once again. The exercise we recommend is pretty simple. Think of some situations in which you felt misunderstood. What type of filter or filters could have been distorting things? What could *you* have said that would have derailed the hurt and pulled the two of you back together? If you can practice some of those kinds of statements in your mind, you'll find it easier to come up with them in the moments when things are starting to go sideways.

1. Distractions

2. Emotional states

3. Beliefs and expectations

4. Differences in style

5. Self-protection

Although we are dealing here with intimate relationships, you could profitably do this exercise in relation to your communication with anyone important in your life—family, colleagues, supervisors.

Talking Safely Without Fighting: The Speaker-Listener Technique

Communication is the lifeblood of a good relationship; it keeps all the good things flowing and removes blockages that most couples experience day-to-day. In fact, in our most recent research, couples reported that tools for communicating well were the single most beneficial aspect of what we teach in our PREP workshops. However, knowing how important communication is and being able to do it well are very different things. Every couple we've talked to agrees that good communication is a very important goal for their relationship, yet most couples have never learned to communicate well when it counts most.

WHEN TALKING SAFELY COUNTS MOST

When do most couples have the greatest difficulty talking well?

- When having a disagreement or a conflict—about money, chores, child rearing, in-laws, and the like. These are conflicts in which the odds of escalation and invalidation are high.

- When talking about something very sensitive that's difficult to talk about using your normal communication styles—about feeling lonely in the relationship or

about sex and sensuality, for example. These are talks
in which invalidation cuts deep.

What do these two situations have in common? One or both
partners may fear that the conversation will not go very well; there
is fear of conflict, fear of frustration, fear of rejection, or some combination of these. The antidote to these kinds of fear is feeling safe.
Every couple has to have a safe way to talk about everyday disagreements and the deeper, more sensitive issues. It doesn't have to
be our way, but it has to be some way. Read on as we get to the heart
of how to talk without fighting.

When You Are in Conflict

Mike and Tracy are a couple who, whenever they started talking about
one of their everyday issues—whether it was money, children, or
chores—they would quickly acceler-
ate into using one of the destructive
patterns of fighting. They were still
very much in love, but they recognized the danger signs and knew that
they needed a better way to deal
with the inevitable conflicts that
came from being married three years,
raising a young child, and having
two full-time careers. Like so many couples, they needed to learn how
to talk safely without fighting when they were upset about their issues.

*The deepest kind of intimacy
develops when one partner
shares something he or she feels
vulnerable about, and the other
partner responds in a positive
and accepting manner.*

We spent the chapter on the danger signs as well as most of the
chapters on gender differences and filters talking about the theme
of safety and about how conflicts are played out between partners.

When You Are Talking About Sensitive Themes

Talking safely about sensitive, deeper issues promotes those feelings of intimacy that come from knowing you can share who you
are *and* be accepted by your partner. That's the essence of being a

great friend to your partner. In our chapter on friendship, we will help you build on your natural tendencies to talk as friends and share intimate feelings about topics that feel safe and are fun to talk about. In this chapter, we are talking about situations in which one or both of you might get upset in a way that would damage your ability to talk constructively and safely about a sensitive topic. At these times, you need ways to communicate that allow you to express what you might otherwise fear saying. The Speaker-Listener Technique we teach you here can be a powerful way to help you talk safely, not only about conflicts but about any sensitive topic.

Taking the Risk

James Cordova of the University of Illinois at Urbana-Champaign conducts research on intimacy. He suggests that the deepest kind of intimacy develops when one partner shares something he or she feels vulnerable about, and the other partner responds in a positive and accepting manner. That response of warm acceptance does something very powerful that transforms a relationship. It makes it more likely that each partner will continue to risk being emotionally vulnerable in the future, in large part because there is a growing expectation that it is safe to do so.

As a couple, you can get on a roll with these kinds of experiences. Safety begets more intimacy, and shared intimacy fosters deeper feelings of safety. Most couples remember very well the power of this snowballing positivity from the days of falling in love. It's a kind of positive escalation.

Have you grown to fear taking this kind of risk in your relationship? That's a worrisome sign of distance creeping in. To stay deeply attached, you need to keep the ability to share intimacy.

By safe, we do not mean risk free. If you are going to share what you are concerned with, hurt by, or hoping for, you are going to take the risk of being hurt by your partner. There is a direct relationship between risk and reward in much of life—especially in marriage. For many couples, what they are risking is the erosion of love that occurs when one's spouse, the person from whom people expect the most respect and acceptance, comes to be associated with pain and rejection.

You cannot be accepted deeply without offering something deep for your partner to accept. There's the rub. You can take the risk, share deeply, and be rejected. This hurts a lot, because you have chosen to risk a deeper part of yourself in the relationship. If your sharing goes well, you find a deep, soul-satisfying acceptance of who you are, no matter how flawed.

THE VALUE OF STRUCTURE

For your relationship to grow as you talk as friends, reveal inner feelings, and handle unavoidable marital conflicts, you need to work together as a team to keep the damaging patterns—escalation, invalidation, withdrawal, and negative interpretations—from happening. One way to do this is to use agreed-on strategies and techniques to help you in important conversations. We call this adding structure to your interaction. Structure can bring some degree of predictability and order to what can be chaotic and emotional topics. It is one of the best means of regulating the inevitable negative emotions that we all experience in marriage.

There are many places where you already take this principle of structure for granted. For example, if you work in a moderately large (or larger) company, there are likely to be some fairly clear rules about how, when, and to whom certain kinds of things can be communicated. The clearer the rules and agreement with them, the better the business is likely to run. If the rules are unstated or unclear, especially regarding how to handle conflicts, people will be more on edge and less secure about what to expect. It's the same in your relationship—we want you to agree in advance how and when you will talk when you really need to.

Please note that the structure is not an end in itself. As is true in many people's workplaces, some structure makes it easier to get the work done efficiently and as a team. But structure is only a tool for getting to the final product. Adding structure to your interaction is just like using scaffolding when constructing or renovating a building. The scaffolding is not part of the building; it's a means to the end of getting the job done safely. You might have noticed that the couple on the front cover of this book is standing on scaffolding. We want to help you reach places that are otherwise hard for many couples to get to.

Another great example of how structure can be useful is in sports. Any sport has a set of rules that define what is OK and what is not OK, what is in bounds and out, and when the action starts and when it should stop. Without the structure that the rules provide, all you would have is chaos. The rules do not define what's great about the sport; they simply make it possible for two teams to engage in it. Our approach allows you and your partner to use some agreed-on rules to level the playing field. Both of you can listen, and both can be heard.

In essence, we are asking you to consider how structure makes various kinds of interaction safe in ways you already readily accept in life, and then to apply that way of thinking to some aspects of your relationship. With adequate structure, you can manage conflict and talk about sensitive issues with less chance of damage to your relationship. When less is at stake, or when there is a good feeling about a difficult issue, you don't need much structure. Just communicate in whatever way you are most comfortable. But at other times, a bit of structure can get you through without damage, and maybe with greater closeness.

We have found a very effective way to teach couples how to talk openly and safely: the Speaker-Listener Technique. It's a way to communicate more safely and slowly when discussing something that one or both of you don't feel very safe talking about.

THE SPEAKER-LISTENER TECHNIQUE

The Speaker-Listener Technique offers you an alternative way of communicating when issues are hot or sensitive, or likely to get that way. Any conversation in which you want to enhance clarity and safety can benefit from this technique. Most (although not all) couples can decide whether to go out for Chinese food without this technique, but fewer can handle emotionally sensitive issues around money, sex, or in-laws, for example, without the safety net that such a technique can provide. Furthermore, one of the best things you can do for your relationship is to develop the confidence that you can deal with whatever issues come your way in life, as a team and without fear.

We have found particular success with the Speaker-Listener Technique because it is so simple and very effective. Most couples we've worked with over the years really appreciate this technique. In our research, it's the number one technique that couples report helps them the most. We ask you to give this a thorough tryout in your relationship. If you decide it's not for you, so be it. If you have another way of talking when in conflict or when it's hard to be vulnerable, that's great. If you do not, here you go. Try it out, and then make it yours with practice. Start by studying the rules for how to use the Speaker-Listener Technique (see box).

The Speaker-Listener Technique

Rules for Both of You

1. *The Speaker has the floor.* Use a real object to designate the floor. We're pretty concrete; we have actually given couples pieces of linoleum, so when someone says they have the "floor," they really mean it! You can use any-

thing, though: the TV remote, a pen, a paperback book. The point is that you have to use some specific object, because if you do not have the floor, you are the Listener. As Speaker and Listener you follow the rules for each role.

2. *Share the floor.* You share the floor over the course of a conversation. The Speaker is the first one to hold the floor. After the Speaker talks, you switch roles and continue, the floor changing hands regularly. This is a trust issue: you trust that you will have the floor when you need it, so you can pass it to your partner when he or she needs it.

3. *No problem solving.* When using this technique, you are going to focus on having good discussions, not on trying to come to solutions. When you focus on solving a problem, you are far less likely to really hear what each other thinks about that problem. We have more to say on that in the problem-solving chapter, but for now, take our advice and learn to avoid trying to solve problems prematurely.

Rules for the Speaker

1. *Speak for yourself. Don't mind-read.* Talk about your thoughts, feelings, and concerns, not your perceptions of the Listener's point of view or motives. Try to use "I" statements, and talk about your own point of view and feelings. "I was upset when you forgot our date," is an "I" statement. "I think you don't care about me" is not.

2. *Don't go on and on.* You will have plenty of opportunity to say all you need to say. To help the Listener listen actively, it's very important that you keep what you say in manageable pieces. If you are in the habit of delivering monologues, remember that having the floor protects you from interruption. You can afford to pause to be sure your partner understands you.

3. *Stop and let the Listener paraphrase.* After saying a bit, stop and allow the Listener to paraphrase what you just said. If the paraphrase was not quite accurate, you should politely and gently restate what you meant to say in a way that helps your partner understand. This is not a test! You want to make it possible for your partner to understand you as well as he or she can.

Rules for the Listener

1. *Paraphrase what you hear.* You must paraphrase what the Speaker is saying. Briefly repeat back what you heard the Speaker say, using your own words if you like, and make sure you understand what was said. When you take the time to restate what you heard, you show your partner that you are listening. If you truly don't understand some phrase or example, you may ask the Speaker to clarify, but you need to limit yourself to just asking for explanations.

2. *Don't rebut. Focus on the Speaker's message.* While in the Listener role, you may not offer your opinion or thoughts. This is the hardest part of being a good Listener. If you are upset by what your partner says, you need to edit out any response you may want to make and *pay attention* to what your partner is saying. Wait until you get the floor to make your response. You will have your chance, and when you do, you'll want your partner to extend the same courtesy to you. When you are the Listener, your job is to speak only in the service of understanding your partner. Any words or gestures to show your opinion are not allowed, including making faces!

Before showing how this technique works in a conversation, we want to give you some ideas about what good paraphrases can sound like. Suppose your spouse says to you, "I had a really tough day. Mom got on my case about how I handled the arrangements for Dad's party. Ugh!" Any of the following might be an excellent paraphrase:

"Sounds like you had a really tough day."

"So, your mom was critical of how you handled the party, and really got on you about it."

"Bad day, huh?"

Any one of these responses conveys that you have listened and displays what you have understood. A good paraphrase can be short or long, detailed or general. At times, if you are uncertain of how to get a paraphrase started, it can help to begin with "What I hear you saying is . . ." Then you fill in what you just heard your partner say. Another way to begin a paraphrase is with the words "Sounds like you think [feel, want] . . ."

When using the Speaker-Listener Technique, the Speaker is always the one who determines if the Listener's paraphrase was on target. Only the Speaker knows what the intended message is. If the paraphrase is not quite on target, it is very important that the Speaker gently clarify or restate the point—not respond angrily or critically. Remember that you and your partner may be dealing with filters that make it difficult to paraphrase accurately. This is your best opportunity to correct any misperceptions or misunderstandings before they interfere with your communication efforts.

When you're in the Listener role, be sincere in your effort to show you are listening carefully and respectfully. Even when you disagree with the point your partner is making, your goal is to show respect for—and validation of—his or her perspective. That means waiting your turn and not making faces or looking angry. You can completely disagree with your mate about something and still show respect. Just wait until you have the floor to make your points.

Sometimes just keeping track of who has the floor—who's the Speaker right now and who's the Listener—is enough to get a couple back on track. Natalie Jenkins, who leads our efforts to reach couples and professionals with the PREP approach, tells audiences a wonderful story about how she got this point across to her daughter and son one day when they were having a nasty argument. After she helped these two youngsters stop escalating, she noticed their toy Mr. Potato Head on the shelf nearby. Natalie, not being one to miss opportunities, took Mr. Potato Head and pulled off his two ears and his tongue. (He couldn't scream—she had his tongue!)

You can completely disagree with your mate about something and still show respect.

Natalie gave the tongue to one of them and the ears to the other, and said, "when you have the tongue, you can speak. When you have the ears, you need to just listen to what the other is trying to tell you." They got the message. Communication works a whole lot better when it's clear whose turn it is to get his or her point across. In her work with adults, Natalie has also noted that we were given two ears and one mouth. Does that suggest where the emphasis needs to be when communicating with others?

When you are using the Speaker-Listener Technique, if the Speaker wishes to ask a question, the most structured way to handle that is to ask the question, have the Listener paraphrase the question to make sure he or she heard it clearly, and then pass the floor so that the Listener becomes the Speaker and can answer the question. We recommend you practice it this way, at least at the start. After you get comfortable with the flow of the technique, you can decide later how to customize it for the two of you.

Using the Speaker-Listener Technique

Here is an example of how this technique can change a conversation that is going nowhere into a real opportunity for communication. Peter and Tessie are in their mid-thirties, with four kids ages two to ten. For years they have had a problem dealing with issues. Peter consistently avoids discussing problem areas, and if cornered by Tessie, he withdraws by pulling into himself. They know they need to communicate more clearly and safely on tough topics and have agreed that the structure of the Speaker-Listener Technique can help.

In this case, Peter and Tessie have been locked in the pursuit-withdrawal cycle about the issue of son Jeremy's preschool. However, they have been practicing the Speaker-Listener Technique and are ready to try something different. Let's see what happens.

TESSIE: I'm really getting tired of leaving Jeremy's preschool up in the air. We have got to deal with this, now.

PETER: (*not looking up from the TV*) Oh? I'm not up for this now.

TESSIE: (*walking over and standing in front of the TV*) Peter, we can't just leave this decision hanging in the air. I'm getting really ticked off about you putting it off.

PETER: (*recognizing that this would be a wise time to act constructively and not withdraw*) Time out. I can tell we need to talk, but I have been avoiding it because it seems that talking just leads to us fighting. I don't want that. Let's try that Speaker-Listener Technique we've been practicing.

This is not a "normal" way to communicate, but it is a relatively safe way to communicate on difficult issues. Each will get to talk, each will be heard, and both will show commitment to discussing the problems constructively. If you tend to withdraw, this technique can help you move constructively toward your partner when he or she is pursuing something. This movement attacks the foundation of the pursuer's belief that the withdrawer does not care about the relationship.

The conversation proceeds, with Peter picking up a piece of carpet they use for the floor.

PETER (SPEAKER): I've also been pretty concerned about where we send Jeremy to preschool, and I'm not even sure this is the year to do it.

TESSIE (LISTENER): You have been concerned, too, and you're partly not sure he's ready.

PETER (SPEAKER): Yeah, that's it. He acts pretty young for his age, and I am not sure how he would do, unless the situation were just right.

Note how Peter acknowledges that Tessie's summary is on the mark before moving on to another point.

TESSIE (LISTENER): You're worried that he wouldn't hold his own with older-acting kids, right?

Tessie is not quite sure she has understood Peter's point, so she makes her paraphrase tentative.

PETER (SPEAKER): Well, partly that's it, but I'm also not sure if he's ready to be away from you that much. Honestly, part of what I think I'm reacting to is that this transition was very hard for me when I was a kid. I had a lot of trouble in school because I was so young. Maybe I'm overreacting, but I still feel pretty anxious about it.

Note how Peter gently clarifies. He's moving forward in the conversation, rather than backward. In general, whenever the Listener feels that clarification is needed, the Speaker should use his next statement to restate or expand on what he is trying to get across.

TESSIE (LISTENER): So, you are feeling torn about him needing me a lot, but really more important, this brings up things you felt really vulnerable about as a kid, and that makes it that much harder.

PETER (SPEAKER): Yes. That's right. Here, you take the floor. (He hands Tessie the floor.)

TESSIE (SPEAKER): Well, I appreciate what you are saying. Actually, I hadn't realized your feelings were this deep about this. I was worried that you didn't care about it.

As the Speaker now, Tessie validates the comments Peter has made.

PETER (LISTENER): Sounds like you're glad to hear that I am concerned, and you were afraid that my not wanting to deal with it meant I didn't care about you.

TESSIE (SPEAKER): Yes. This really helps a lot to understand you. I agree that this is not an easy decision.

PETER (LISTENER): It's making you feel better that we are talking this through.

TESSIE (SPEAKER): Big time. It also confirms something I had thought anyway, that if we did put him in preschool this year, it would have to be just the right place. We'd both have to feel really right about it.

PETER (LISTENER): You're saying that it would have to be just the right preschool for it to be worth doing this year.

TESSIE (SPEAKER): Exactly. I think that it might be worth trying if we could find a great environment for him.

Tessie feels good with Peter listening so carefully, and lets him know it.

PETER (LISTENER): So you would try it if we found just the right setting.

TESSIE (SPEAKER): I *might* try it; I'm not sure I'm ready to say I *would* try it.

PETER (LISTENER): You're not ready to say you would definitely want to do it, even with a perfect preschool.

TESSIE (SPEAKER): Right. Here, you take the floor again.

As you can tell, they have been practicing quite a bit. They are both doing an excellent job following the rules and showing concern and respect for each other's viewpoints. Couples can have discussions like this on difficult topics, even when they disagree. The keys are to make the discussion safe and to show respect for your partner's thoughts, feelings, and opinions. With practice, the process can become far more natural than it will seem to be at first.

We would like you to note something very important in the conversation between Peter and Tessie, something we've seen hundreds of time with couples. What initially seems to be a simple conflict and disagreement (albeit about something very important) really has a lot more to it than appears at first glance. It's only because they are talking safely here that they get to two key pieces of information. One is that Peter is more deeply affected by this subject because of how it was handled when he was a child. The other is that Tessie was starting to make a pretty negative interpretation of why he was avoiding, thinking that maybe he just didn't care about her.

In summary, the couple's discussion is a conflictual talk made safe in a way that leads to an intimate talk about more sensitive themes. This does not always happen, of course, but it happens a lot when couples have a safe way to talk. There are many ways to be intimate and close in your relationship (and we'll get to almost all of them in later chapters), but this is one of the most powerful ways of all. Here, because it's safe, Tessie and Peter come closer together on an emotional level when the issue could have driven them farther apart.

Their conversation demonstrates exactly the best possible way to use the Speaker-Listener Technique. Because their conflict talks go so well with the technique, couples like Peter and Tessie start to talk about sensitive issues as a way to feel more intimate and closer to each other. Being vulnerable to each other and feeling safe and good about that are added benefits of using the Speaker-Listener Technique.

Some helpful hints: to ease into the use of the technique, you will find it helpful to focus on nonrelationship issues at first. The point of your first practice sessions is to learn to talk in this new way, not to resolve relationship issues. By talking about the last movie you saw, your dream vacation, or the project you are doing at work, you keep some of the stress out of the conversation until you are more skilled with the process. In the exercises at the end of the chapter, we will take you through a progression of issues, moving at the speed at which you are comfortable, as you gain confidence in your skills.

The Advantages of Using the Speaker-Listener Technique

The Speaker-Listener Technique has many advantages over unstructured conversation when there is any fear that the talk won't go well. Perhaps most important, it counteracts the destructive styles of communication described in Chapter Two.

1. *Escalation*. The structure of the technique makes it much harder to get into escalation. In fact, it is nearly impossible to escalate if you both follow the rules and work at showing respect. It is difficult to scream at one another if you have to stop every few sentences and ask for a paraphrase! The momentum of escalation is stopped dead.

2. *Invalidation*. The simple process of paraphrasing intervenes effectively with invalidation because the Speaker gets immediate feedback that she was heard. You can enhance the validation by saying "I understand" or "I see what you mean" at the end of a paraphrase or when you get the floor. This does not mean that you agree, just that you can see the issue from the other's perspective. Save agreement or disagreement for your turn as Speaker. This principle bears one more repeat: you do not have to agree with your partner to be a good listener.

You do not have to agree with your partner to be a good listener.

3. *Filters and negative interpretations*. The Speaker-Listener Technique makes it much easier to identify filters as soon as they come up. They will be evident in the paraphrases. The Speaker will have a nonthreatening opportunity to say, "That's not quite what I said. I said [such-and-such]. Could you paraphrase again, please?" In this way, filters are recognized right away, and the distortions they cause can be addressed. Using the technique can help you catch and correct those very destructive negative interpretations.

4. *Pursuit and withdrawal*. For the spouse who tends to withdraw from conversations in which conflict is possible, the structure makes

it much safer to remain in the conversation. With a clear sense that both of you are committed to keeping things from getting out of hand, withdrawers have less to be anxious about. Conflict is less likely to occur in an unmanageable way. For the spouse who is usually in the pursuer role, structure in conversations ensures that he or she will be heard and that issues are going to be addressed. Pursuing is less useful or necessary, as the withdrawer feels safer and more willing to address issues. This gets you both closer to a win-win situation and out of hopeless win-lose cycles.

Our research shows that couples benefit from learning to use structure when handling conflict. Agreed-on rules like the Speaker-Listener Technique add some degree of predictability, which reduces anxiety and avoidance, helping both of you win rather than lose when dealing with conflict. You need to work together to fight negative patterns rather than fight each other.

One Last Pause for Thought

We want to add one more skill to this chapter. In Chapter Eight you will learn a set of ground rules to help implement the skills we teach in your day-to-day life. Here we will introduce an idea that flows from our ground rule concepts and can help you put the Speaker-Listener Technique into practice.

When conflict is escalating in a discussion, or when a conversation is just not going well, we recommend that couples call a "Pause." Just as when you push the pause button on your VCR or DVD player, you freeze the action. Both of you agree to halt the negative interaction and start over—after taking a break or right away—using the Speaker-Listener Technique.

At times, it may make sense just to say, "Let's hit the rewind button and start again." For example, one couple we know had a fight over the phone in which all four danger sign patterns were used within two minutes. The husband was about to angrily hang up on his wife because he momentarily felt there was no other way to stop her yelling at him. But he saved the day by saying to himself, "I need to Pause—I know I'll feel terrible if I hang up on her." Instead, after a few deep breaths, he said as nicely as possible, "Honey, this isn't going anywhere. Let's take a break, and let me call you back in ten minutes, OK? Remember, no matter what, I love you." She agreed, and ten minutes later he called back and started by saying, "Honey, let's pretend we didn't have the previous call. I'll hit the rewind button and we can start again, OK? . . . OK, tell me about your day." That's the Pause that refreshes.

Taking a Pause works well within the technique as well. If the Speaker is going on a bit too long, the Listener can signal a Pause so that he can paraphrase more accurately. If the Listener starts to inject his own opinions or rebuttals into his paraphrase, the Speaker can call a Pause and remind her partner of the rules. Using the Pause gives time for thought, serving to break negative cycles and redirect the conversation along more positive paths.

For the Skeptical at Heart: Common Questions or Objections

• "It's so artificial." Probably the number one criticism we hear about this technique is that it's artificial and just not natural. It's not a normal way for people talk to one another. Very true. Note, however, the assumption that is embedded in this criticism—that how we naturally talk to one another is usually superior to ways we've learned to talk with one another. If you have children, you already know how often you show that you don't really believe that. There are many "natural" ways children communicate with others, ways that you try to help them overcome by teaching them principles and rules for how to treat others.

If you and your partner naturally do those negative behaviors we call danger signs when discussing conflicts and problems, what's so hot about being natural? The danger signs are exceedingly natural for many people. Try being unnatural for a bit. You might really like it.

• "It goes so slowly when we talk like this." Yes, it does. That's a big part of why it works. Stop to think about all the time couples waste fighting over and over again about the same issues without the partners really hearing one another. That's very sad and very unproductive. Yes, a talk with this technique is on the slow side, but that may be the fastest you've ever dealt with a difficult topic in your relationship. Sometimes the fastest route is to drive in the slow lane.

- "We have trouble sharing the floor." So, one or both of you tend to want to hang on to the floor once you have it? We have a simple suggestion to solve this. Add a rule that you will switch the floor after every three or four statements of the Speaker that are paraphrased by the Listener. This ensures that each of you will know that your turn to talk is coming up soon. You will be a better listener when you know you are going to have a chance to respond with your point of view soon.

Although it may be frustrating to have to pass the floor when you are in the middle of building a point, rest assured; you will get the floor back quite soon. Too often people feel they have to get everything in before the door shuts, while their partner is finally listening. If the two of you get in a habit of talking more and doing a good job of it, that feeling will go away. Don't try to get so much through each open door that you make it unpleasant for your partner to keep that door open whenever you are around.

This is really a simple one, although as we've said elsewhere, simple is not always easy to do. Share. Take turns. It's not magic; it's being polite. It's about honoring your partner.

- "I really hate rules." Many of you can relate to this one. Some people really dislike structure more than others. Some people feel truly confined when trying to follow these kinds of rules. We value that input. Keep in mind something we cannot stress enough: we do not recommend talking like this when you are just being together as friends and not talking about things that are difficult. That would be unnatural and constraining in ways that we don't think would benefit your relationship.

Suppose, though, that one of you really doesn't like this structural idea, for any kind of talk. We have a couple of points in response to your concern. First, the primary point in this chapter is that every couple needs to have a way to talk about the most difficult things. If you have another way, or develop another way, you'll do fine. You can safely ignore our ideas in this chapter and move on to the next—as long as the two of you agree that you have another way to talk safely and you both agree on what that other way is. If this describes the two of you, we bet you've already figured out some ways to talk without fighting that work well for you.

Second, we've noted over the years that if one partner is not so wild about trying this and working at it, it's usually the one who is otherwise more comfortable with conflict. That does not necessarily mean he or she is handling conflict well; rather, we're talking about the partner who is less negatively affected by the conflict. If that sounds like you, give a lot of thought to using the Speaker-Listener Technique. *You* might not feel intimidated by talks about anything. But if one of you benefits a lot from using structure to make it safe to talk, both of you will gain in your relationship.

To feel safe when communicating, one of you likely needs the structure more than the other. Like the rules in almost any setting, these level the playing field to make the "game" fairer to both of you in terms of how things will proceed.

- "I've heard that 'active listening' doesn't work." In part, the Speaker-Listener Technique is based on what some call active listening. Paraphrasing is a key example of being very active in the listening role. John Gottman and his associates have suggested that because couples do not naturally talk this way it's not worth trying to teach any couple to talk this way. Further, he has suggested that asking people to communicate in this way when they are upset about things is forcing them to perform emotional gymnastics—something that's just plain hard to do.

Because more people have become aware of some disagreement on this subject between two prominent teams of marital researchers, we need to tell you explicitly what we think. First, to be clear, for many years we've been doing kinds of research similar to (and different from) what John Gottman does. There is far more agreement on what hurts and helps couples than the public debate about active listening conveys. Second, as we said earlier, pointing out that people don't naturally communicate in this way is not much of a criticism at all. You have already done many things today that were not natural to you at some earlier point in life, but your life is better for having learned those things.

Third, we agree with John that couples cannot do this well when they are very upset and negatively aroused. If you are so upset that you cannot talk respectfully to one another, even when trying to follow a few agreed-on rules, you need to have a Time Out rather than talk. Those times are what Time Out is for. (We discuss Time Outs further in Chapter Eight.) These are also great times to work on calming yourself down, as we discuss in Chapter Six.

Fourth, our confidence in the value of this technique for most (not all) couples comes from many years of research. We've learned several things: (1) couples can learn how to do this; (2) couples who practice the technique for some period of time (see our recommendations about the need for practice) can show improvements in communication about issues up to five years later; and (3) couples say this technique is the single most valuable thing they have learned in PREP workshops, suggesting that couples themselves see great value in this model. In fact, in many studies of what couples feel they need in order to help their relationships, communication skills ranks in the top two—and usually it's number one.

Don't take our word for it. Don't take Dr. Gottman's. Find out for yourselves what works for you. As we said before, the real key here is that the two of you need some way to talk well about those subjects that are hard to talk about. The Speaker-Listener Technique is one powerful, relatively simple way. There are others. You need only one. If you don't have one already, try ours.

• "What if my partner isn't interested?" Some of you will be in relationships where your partner is not as committed to working on these issues. We feel strongly that any change in either partner will have a positive effect on the relationship. Your effort to try these skills and bring safety and structure to your communication will be helpful and will perhaps even encourage your partner to participate, as he or she comes to feel validated and accepted by you.

A Final Word on the Importance of Practice

Practice is everything with this technique. Practicing it regularly for some time can help all of your communication in your marriage—not just when you are using all the rules of the technique. We think this is partly due to the fact that one of the things you are practicing when you practice the Speaker-Listener Technique is the inhibition of the danger signs. You are also practicing respect, in that there are two viewpoints in any important talk, and both need to be heard.

Many couples keep "floor" magnets (on which we've printed the rules) on their refrigerators so that the rules and the object they use for the floor are handy. We call these partners "floor on the fridge" couples. They've gotten used to the technique. It works well for them, and they've agreed to use the model when things get hot, sensitive, or just plain very important. In fact, one husband told us that when he comes home and sees that the floor is not on the fridge, he knows his wife is waiting for him and ready to use the Speaker-Listener Technique. Sometimes that's not what he wants to see, but he knows the talk will be as safe as they can make it. Practicing regularly makes it all the easier to engage those skills when you call on them.

Other couples practice enough so that they incorporate the key aspects of the rules into their style of talking generally—whether or not they are using the rules more fully and obviously. For these couples, there is a mutual sensing of when conversations are getting touchier, and they learn to shift into a modified version of the technique. For example, they might not use an object for the floor, but they begin something of a careful turn-taking process—again, because they've practiced. So even if you don't think you want to communicate this way very often, practicing these skills for some time can produce big benefits.

Although it is true that the other exercises in this book can help you learn the material, the ones here are absolutely essential. In the exercises ahead, we will outline how the two of you can learn how to really benefit from the ideas in this chapter. If you want to strengthen your marriage and reduce your chances of divorce, learn to move toward each other and deal constructively with those issues that have the potential to drive you apart. We will cover many other important principles in this book, but none is more critical.

Talking Points

1. You can choose to use the Speaker-Listener Technique to talk about any conflictual or sensitive issues.

2. Talking safely about sensitive, deeper issues promotes those feelings of intimacy that come from knowing you can share who you are *and* be accepted by your partner.

3. Our research shows that couples benefit from learning to use structure when handling conflict. Agreed-on rules like the Speaker-Listener Technique add some degree of predictability, which reduces anxiety and avoidance, helping both of you win rather than lose when dealing with conflict. Rather than fight each other, you need to work together to fight negative patterns.

 EXERCISES

The Speaker-Listener Technique does not work miracles, but it does work well. If it is going to be useful, you have to practice. Like any new skill, you're likely to be a bit unsure at the start. You need to learn this technique so well *together* that the rules are automatic when you have something really difficult to discuss.

If you were learning to play tennis, you would not try to perfect your backhand at center court in Wimbledon. Instead you would hit backhands against the back wall for hours to get it just right.

Trying to learn a new skill in a high-stress situation is not advisable. Here we suggest a good method to learn the Speaker-Listener Technique most effectively.

Starting Out

Practice this technique *several* times a week for fifteen minutes or so each time. If you do not set aside the time to practice, you will never find this powerful technique very helpful.

For the first week, try the technique with only *non*conflictual topics. Talk about anything of interest to either of you: your favorite vacation ever, news, sports, your dreams for the future, concerns you have at work, and so on. Your goal here is not to resolve some problem but to practice new skills. When you practice with these topics, it doesn't matter what topic you chose, only that you try to stick to the technique.

Moving On to Conflictual Topics

1. After you have had three successful practice sessions about non-conflictual topics, choose minor conflict areas to discuss. Sometimes couples are poor at knowing what will and will not trigger a fight. If things get heated on a topic you choose, drop it. (It won't go away, but you can deal with it when you have practiced more together.)

Practice several discussions in which you both exchange some thoughts and feelings on these issues. Don't try to solve problems; just have good discussions. This means that your goal is to understand each other's point of view as clearly and completely as possible.

Problems are sometimes solved in the process because all that was needed was for both of you to understand where the other was coming from. That's OK, but don't set out to solve problems or intentionally try for solutions. You are focusing on good discussions right now. You'll learn and practice problem solving in another chapter.

2. When you are doing well with smaller issues, move up to tougher and tougher issues. As you do, remember to work at sticking to the rules. The technique works if you work at it.

6

Controlling the Home Fires: Handling Issues and Events Well

Have you ever seen a wildfire out of control? The consuming fire can be a frightening sight. However, a fire that is under control can be a useful tool and even a pleasant experience. For example, many wilderness areas use controlled burns to destroy dry wood and brush and to prevent out-of-control fires from starting. When clear boundaries are set and careful controls are in place, the danger of fire can be minimized. Better than that, it can then be used as a productive and helpful tool. A fire in your living room fireplace can be warming, soothing, and romantic.

That's a lot like how relationships are for most of us. There are, at times, explosions of energy and great flames touched off by a tiny spark, leading to an out-of-control blaze of conflict. At other times, well-handled conflict can provide light and warmth in a relationship, leading to increased feelings of intimacy and closeness.

The sparks in relationships can be any of the day-to-day happenings in couples' lives. We call these *events*. Of course, we're talking here about the kind of sparks that lead to fighting, not the kind that fuel passion. The blazes that are triggered by events are related to the *issues* in your relationship. All couples experience events, and all couples have difficult issues. What is damaging is your regularly having events or sparks touching off explosive issues. In this chapter, we'll go deeper than we have up to this point in helping you understand some of the conflicts that affect you, and what to do about them.

ISSUES AND EVENTS

When we asked people what starts most of their arguments, the top two answers were money and children. In another study from our research center, the top three areas that couples reported led to conflicts were money, sex, and communication. Other common conflict areas are in-laws, recreation, alcohol and drugs, religion, careers, and housework. These are all in the category of what we call *issues*. All couples have issues.

Have you ever just sat there thinking, "Gee, I think I'll start a fight with my partner about money at, say, seven-thirty tonight. Yeah, that's right. That's a plan." Of course not. That's not how fights start. Things heat up when some event triggers the bigger issue. An example will help you see what we mean.

Ellen and Gregg have a serious money issue. One day, Ellen came home from work and put the checkbook down on the kitchen counter as she went to the bedroom to change. Gregg took a look at the checkbook and became livid when he saw an entry for $150 made out to a department store. When Ellen walked back into the kitchen, tired after a long day at work, she was looking for a hug or a "How was your day?" Instead, the conversation went like this:

GREGG: What did you spend that hundred and fifty dollars on?
ELLEN: (*very defensive*) None of your business.
GREGG: Of course it's my business. We just decided on a budget, and here you go blowing it. How are we ever going to solve our money problem if you can't control your spending?
ELLEN: If you'd have the guts to ask for a raise, we wouldn't be having problems with money.

All of a sudden they were off into a huge argument about money. But it happened in the context of an event—Gregg looking at the checkbook and seeing that Ellen spent $150. Because money is such a hot issue for them, just about any money-related event could trigger arguments about it. Any small event around money can trigger the negative emotions associated with their money issue, at virtually any time; and their argument, fueled by the patterns we call the danger signs (Chapter Two), can easily explode into a wildfire.

Regulating Negative Emotions: A Skill for Life

One of the most important skills that anyone can learn in life is how to manage her own negative emotions. So much of how life will go for a person depends on how well she can do this. Without being able to control how she handles negative emotions, a person will go through life reacting with anger, sadness, and hostility depending on the whim of the events in her life. Psychologists call what we're discussing here *negative affect regulation*.

The two most important skills in marriage are to be able to regulate your own negative emotions when you are upset and to be able to regulate your negative emotions when your partner is upset. We believe that there are some ways that husbands tend to have a harder time regulating their own negative emotions when their wives are upset. If that sounds like you, it is critical for you to learn to soothe yourself (such as by taking a deep breath) and remind yourself that withdrawing or getting upset is not going to help matters.

Many husbands act as if their wife's anger is the problem. That really isn't so. Unless she's expressing her anger in a hostile and invalidating way, it's neither wrong nor uncommon for one mate to feel angry toward the other from time to time. Husbands, the most powerful thing you can usually do to help your wife calm down when angry is to really pay attention to what she's saying.

> Wives, it's more likely your husband will really hear you if you can regulate your own emotions, calm down a bit, and express your concern clearly but more gently than you might otherwise have done.
>
> Gentleness and respect. They are what works best.

Events like this are common to all couples. There was some irony to Ellen and Gregg's situation, as it turned out that Ellen had actually spent the $150 on a new sweater for Gregg because he had just received an offer for a new job. In the midst of a heated argument, she didn't feel much like bringing this up. She told him later, while still angry, thinking that would put him in his place. Their inability to put the brakes on this argument ruined the next several days for them.

Here's another metaphor from Mother Nature that many couples find useful. Have you ever visited Yellowstone National Park? Issues and events work like the geysers in Yellowstone. Underneath the park are caverns of hot water under pressure. The issues in your relationship are like these underground pockets of steam and heat in Yellowstone. The more troublesome issues contain the greatest amount of heat in the form of negative emotions. The pressure keeps building up when you aren't talking about your issues in a constructive manner. Then the smallest events, sometimes so small they are embarrassing to mention, trigger a sudden eruption in your relationship. Most couples also have an Old Faithful; you know, one of those big issues that keep coming back time and time again.

Most couples deal with issues only in the context of events. In other words, the only time an issue gets attention is when you are fighting about it.

This leads us to one of the most important points in the book: most couples deal with issues only in the context of events. In other

words, the only time an issue gets attention is when you are fighting about it.

For Ellen and Gregg, there is so much negative energy stored up around the issue of money that it's easily triggered. They never sit down and talk about money in a constructive way, when no event has occurred. Instead, they argue about money when a check bounces, a large bill comes, or the hot water heater breaks. They never get anywhere on the big issue because they spend their energy dealing with the crises of the events. These are not times they are likely to handle things well.

What about you? Do you set aside time to deal with issues ahead of the times when events trigger them? You're not alone if you usually don't. We admit that it's hard to be proactive, and it's especially hard to decide to talk about a conflict area when things are going well. But we all pay a price in terms of the erosion of love and happiness if we go through life just waiting for the next fight to erupt. Like the couple in the Yellowstone drawing here, you start to feel as though you are walking on eggshells. If you feel anxious most of the time about conflicts breaking out, you'll have a very tough time keeping the feeling of safety and security in your relationship. Remember, it's crucial to be safe at home.

Compared with the trivial events that can start fights, the issues that couples must face can be really significant. You need to deal with your issues under your control; do not allow your issues to control you!

Tim and Samantha had avoided discussing her strong negative feelings about the intrusion of his relatives on their time together as a couple. One evening, they went to a baseball game—the first time they'd been out for three or four weeks. On the way, Tim received a phone call on the mobile phone from his mother. When the lengthy phone call ended, Samantha confronted Tim.

SAMANTHA: Why do you always let her interfere with our relationship? This is our evening out.
TIM: (really hot under the collar) There you go again, blasting me
   when we're going out to have fun for a change.
SAMANTHA: (sounding indignant) Well, I didn't know we were planning on bringing your mother with us.
TIM: (words dripping with sarcasm) Ha, ha. Real funny, Sam.

And their evening was destroyed. They never even made it to the ballpark. They spent the night arguing about his mother calling and whether or not she was too involved in their lives.

As in this case, events tend to come up at inopportune times— you're ready to leave for work, you're coming home from work, you're going to bed, you're out to relax, the kids are around, friends have come over, and so forth. Things come up that disturb you, but at what are often the worst times to deal with issues.

How to Deal with Triggering Events

It's very important to try to work both individually and together to stop events from dragging you into big arguments about issues— fights that tend to erupt at the worst of times. The key to this is saying to yourself, "We don't have to deal with this right now. This isn't the time. We can talk later." It is natural for annoying events to happen. You need to have the ability to let annoying events bounce off you. We all do this all the time in other relationships, especially with friends and at work. For example, how often does a coworker or boss say something to you in a somewhat hostile tone in a meeting or around others, but you *decide* it's not the time to deal with it and *choose* to move on? When you do this kind of internal editing at home or at work, it doesn't mean you are denying that something important just happened or that you feel angry. But there are times to deal with things and times to drop them or let them roll off you.

Let's return to Samantha and Tim. There are any number of ways they could have used the issues-and-events model to save their evening. Tim could have said to his mom, "Mom, this isn't a good time to talk. Let me call you back." Or "Mom, my cell service is acting up again; you're breaking up. I'll call tomorrow." Even if Tim didn't recognize that his mother's calling was a provocative event for Sam and took the call, Sam could have said to herself, "Here he goes again. He seems to care more about her than me—but I really want to have a nice time tonight, and I'm going to let this go for now and talk about it some other time."

Let's give them a second chance and assume neither of them realized that an event was about to trigger an issue. The following interaction ensued after Tim's call with his mother ended:

SAMANTHA: I feel really angry that you took that call from your mother.

TIM: What did you expect me to do?

SAMANTHA: (*taking a deep breath*) Honey, I have a lot to say, but let's Pause for now. Why don't we talk about this tomorrow, so we can enjoy seeing the Rockies beat the Dodgers tonight. We need to talk this out, but this isn't the time.

TIM: You're right. I'm sorry I took the call—but for now let's be friends and have some fun!

Here Tim and Samantha, although they are both annoyed with each other and the situation, decided to let the topic drop and went on to the ball game, where they ended up having a very nice evening. (The Rockies won in extra innings.) You can see that Samantha is thinking that Tim's mother is more important to him than she is. Whether or not that's a negative interpretation, you can see that they will have a very tough time breaking through to a better understanding if they only talk about this kind of important and emotionally loaded issue in the context of an event like the cell phone call. When they didn't allow the event to drag them into a big issue fight, Tim and Samantha went from striking out with the bases loaded to hitting a home run.

If a couple is working at managing issues rather than being managed by them, they can cut short what otherwise could erupt into huge battles. Even though they briefly escalated, in the second scenario Tim and Sam were able to calm things down. This is what we mean by separating issues from events. As we discuss later, this will work only if you have developed some trust that issues won't just be dropped, and you actually do get around to talking about them. For Tim and Sam, as for most couples, separating issues from events saved their evening and, in the long run, maybe even their marriage. Managing conflict is not always easy, but it's one of the most important and wisest things you can do to have a great relationship—and it's under your control.

Marge and Bill are in a situation similar to that of Sam and Tim, which Marge handles quite differently from the start. Bill tends to spend a good chunk of his evenings surfing the Web, checking in with his office online and using the Internet for stock market research. Several nights last week, Marge tried to ask Bill some questions about arrangements for a family reunion. He kept brushing her off, saying they would talk some other time.

This bothers her. She starts to wonder about the amount of time he spends on the computer. She even starts to think that maybe he's bored with her or no longer cares. Marge realizes suddenly that her filters—her negative interpretations—are taking over, even causing her to question Bill's love for her. She handles this potentially out-of-control blaze by saying to herself, "I know he's working on the family finances, or relaxing after a tough week—if this keeps happening, I'll talk to him about it at a couple meeting or when I have his full attention." (We discuss couple meetings in Chapter Eight.) What a great way to get control: to directly face your interpretations and remind yourself of the evidence to the contrary.

If one of you needs to get some feelings out right away in order to cool down, you could agree to briefly let some of the feeling out but to move the fuller discussion of the issue to a time when you'll both handle it better. This is one of those trust issues again. One reason people focus on events and let them turn into issue arguments is that they don't believe that "later" will happen. So for them there's no payoff in waiting, and they jump in with both feet. If you are one of these people, listen carefully: this strategy is doomed to failure. You will not feel better just venting negative feelings, and you are adding fuel to smoldering fires. The key is to soothe yourself now and read on to learn how to work together to make "later" happen.

Types of Talk

Recently, we have come to believe there are only three types of talk couples engage in. We call the first type of talk casual talk. This type of talk is necessary to get through the nitty-gritty events and details of life. Who is going to pick up the kids? What time are you going to be home from work? This talk should be polite and respectful, and even cheerful at times.

We call the second type of talk conflict talk. Conflict talk is necessary for dealing with the inevitable conflicts, issues, and disagreements that are a part of marriage. In our view, this type of talk should be engaged in only when both of you are ready. It should be done with an eye to safety and respect—to talking without fighting. In learning the tools we present in this book, couples gain confidence that they can deal with issues as they come up in life. Increased confidence leads to the ability to better tolerate differences with your partner.

The third type of talk is the most important. It's the type of talk that reflects the reason most people want to get married and stay married. We call it friendship talk. Friendship talk builds and maintains intimacy, connection, attachment, and security—all the good stuff. It's the type of talk we think couples should be engaging in naturally and most of the time when they are together. For most couples, friendship talks were a major part of how they fell deeply in love in the first place. If you stop having them, you can lose touch with why you liked your mate in the first place. That's not a good thing. We'll elaborate on these themes in Chapter Nine.

HIDDEN ISSUES

Most of the time, the issues that are triggered by events are very clear, because they are about the topics most us deal with every day— money, chores, children, and so on. In the case of Ellen and Gregg, his looking at the checkbook touched off the issue of money. That's not hard to figure out. But at other times, you'll find yourselves getting caught up in fights around events that don't seem to be attached to any particular issue. Or you find you aren't getting any- where when talking about particular problems, as if your relation- ship were a car stuck on ice, spinning its wheels.

Hidden issues often drive the really frustrating or destructive arguments couples have. For example, Samantha and Tim ended up arguing about his mother and his taking calls from her at any time. But the real issue may be that Samantha feels she isn't important to him.

When we say these issues are often hidden, we mean that they are usually not being talked about openly. Hidden issues are very important: they reflect the unexpressed expectations, needs, and feelings that, if not attended to, can cause great damage to your marriage. Hidden issues better explain the fury that seemingly innocent events can trigger.

Hidden issues reflect the unexpressed expectations, needs, and feelings that, if not attended to, can cause great damage to your marriage.

We see several types of hidden issues in our work with couples: *power, caring, recognition, commitment, integrity,* and *acceptance.* There may be others that typify your relationship, but these six capture a lot of what goes on in relationships.

Hidden Issues of Control and Power

When you are dealing with control issues, the questions relate to status and power. Who decides who does the chores or how to spend family funds? Are your needs, your desires just as important as your partner's, or is there an inequality? Is your input important, or are major decisions made without you? Who's in charge? Do you feel controlled?

Control and power issues can surface in your relationship when various decisions come up—even small ones. A power struggle can result over just about anything. It's no accident that in study after study, money is rated the number one problem area. So many decisions in our lives revolve around money. If you have significant power or control issues in your marriage, it's likely that you struggle a lot with money as well as with any number of other issues.

Hidden Issues of Caring

The main theme of hidden issues of caring relates to the extent to which you feel loved and cared for by your partner. Such issues are often triggered when people feel that their partner isn't meeting important emotional needs.

Jill and Nelson repeatedly fought over who should refill the orange juice container. The real issue fueling their arguments wasn't O.J., but rather a hidden issue of caring. Nelson had always thought of his mother's refilling the O.J. container as a demonstration of her love and caring for him. Because Jill wouldn't do it, he felt she didn't love him.

For her part, Jill was thinking, "Who's he to tell me to make the orange juice? Where does he get off saying I have to do it?" She resisted doing the task simply because she didn't accept being told what to do. Without verbalizing it, she was expressing a hidden control issue.

For them, effectively discussing this conflict brought them closer; having exposed the hidden issues, they no longer found the O.J. to be so important.

NELSON (SPEAKER): So for me, it really isn't about wanting to control you. I guess I connect refilling the O.J. with showing love, so that I've put this pressure on you to do it to be sure that you love me.

JILL (LISTENER): *(summarizing in her own words)* So for you, the key issue is wanting to know I care, not wanting to control me?

NELSON (SPEAKER): *(He goes on to validate her, as well.)* Exactly, and I can see how you'd be feeling controlled without knowing that. *(He hands Jill the floor.)*

JILL (SPEAKER): You're right. I've really felt you wanted to control me, and that's a real hot button given what I went through when I was married to Hank.

NELSON (LISTENER): It really did seem to you that I just wanted to control you, and that's an especially sensitive area for you.

JILL (SPEAKER): You got it. I want to be your partner, not your servant.

NELSON (LISTENER): *(He captures what she's saying in his own words.)* Sounds like you want us to be a team.

JILL (SPEAKER): Yep!

As you can see from the tail end of their conversation, learning to talk about the bigger concerns paved the way for greater connection instead of alienation over an empty O.J. container. This is another example that hints at how hard it would be to solve the problem about the event—refilling O.J.—unless you were communicating well enough to get the hidden issues out in the open.

Hidden Issues of Recognition

Whereas issues of caring involve concerns about being cared for or loved, recognition issues are more about feeling valued by your partner for who you are and what you do. Does your partner appreciate your activities and accomplishments? Do you feel that your efforts in your marriage are ignored?

Burt and Chelsea recently started a business together, shortly before getting married in Las Vegas on short notice. In fact, they met working for the same mortgage company and have worked together throughout their two-year relationship. In a therapy session just six months after their marriage, Chelsea says, "I feel like we got married that way just for the financial advantages. Burt is always going on about the financial stress of the business and our new house, but when I offer to help out more at the office, he always turns me down. But then, when he's really feeling stressed, he yells at me for not helping out more!"

Such examples are common. Many men tell us they don't feel that their wives place much value on their work to bring home income for the family. Likewise, we hear many women say that they don't feel their husbands appreciate what they do at home for the family—whether or not they work outside the home. In both these cases, spouses may try hard to get recognized for what they bring to the family, but eventually burn out if their mate fails to express appreciation. How long has it been since you told your partner how much you appreciate the things he or she does?

Hidden Issues of Commitment

Commitment themes reflect concerns about the extent that you are going to be together—no matter what. The key here is each person's sense of the long-term security of the relationship: Are you going to stay with me? One couple we worked with, Alice and Chuck, had huge arguments about separate checking accounts. Whenever the bank statement arrived, he would complain bitterly about her having a separate account.

The real issue wasn't the money. For Chuck, the hidden issue was one of commitment. He had been married once before, and his ex-wife had a separate account. She decided to leave him after fifteen years of marriage, which was easier to do because she had saved up several thousand dollars in this account. Now, when the statement for Alice's account would arrive, Chuck associated it with thoughts that Alice could be planning to leave him. Alice was planning no such thing, but because Chuck rarely talked openly about his fear, she wasn't really given the opportunity to alleviate his anxiety by affirming her commitment. The issue kept fueling fast-burning conflict during these events.

When your commitment to one another is secure, it brings a deeper kind of safety to your relationship than that which comes from good communication. This is safety that comes from the lasting promise to be there for one another, to lift one another up in tough times, to cherish each other for a lifetime. Do you worry about your partner's long-term commitment to you and the marriage? Have you talked about this openly, or does this issue find indirect expression in the context of events in your relationship?

Hidden Issues of Integrity

Integrity is triggered as an issue when you think your partner is questioning your motives, values, or standards. Whether this questioning is real or you have imagined it, you feel judged, and this fuels a desire to defend yourself. When Byron and Gladys argue, both are very certain they know what the other meant. Most often they're sure that what the other meant was negative. Both are therapists, so you'd think they'd know better! They have a serious problem making negative interpretations. Here's a typical example:

GLADYS: You forgot to pick up the dry cleaning.

BYRON: *(feeling a bit indignant)* You didn't ask me to pick it up; you asked me if I was going by there. I told you I wasn't.

GLADYS: *(really angry at what she sees as his lack of caring about what she needs)* You *did* say you'd pick it up, but you just don't give a damn about me.

BYRON: *(feeling thoroughly insulted)* I do care, and I resent you telling me I don't.

Gladys's caring issue is pretty out in the open here, although they are not exactly having a constructive talk about it. Byron feels insulted at her calling him an uncaring, inconsiderate husband who never thinks about her needs. That really offends his sense of himself as a good and loving husband. Her mind reading triggers his defensive reaction. Each winds up feeling invalidated.

This example illustrates why structure and safety are really needed to keep the flames of conflict contained. When Byron feels attacked in his view of himself as a husband, the blaze can really flare out of control. Next time you are tempted to attack your partner's self-image, values, or motives, be aware that you are fanning the flames.

Acceptance: The Bottom Line

There seems to be one primary issue that can overlay all the others listed here: the desire for acceptance. Sometimes this is felt more as a fear of rejection, but the fundamental issue is the same. At the deepest level, people are motivated to find acceptance and to avoid rejection in their relationships. This reflects the deep needs we all have to be respected, connected, safe, and accepted by our spouse.

This fundamental fear of rejection drives so many other hidden issues. Unfortunately, the fear is valid. Marriage involves imperfect people who can deeply hurt one another. You can see this fear of rejection come up in many ways. For example, some people are afraid that if they act in certain ways their partner is going to reject them. Often people ask for something indirectly because they don't want to risk making their desires clearer—and becoming more vulnerable by expressing their desires more openly. For example, you might say, "Wouldn't you like to make love tonight?" rather than "I would like to make love with you tonight." When a self-protection filter causes you to phrase your desires in this way, your worries were triggered by the fear of rejection.

There are a number of other ways in which people act out their hidden issues of acceptance and rejection. Consider the example of Craig and Louise and their problem with his yearly hunting trip.

Craig and Louise have been married for seventeen years, and things have gone well for them all along. They have four kids, ages seven through fifteen. There are few things they don't handle well. They talk regularly about the more important issues, which keeps things running pretty smoothly. However, there is one problem they've never really handled.

Once a year, every year, he goes hunting with his friends for two weeks. The men rent a cabin in the mountains and virtually disappear for two weeks. The following argument is typical. It was late, and Craig was packing to leave at five in the morning.

LOUISE: I really hate it when you leave for this trip every year. You leave me to handle everything by myself.

CRAIG: (feeling a bit defensive) You knew when we got married that I did this every year. I don't know why you have to complain about it every time.

LOUISE: (going on the attack) I just don't think it's very responsible to leave your family alone for two weeks. The kids need you around more than that. They get very irritable while you're gone.

CRAIG: (He's thinking, "Why do we have to do this every year? I hate this argument." He's getting angry.) I do a lot with them. You need to deal with this better—I'm not about to give this up.

LOUISE: (angrier herself) If you cared more about your family, you wouldn't have this need to get away from us for two weeks every year.

CRAIG: (*getting up to leave the room, feeling disgusted*) Yeah, you're right. You're always right, "my dear."

LOUISE: (*yelling as he walks out*) I hate it when you talk to me like that. You can't treat me like your dad treats your mom; I won't stand for it.

CRAIG: (*shouting from the other room*) I'm not like my father, and you aren't telling me what to do. I'm going, I'll keep going every year, and you might as well just get used to it.

What's really going on here? Getting ready for the trip is the event. They have this same nasty argument every year, usually the night before he leaves. It's as much a part of the tradition as the trip is. Neither likes it, but they haven't found a way to handle the situation differently.

You can see many of the hidden issues being triggered for Craig and Louise. Deep down, she worries whether Craig really cares about her when these trips come up. She feels lonely when he leaves, and this is hard to handle because she sees him looking forward to being gone. She wonders if he's delighted to get away from her. She feels nearly abandoned—reflecting some commitment issues that also get triggered. Her focus on the kids is a smoke screen for her real concerns.

Craig likes to be in control of his life, so that's one hidden issue triggered here. "No one's going to tell me what to do!" Also, as they argue unproductively, an integrity issue comes up. He feels she's calling into question his devotion as a husband and father. He sees himself as very dedicated to the family and just wants this two-week period each year to be with the guys. He doesn't think that's asking a lot.

You can see acceptance underneath it all as the most basic hidden issue driving the issues of power, caring, commitment, and integrity in their argument. Neither believes that the other accepts who he or she is, and that is very confusing. After all, they really do have a great relationship, and each generally feels good about the other. Yet the need for acceptance is so basic for all of us that it can get triggered by almost any event or issue—if we let it.

Recognizing the Signs of Hidden Issues

You can't handle hidden issues unless you can identify them. There are four key ways to tell when there may be hidden issues affecting your relationship.

Wheel Spinning

When an argument starts with you thinking, "Here we go again," you should suspect hidden issues. You never really get anywhere on the problem because you often aren't talking about what really matters—the hidden issue. We have all had these arguments in which we have said everything many times before and now feel hopeless as the cycle starts yet again.

Trivial Triggers

When trivial issues are blown up out of all proportion, you should suspect hidden issues. The argument between Jill and Nelson we saw earlier is a great example. Needing to refill an empty orange juice container seems like a trivial event, but it triggers horrendous arguments driven by the issues of power and caring.

Avoidance

When one or both of you are avoiding certain topics or levels of intimacy, or feel walls going up between you, you should suspect hidden issues. For example, we have talked with many couples from different cultural or religious backgrounds who strongly avoid talking about these differences. We think that this behavior usually reflects concerns about acceptance: Will you accept me fully if we really talk about our different backgrounds? Avoiding such topics not only allows hidden issues to remain hidden but also puts the relationship at greater risk, as the couple never deals with important differences that can have great impact on a marriage.

Other common but sometimes taboo topics in marriage can include issues of sex, personal appearance, feelings about ex-spouses, jealousy, and so on. There are many such sensitive topics that people avoid dealing with in their relationships out of fear of rejection. What issues do you avoid talking about?

Scorekeeping

When one or both of you start keeping score, you should suspect hidden issues. Scorekeeping could mean you are not feeling recognized for what you put into the relationship. It could mean you are feeling

controlled and are keeping track of the times your partner has taken advantage of you. Whatever the issue, scorekeeping can be a sign that there are important things the two of you aren't talking about— just documenting. Scorekeeping reflects that you are working against each other at times, rather than being teammates. We'll talk more about the dangers of scorekeeping in Chapter Fourteen.

Handling Hidden Issues

What can you do when you realize hidden issues are affecting your relationship? You can recognize when one may be operating and start talking about it constructively. This will be easier to do if you are cultivating an atmosphere of teamwork using the kinds of techniques we've presented thus far. We strongly recommend using the Speaker-Listener Technique when you are trying to explore such issues.

When dealing with hidden issues, it's very important to focus less on problem solving and more on hearing each other's thoughts and feelings. There is no more powerful form of acceptance than really listening to the thoughts and feelings of your mate. This type of validation is critical to emotional intimacy in relationships.

Let's return to Louise and Craig. Perhaps a more open and sensitive discussion of their issues might include the following exchange:

LOUISE (SPEAKER): Craig, I really don't understand why this trip is so important to you, especially when you know it upsets me.

CRAIG (LISTENER): So you're saying you're confused about why I go away when I know it bothers you.

LOUISE (SPEAKER): That's right. You're usually so considerate of my feelings, but when you leave anyway, I feel really hurt and abandoned.

CRAIG (LISTENER): OK, you think I usually care about your feelings, but when I leave, you feel hurt and abandoned. (*Louise hands Craig the floor.*)

CRAIG (SPEAKER): I feel sorry that you still feel hurt, when you know that I really love you and would never leave you. It's just that my relationship with my friends is also really important to me, and I'd think you would respect that.

LOUISE (LISTENER): You're saying that you really do love me and don't mean to hurt me, but you want me to respect your relationship with your friends.

CRAIG (SPEAKER): Yes, that's it. I don't understand why I can't be with them and still love you and the kids. It feels like you think I can't do both.

LOUISE (LISTENER): You think I don't believe you can love us and your friends, that it has to be only one or the other.

You can hear how different this conversation is from their earlier argument. The use of the Speaker-Listener Technique adds the structure and safety that this couple needs if they are to risk talking about their real feelings. After several good discussions of this type, next year's trip might get off to a much better start.

We are often asked about how to solve hidden issues. Often you don't solve hidden issues as much as you soothe them through mutual understanding and respect. These deep feelings are part of who you are, your view of the world, and the result of your life experiences. They are not things that need to be "solved." When you really hear each other, what has in the past been frustrating—and perhaps causing confusing filters in many talks you have—can turn into opportunities to know one another more deeply.

Our goal in this chapter has been to give you a way to explore and understand some of the most frustrating happenings in relationships. You can prevent lots of damage by learning to handle events and issues with the time and skill they require. Using the model presented here along with all the skills and techniques presented in the first part of the book will help you do just that.

For all too many couples, the hidden issues never come out. They fester and produce sadness and resentment that eventually destroy the marriage. It just doesn't have to be that way. When you learn to discuss deeper issues openly and with emphasis on validating each other, what had been generating the greatest conflicts can actually draw you closer together.

Talking Points

1. Events are day-to-day happenings in everyone's life that can act as sparks for conflict about deeper issues. It is your responsibility to separate talks about events from talks about issues.

2. Issues are part of everyone's life as well. The goal is to talk about issues when you aren't in a state of crisis, so that you can deal with them more effectively.

3. Hidden issues are even farther under the surface and can blaze out of control when not recognized and addressed. Of the six types of hidden issues, acceptance, or the corresponding fear of rejection, is probably the most pervasive.

 # EXERCISES

We recommend that you work through the first two exercises individually; the third gives you the opportunity to sit down and talk together about your impressions.

Signs of Hidden Issues

We're going to repeat the list of signs that hidden issues may be affecting your relationship. Do you notice that one or more of these signs come up a lot in your relationship?

- Wheel spinning

- Trivial triggers

- Avoidance

- Scorekeeping

What Are Your Hidden Issues?

Next we'd like you to consider which hidden issues might operate most often in your relationship. In addition to the hidden issues listed here, there may be some big issue you'd like to add. Consider each issue and to what degree it seems to affect your relationship negatively. Also, how hidden are they for you?

Note if there are certain events that have triggered or keep triggering the issues. You can list these events on the right-hand side of your list of issues or on a separate piece of paper.

- Power and control

- Caring

- Recognition

- Commitment

- Integrity

- Acceptance

Talking About Your Hidden Issues

Plan some time together to talk about your observations and thoughts. For most couples, there are certain hidden issues that repeatedly come up. Identifying these can help you draw together as you each learn to handle those issues with care. Also, as you discuss these matters, you have an excellent opportunity to get in some more practice with the Speaker-Listener Technique.

7

New Perspectives on Problems and Problem Solving

All couples have problems, and even the happiest couples don't ever solve some of their key problems. Let's repeat that in case it was not clear: some of the happiest couples we've seen still struggle with significant relationship issues over many years. We stress this idea because we'd like to adjust your expectations to be more in line with reality.

Many partners believe there is something wrong with their marriage if they have problems that are not readily solvable. This belief can be very damaging to a relationship. One of the pathways to unhappiness or divorce lies not so much in having problems but in believing that there is something seriously wrong with your relationship because you've not resolved all your problems. At the end of the chapter, we'll tell you more about how you can have a great relationship despite unresolved problems.

Understanding one another is more important for maintaining respect and connection than is solving every problem that life throws your way.

There are times, however, when you'll want to do the best job you can together to solve a particular problem in a way that satisfies both of you. That's the focus of this chapter. We present a straightforward approach to problem solving that can help you through those times when you really need practical, workable solutions.

We have resisted the temptation to present our problem-solving model until this point because most couples try to solve problems prematurely—before they have thoroughly discussed the issue at hand and understood—not necessarily agreed with—each other's perspective. Understanding one another is more important for maintaining respect and connection than is solving every problem that life throws your way. And for many problems, just understanding each other better is all the solution you need.

PREP and the Cold War

The problem-solving model we present in this chapter works for more than just marital problems. When Howard was teaching a course at the University of Denver called Understanding Human Conflict, he told the story of famous summit meetings during the first Bush administration between the president and Mikhail Gorbachev, the Soviet prime minister. During the first part of the meeting, problem solving was banned. Instead, each side presented its views on three major issues (for example, disarmament, human rights). The key task for both sides, up front, was to do the best job they could to understand the other side's perspective. Only then did they move on to problem solving.

You may recall that this summit conference was credited by many as marking the beginning of the end of the Cold War. What you may not know is that Gorbachev was carrying in his back pocket a copy of the classic book on negotiating, *Getting to Yes*, by Roger Fisher, William Ury, and Bruce Patton. By placing a floor on your fridge (see Chapter Five), you too can remind yourself of the power of this simple model and thaw your own cold wars.

THREE KEY ASSUMPTIONS

There are three assumptions, all of which are confirmed by research, that we want to explore in detail before presenting the specific steps that can help you effectively solve many common problems in your relationships:

1. All couples have problems.

2. Couples who are most effective at problem solving work together as a team.

3. Most couples rush to find quick solutions; in their haste, they do not take into account the real concerns of each partner and thus fail to produce lasting solutions.

No Getting Around Having Problems in Life

Although the nature of the problems changes for couples over time, all couples encounter problems. There are some problems that are likely to remain much the same over the long term. For example, let's say personality differences lead to fairly frequent conflicts between the two of you. Perhaps one of you is more compulsive and neat and the other more carefree. Or one of you is super-shy and the other the life of the party. Such differences are often what attracts partners in the first place, but they can also become sources of conflicts over the details of life. These kinds of problems are not likely to go away over time. (What does tend to change in great relationships is that the partners develop the ability to accept one another in spite of the differences.)

In contrast to these kinds of problems, some are very specific and need real solutions. Maybe it's July, you've moved to a new neighborhood, and you disagree about whether or not your children should go to the school down the block or to the new charter school a few miles away. That's a problem that requires a real decision right now. The ideas in this chapter are ideal for such situations, when the two of you need a little extra structure to deal with the problem most effectively.

What you argue about will differ depending on your stage of life, your type of job, where you live, and so on. For example, we've worked a lot with military couples over the years. They have particularly intense issues related to such problems as where they will live in a few years, and deployments, whereby one partner might go away for months at a time—and sometimes on dangerous missions. Frequent, extensive travel can really stress a couple out over problems with who's in charge, whom the children should obey most, who pays the bills, the risk of affairs, and so forth.

In one of our long-term studies of marriages, a colleague of ours at the University of Denver, Ragnar Storaasli, found that engaged couples tended to report that their key problem areas are with jealousy and in-laws. These issues reflect a core task that couples have early in a relationship: to establish boundaries with those outside the relationship. By the first year of marriage, couples reported other problems as being most important, such as communication and sex. These are issues central to how a couple interacts. Whether in a new or older relationship, most couples report money as a top problem, no matter how much they have. Money is a ripe area for conflict.

In a related study, we found that for couples in their first marriages, the top argument starters were money and child rearing; other issues (chores, time together, in-laws, jealousy, alcohol and drugs, and so on) were mentioned far less often. For couples in a second marriage, the order was reversed: child rearing was rated as the most frequent argument starter, and money came in second. So for those of you in second marriages, you are especially likely to argue about how to handle the complex issues of raising children that come with blended families. Empty nest couples, whose children are grown, are most likely to argue about communication, conflict, and sex, according to a survey by our colleagues Dave and Claudia Arp, coauthors with us of *Fighting for Your Empty Nest Marriage*.

Who's on My Side?

You have a choice when dealing with any problem. Either you will nurture a sense that you are a team working together against the problem or you will operate as if you are working against each other. This principle holds with all problems, great or small.

Jeremy and Lisa are a newlywed couple in their late twenties who have nurtured their teamwork, as illustrated by the following conversation. They were talking about how to handle the feeding of their newborn baby, Brent, while Lisa is away at work at the local hospital where she is a pediatric nurse. Jeremy recently lost his job as an executive when his firm merged with another, but was confident of finding another position in the near future.

LISA: The biggest concern I have is about breast feeding.

JEREMY: What do you mean? Can't he do that when you're at home—with me giving him a bottle during your shift?

LISA: No. That's not going to work because I'll swell up while away. I make milk whether or not he drinks it, you know.

JEREMY: I had no idea that would be a problem. You mean you can't go through your shift without him nursing?

LISA: Not without exploding.

JEREMY: Ouch! What can we do to make this work out?

LISA: Well, either Brent nurses on my break or I need to pump.

JEREMY: What's better for you? I could help either way.

LISA: Would you be willing to bring him over to work at lunchtime? If he'd nurse well then, that would tide me through the day, and you could give him bottles the rest of the time.

JEREMY: Sure. I'd be glad to bring him over. No biggie with me out of work for now.

LISA: That would help a lot. I'd also get to see him during the day. Let's give it a try this week.

Notice how natural it is for Jeremy and Lisa to foster a sense of respect and cooperation. This is the way they have learned to approach all kinds of problems—as challenges to be met together.

Contrast the tone of Jeremy and Lisa's discussion with that of Shandra and Eric. Shandra, the owner of her own dry cleaning business, and Eric, a real estate agent, are the parents of two middle schoolers. They have repeated arguments about housework, which generally go like this:

SHANDRA: *(calmly)* We need to do something about keeping the house looking better. It's such a mess most of the time . . . it's depressing to be here.

ERIC: *(a bit annoyed)* Look, that's your job. My work requires me to be out a lot more than you. I just don't have the time, and you know it! Keeping the place picked up is more your job than mine.

SHANDRA: *(hurt and angered)* Says who? There's a lot more to do than you seem to think. And did you forget that I work, too? Besides, you don't even clean up after yourself!

ERIC: I'd do more around here if you could generate more money in your business. You know, when you're home, you spend lots of time watching the tube—you could use your time better.

SHANDRA: *(anger growing)* I need some breaks, but that's not the point. I work just as hard as you outside the home, and you should . . . you need to do more of your share.

ERIC: I'm not going to give up my free time because you aren't using yours well. We had a deal, it's fair, and that's all I have to say. *(He turns away and walks out of the room.)*

The only results of this discussion are that Shandra is more discouraged and Eric is annoyed that she even brought up the problem. There is a definite lack of teamwork. Eric refuses to accept any role in dealing with this problem. He sees Shandra as trying to take something away from him, not as a partner working to make life as good as it can be for both of them. Likewise, Shandra sees Eric as the problem, not as a teammate who is working with her to solve the problem.

All too often, people approach problems as if their partner were an enemy to be conquered. For such couples, problems are approached as if there will be a winner and a loser. Who wants to lose? The good news here is that you don't have to be locked into the cycle of one person trying to win at the expense of the other. You can decide to work as a team.

The Team's the Thing

Allan Cordova has conducted research at the University of Denver on teamwork with couples in the transition to parenthood. Whether or not a couple is having a baby, teamwork is crucial. Here's what he told us about his research as well as other studies in this area:

Research suggests that teamwork—how coordinated, committed, and "in sync" couples feel and act—is a cornerstone of marital adjustment. The stakes of thinking and acting like a team may be the highest under stressful circumstances, such as when trying to talk about a hot topic. But being a team may mean different things for husbands and wives. In my work, I've found that couples who score higher on measures of teamwork are couples who also score highly on general marital satisfaction, commitment, confidence in the ability to constructively solve relationship problems, and communication quality.

In another teamwork study conducted by R. Carols and Don Baucom, women responded more positively to specific, recent supportive events, whereas men tended to be relatively more affected by more general and historical relationship support. Similarly, in my research, I discovered that both men's and women's marital happiness was related to "feeling" like a team. But for women, and not for men, marital happiness was also related to the frequency of actual teamlike behaviors (for example, doing a chore you don't normally do in order to help out your spouse; saying "thank

you" to acknowledge your mate's efforts). This may mean
the difference between "talking the talk" (saying you feel
like a team player) and "walking the walk" (acting like a
team player).

Among other things, what all this means is that part
of teamwork is following through on things you've
agreed to do. Are you walking, or are you just talking?

Why the Big Rush?

Many well-intended attempts at problem solving fail because couples don't take the time needed to understand each other's concerns.
This is particularly true when one partner is upset about something.
All too often, we want to fix what's wrong—and all too often our
efforts wind up making our partner even more upset. If you are deciding which movie to see, not much is at stake in rushing to a solution—except maybe sitting through a boring film. If you are deciding
something more important, such as how to parent or how to divide
up the household responsibilities, it's critical that you take the time
to listen first and then decide if resolution makes sense.

Do Men Want to Solve More Than Women?

First off, we need to tell you that Howard and Scott
would have answered this question ages ago, but Susan
keeps wanting to talk about it! But seriously: countless
men have told us that when they perceive their wife's
concerns as being unfixable, they feel helpless, which
leads them to withdraw. This scenario can come up a lot,
because in many marriages, women are the ones who

more frequently bring up the issues that they think need to be dealt with. But that does not mean that their greatest goal is necessarily to solve the problem. When we ask wives what they want, the answer is simple: "I want my husband to listen to me, not fix things for me." It's not just men who want to fix things; we are a problem-solving-oriented society that rewards people who are good fixers. Both men and woman tend to go for the problem-solving jugular, and feel helpless and hopeless when that doesn't work. It's better to resist this urge and listen as a friend might to what is upsetting your partner.

Two major factors propel couples to rush to solutions: time pressure and conflict avoidance.

Time Pressure

We live in a "give-it-to-me-now" world of instant solutions to problems and desires. This might work fine when it comes to wanting a certain brand of shaving cream or a particular color of draperies at the store, but it's not how relationships work. When it comes to the problems with which most couples struggle, hasty decisions are often poor decisions. You may have heard the expression "You can pay me now or pay me later" in regard to car maintenance, and it's all the more true when dealing with problems in relationships.

Conflict Avoidance

Sometimes people rush to solutions because they can't stand to deal with the conflict. Frances and Bjorn have been married twenty-four years, with one child through college and one a senior in high school. Bjorn is an insurance salesman, and Frances works nearly full-time as a volunteer with a local religious charity. They've always had enough money, but things have gotten much tighter with college bills piling up. An issue for Bjorn is that Frances devotes so much time to a job that doesn't pay. The following interchange is typical of their attempts to solve the problem.

BJORN: *(testy)* I noticed that the Visa bill was over three thousand dollars again. I just don't know what we are going to do to keep up. It worries me. I'm doing all I can, but . . .

FRANCES: *(gives no indication that she is paying attention to Bjorn)*

BJORN: *(frustrated)* Did you hear me?

FRANCES: Yes. I didn't think we spent that much this time.

BJORN: How many clothes did Jeanne need, anyway? *(really annoyed now)*

FRANCES: *(annoyed but calm)* Well, we figured she needed one really nice outfit for applying for jobs. I guess we got more extras than I thought, but they were all things she can really use. It's really important to her to look good for interviews. And you know, the sooner she gets a job, the better off our budget will be.

BJORN: *(settling down a bit)* I can understand, but this kind of thing adds to my worry. *(long pause)* We aren't saving anything at all for retirement, and we aren't getting any younger. If you had some income coming in for all your work, it would help a lot.

FRANCES: Why don't we just get rid of that credit card? Then you wouldn't have to worry about it anymore.

BJORN: We could do that, and also plan to put aside an extra hundred-and-fifty dollars a month in my retirement plan. That would help a lot to get us going in the right direction. What about a part-time job?

FRANCES: I can think about it. What I'm doing seems a lot more important. For now, let's try to get rid of the credit card and save more. That sounds good. Let's try it out.

BJORN: OK, let's see what happens.

End of discussion. The one good thing about this conversation is that they had it. However, what are the chances that they came to a satisfactory resolution of their money problem? Two months later, nothing had changed, no more was saved, the credit card was still being used, interest was accruing, and they were no closer to working together on the budget.

This example illustrates what couples do all the time: make a quick agreement so that they can avoid conflict. Solutions arrived at in this manner rarely last because not all the important information is "on the table." In our example, Bjorn and Frances didn't really address his central concern about her volunteer job. Furthermore, they drew up no specifics about how they would implement their agreement.

When you settle prematurely on a solution, you are likely to pay for the lack of planning with the eruption of more conflict about the issue later on.

HANDLING PROBLEMS WELL

Our approach to solving problems is structured. In other words, we recommend a specific set of steps. As we've said earlier, it's when you are dealing with things that are difficult to handle that you're most likely to benefit from added structure. We have featured these steps in our materials for couples for many years now. Similar models are contained in such works as *We Can Work It Out* (1993), by Notarius and Markman, and *A Couple's Guide to Communication* (1976), by Gottman, Notarius, Gonso, and Markman—from which we have adapted a few ideas.

Although these steps are very straightforward, don't be misled by the simplicity of the approach. You must be willing to work together and to experiment with change; you must be creative and flexible. We think of this structure as like a scaffold around a building under construction. You need the support to complete the project. Full discussion clarifies the issues, removes conflict, and increases the feeling of teamwork. Solutions flow naturally from working together against problems rather than working against each other.

The following shows the steps to handling problems well:

I.   Problem Discussion

II. Problem Solution

    A. Agenda setting

    B. Brainstorming

    C. Agreement and compromise

    D. Follow-up

We've learned over the years that some couples really like to fol-low explicit steps like these—and greatly benefit. Others don't care for quite as much structure when working on problems. We are going to strongly recommend practicing these steps because we believe that doing so can build your sense of confidence that the two of you can deal with problems in the future. Then, over time, you can decide how and when you want to use the specific guidelines.

As you read what follows, give a lot of thought to the principles reflected in these steps. The themes here are the essence of how people get to great solutions for difficult issues in life.

Problem Discussion

Problem solving is easiest when the two of you have created an atmos-phere of mutual respect and acceptance. Therefore, we strongly rec-ommend discussing problems before trying to solve them. In the Problem Discussion step, you are laying the foundation for a solution to come. Whether the problem is large or small, you should not move on to Problem Solution until you both understand, and feel under-stood by, the other. We recommend you use the Speaker-Listener Technique for this step, to facilitate the kind of good discussion needed before attempting to find solutions to the problem at hand. If another technique helps you talk through your issues, use it here instead.

In many instances, you'll find that after an excellent discussion, there's really no problem solving to be done—just having a good discussion is enough. In fact, in our PREP seminars, we often shock couples by announcing that our experience indicates that approximately 70 percent of the issues couples face do not need to be solved as much as just aired out. It's hard to appreciate this point without experiencing the power of good talk. The fact is, we often want something much more fundamental in our relationships than solutions to problems—we want a friend.

When the first edition of this book was published, Howard had the honor of appearing on *Oprah*. Although they disagreed on some issues, Howard and Oprah found a surprising area of agreement. Howard stated, "We have estimated that as many as 70 percent of the problems couples face don't need problem solving as much as a good, open talk." Oprah didn't merely concur but said it may be even 80 percent or more! Hey, this is better than research.

The couples described in this chapter experienced greater pain and distance because they failed to take the time to discuss the issues before coming to agreements. We have repeatedly seen that when good discussions precede problem solving, problem solving can often go smoothly and surprisingly quickly, even on difficult issues. When you've put all the relevant facts and feelings on the table, you've laid the foundation for working as a team.

Being Clear About What You Are Upset About

Often we complicate our communication by expressing so much anger and general frustration that our real message can be lost in the shuffle. In their book *A Couple's Guide to Communication*, Gottman, Notarius, Markman, and Gonso discuss a great way to make it more likely that your message will be clearly heard by your partner; they call it the XYZ statement. This can be very valuable in or out of a problem-solving context. When you make an XYZ statement, you put your gripe or complaint into this format:

"When you do X in situation Y, I feel Z."

When you use an XYZ statement, you are giving your partner usable information: the specific behavior, the context in which it occurs, and how you feel when it happens. This is highly preferable to the typical alternative: a vague description of the problem, and some character assassination instead of an "I" statement.

For example, suppose you had a concern about your partner making a mess at the end of the day. Which of the following statements do you think gives you a better shot at being heard?

"You are such a slob."

"When you drop your pack and jacket on the floor [X] as you come in the door at the end of the day [Y], I feel angry [Z]."

Or let's say you were angry about a comment your spouse made at a party last Saturday night. Which statement is better at getting your point across?

"You are so inconsiderate."

"When you said that what I did for work wasn't really that hard [X] to John and Susan at the party last Saturday [Y], I felt very embarrassed [Z]."

Unless you are careful, it's all too easy to fall into a nonspecific attack on character. Such statements are guaranteed to cause defensiveness and escalation. The XYZ statements are far more constructive. You identify a specific behavior in a specific context. The "I feel Z" part requires you to take responsibility for your own feelings. Your partner does not "make" you feel anything in particular—you are in charge of how you feel.

Keep in mind that no one really likes to hear a gripe or criticism, no matter how constructively expressed. But unless you are hiding out in avoidance, there are times when you need to voice your concern, and you need to do it without fostering unneeded conflict. The XYZ format will help you do just that.

Problem Solution

We have found that after couples have done the work of Problem Discussion, the following steps work very well.

Agenda Setting

The first step in the Problem Solution phase is to set the agenda for your work together. The key here is to make it very clear what you are trying to solve at this time. Often your discussion will have taken you through many facets of an issue. Now you need to decide what to focus on. The more specific you are at this step, the better your chances of coming to a workable and satisfying solution. Many problems in marriage seem insurmountable, but they can be cut down to size if you follow these procedures. Even a great rock can be removed in time if you keep chipping away at it.

Let's say you've had a Problem Discussion about money, covering a range of issues, such as credit card problems, checkbooks, budgets, and savings. The problem area of "money" can contain many smaller problem areas to consider. So take a large problem such as this and focus on the more manageable pieces, one at a time. It is also wisest to pick an easier piece of a problem to work on at first. You might initially decide who should balance the checkbook each month, then deal with budget plans later.

At times, your Problem Discussion will have focused from start to finish on a specific problem. In this case, you won't have to define the agenda for problem solving. For example, you may be working on the problem of where to go for the holidays—your parents' home or your spouse's. There may be no specific smaller piece of such a problem, so you will set the agenda to work on the whole of it.

Brainstorming

As far as we know, the process referred to as brainstorming has been around forever. However, it seems to have been refined and promoted by NASA during the early days of the U.S. space program. The organization needed a way to bring together the many different engineers and scientists when looking for solutions to the varied problems of space travel. Brainstorming worked for NASA, and it came to be frequently used in business settings. We have found that it works very well for couples, too.

There are several rules regarding brainstorming:

- Any idea is OK to suggest.

- One of you should write the ideas down as you generate them together.

- Don't evaluate the ideas during brainstorming, verbally or nonverbally (this includes making faces!).

- Be creative. Suggest whatever comes to mind.

- Have fun with it, if you can. This is a time for a sense of humor; all other feelings should be dealt with in Problem Discussion.

The best thing about this process is that it encourages creativity. If you can resist the temptation to comment critically on the ideas, you will encourage each other to come up with some great stuff. Wonderful solutions can come from considering the points you've made during brainstorming. Following the rules we've listed here helps you resist the tendency to settle prematurely on a solution that isn't the best you can find. Loosen up and go for it.

Agreement and Compromise

In this step, the goal is to come up with a *specific* solution or combination of solutions that you both *agree* to try. We emphasize "agree" because the solution is not likely to help unless you both agree—sincerely—to try it. We emphasize "specific" because the more specific you are about the solution, the more likely you will be to follow through.

Although it is easy to see the value of agreement, some people have trouble with the idea of *compromise*. We've even been criticized for using the term from time to time. Obviously, compromise implies giving up something you wanted in order to reach an agreement. To some, compromise sounds more like lose-lose than win-win. But we do mean to emphasize compromise in a positive manner. Marriage is

about teamwork. The two of you will see some things differently. You would at times make different decisions. However, many times the best solution will be a compromise in which neither of you gets everything you wanted.

The two of you nurture a great marriage when you can put the needs of the relationship above your individual desires at key times of life.

You're not going to have a great marriage if you insist on getting your way all the time. The two of you nurture a great marriage when you can put the needs of the relationship above your individual desires at key times of life.

Follow-Up

Many couples make an agreement to try a particular solution to a problem. It is just as important to follow up on how the solution is working out. Following up has two key advantages. First, you often need to "tweak" solutions a bit for them to work in the long term. Second, following up builds accountability. Often we don't get serious about making changes unless we know there is some point of accountability in the near future.

At times you'll need a lot of follow-up in the Problem Solution phase. Other times, it's not really necessary: you reach an agreement, the solution works out, and nothing more needs to be done.

Some couples choose to be less formal about follow-up, but we think they are taking a risk. Most people are so busy that they don't plan their follow-up, and it just doesn't happen. There is an old but true saying: if you fail to plan, you plan to fail.

A DETAILED EXAMPLE:
BJORN AND FRANCES

It did not take Frances and Bjorn very long to realize that their problem solving about the credit card, her volunteer work, and their retirement savings was not working. They decided to try the steps we are suggesting.

First, they set aside the time to work through the steps. It may not take a lot of time, depending on the problem, but setting aside time specifically for working toward solutions is very wise. Let's follow the couple through the steps we've outlined.

Problem Discussion

Bjorn and Frances decide to use the Speaker-Listener Technique for their Problem Discussion.

FRANCES (SPEAKER): I can see that we really do have to try something different. We aren't getting anywhere on our retirement savings.

BJORN (LISTENER): You can see we aren't getting anywhere, and you are also concerned.

FRANCES (SPEAKER): *(letting Bjorn know he had accurately heard her)* Yes. We need to come up with some plan for saving more and for doing something about the credit cards.

BJORN (LISTENER): You agree we need to save more, and can see that how we spend on the credit cards may be part of the problem.

FRANCES (SPEAKER): I can also see why you are concerned about my volunteer work—when I could be spending some of that time bringing in some income. But my volunteer work is really important to me. I feel like I'm doing something good in the world.

BJORN (LISTENER): Sounds like you can appreciate my concern, but you also want me to hear that it's really important to you. It adds a lot of meaning to your life. *(Here, he validates her by listening carefully.)*

FRANCES (SPEAKER): Yeah. That's exactly what I'm feeling. Here, you take the floor; I want to know what you're thinking. *(She hands Bjorn the floor.)*

BJORN (SPEAKER): I have been anxious about this for a long time. If we don't save more, we are not going to be able to maintain our lifestyle in retirement. It's not all that far away.

FRANCES (LISTENER): You're really worried, aren't you?

BJORN (SPEAKER): Yes, I am. You know how things were for Mom and Dad. I don't want to end up living in a two-room apartment.

FRANCES (LISTENER): You're worried we could end up living that way, too.

BJORN (SPEAKER): I'd feel a lot better with about three times as much saved.

FRANCES (LISTENER): Too late now. *(She catches herself interjecting her own opinion.)* Oh, I should paraphrase. You wish we were much further along in our savings than we are.

BJORN (SPEAKER): *(This time, he feels he is really getting her attention.)* I sure do. I feel a lot of pressure about it. I really want to work together so we can both be comfortable. *(letting her know he wants to work as a team)*

FRANCES (LISTENER): You want us to work together and reduce the pressure, and plan for our future.

BJORN (SPEAKER): *(suggesting some alternatives)* Yes. We'd need to spend less to save more. We'd need to use the credit cards more wisely. I think it would make the biggest difference if you could bring in some income.

FRANCES (LISTENER): You feel that to save more we'd need to spend less with the credit cards. More important, you think it's pretty important for me to bring in some money.

BJORN (SPEAKER): Yes. I think the income is a bigger problem than the outgo.

FRANCES (LISTENER): Even though we could spend less, you think we may need more income if we want to live at the same level in retirement. Can I have the floor?

BJORN (SPEAKER): Exactly! Here's the floor. *(He hands her the floor.)*

FRANCES (SPEAKER): *(responding to Bjorn's clarification)* Sometimes I think that you think I'm the only one who overspends.

BJORN (LISTENER): You think that I think you're mostly at fault for spending too much. Can I have the floor again? *(Frances hands him the floor.)*

BJORN (SPEAKER): Actually, I don't think that, but I can see how I could come across that way. *(validating Frances's experience)* I think I overspend just as much as you do. I just do it in bigger chunks.

FRANCES (LISTENER): Nice to hear that. *(Here she's validating his comment; she feels good hearing him taking responsibility.)* You can see that we both spend too much, just differently. You buy a few big things we may not need, and I buy numerous smaller things.

BJORN (SPEAKER): Exactly. We are both to blame, and we can both do better.

FRANCES (LISTENER): We both need to work together. *(Bjorn gives Frances the floor.)*

FRANCES (SPEAKER): I agree that we need to deal with our retirement savings more radically. My biggest fear is losing the work I love so much. It's been the most meaningful thing I've done since the kids got older.

BJORN (LISTENER): It's hard to imagine not having that . . . it's so important to you.

FRANCES (SPEAKER): Yes. I can see why more income would make a big difference, but at the same time I would hate to lose what I have. I really like running those programs for the kids—especially when I see one of them open up.

BJORN (LISTENER): You enjoy it, and you are doing something really useful. I can hear how hard it would be for you to give it up.

FRANCES (SPEAKER): Exactly. Maybe there's some way to deal with this so that I wouldn't lose all of what I'm doing but could help us save what we need for retirement at the same time.

BJORN (LISTENER): You are wondering if there is a solution that would meet your needs and our needs at the same time.

FRANCES (SPEAKER): Yes. I'm willing to think about solutions with you.

They discontinue the Speaker-Listener Technique.

BJORN: OK.

FRANCES: So, are we both feeling understood enough to move on to Problem Solution?

BJORN: I am, how about you?

FRANCES: *(She nods her head, yes.)*

Here they are agreeing together that they've had a good discussion and that they're ready to try some problem solving. They are consciously turning this corner together to move into Problem Solution.

Problem Solution

Bjorn and Frances now go through the four steps of Problem Solution.

Agenda Setting

At this step, the important thing is for them to choose to solve a specific piece of the whole issue discussed. This increases their chances of finding a solution that will really work this time.

FRANCES: We should agree on the agenda. We could talk about how to get more into the retirement accounts, but that may not be the place to start. I also think we need a discussion to deal with the issue of the credit cards and how we spend money.

BJORN: You're right. We are going to need several different stabs at this entire issue. It seems we could break it all down into the need to bring in more and the need to spend less. I don't want to push, but I'd like to focus on the "bring in more" part first, if you don't mind.

FRANCES: I can handle that. Let's problem-solve on that first, then we can talk later this week about the spending side.

BJORN: So we're going to brainstorm about how to boost the income.

Brainstorming

The key here is to generate ideas freely.

FRANCES: Let's brainstorm. Why don't you write the ideas down— you have a pen handy.

BJORN: OK. You could get a part-time job.

FRANCES: I could ask the board of directors about making some of my work into a paid position. I'm practically a full-time staff member, anyway.

BJORN: We could meet with a financial planner so we have a better idea of what we really need to bring in. I could also get a second job.

FRANCES: I could look into part-time jobs that are similar to what I'm already doing, like those programs for kids with only one parent.

BJORN: You know, Jack and Marla are doing something like that. We could talk to them about what it's about.

FRANCES: I feel this list is pretty good. Let's talk about what we'll try doing.

Agreement and Compromise

Now they sift through the ideas generated in brainstorming. The key is to find an agreement that both can support.

BJORN: I like your idea of talking to the board. What could it hurt?

FRANCES: I like that too. I also think your idea of seeing a financial planner is good. Otherwise, if I'm going to try to bring in some extra, how do we really know what the target is? But I don't think it's realistic for you to work more.

BJORN: Yeah, I think you're right. What about talking to Marla and Jack about what they're into?

FRANCES: I'd like to hold off on that. That could lead them to try to get me involved, and I'm not sure I'm interested.

BJORN: OK. What about exploring if there are any kinds of part-time jobs where you could be doing something that has meaning for you and make some bucks, too?

FRANCES: I'd like to think about that. It'd be a good way to go if they don't have room in the budget where I am now. I sure wouldn't want to do more than half-time, though. I would hate to give up all of what I'm doing now.

BJORN: And I wouldn't want you to. If you could make a part-time income, I'll bet we could cut back enough to make it all work.

FRANCES: So, how about I talk to the board, you ask Frank about that financial planner they use, and I'll also start looking around at what kinds of part-time jobs there might be.

BJORN: Great. Let's schedule some time next week to talk about how we are doing in moving along for the solution we need.

FRANCES: Agreed. (*They agree on a time to meet for follow-up.*)

Follow-Up

At the end of the week, Frances and Bjorn met to discuss what they were finding out and what to do next. To Frances's surprise, the board member she had talked with seemed eager to try to work out something. In the meantime, she'd gone ahead with looking into various part-time jobs that would meet her needs. Bjorn had scheduled a meeting for them with a financial planner for the following week.

In this case, the solution really was a process made up of a series of smaller steps and agreements. Bjorn and Frances were moving on an issue that had been a problem between them for a long time, mostly because they were working together and no longer avoiding a tough issue.

Later, they went through the steps again and came to a specific agreement about spending less. They decided how much less to spend, and agreed to record all the credit card purchases in a checkbook register so that they would know how they were doing compared to their target. In contrast to their problem solving about income, which was a process lasting several weeks, this specific solution on spending was implemented right away, and not much tweaking was needed.

WHEN IT'S NOT THAT EASY

We'd like to tell you that this model always works this well, but there are times when it doesn't. What do you do then? In our experience with couples, there are a few common difficulties that often come up when dealing with problems. Here we'll make some suggestions for handling them.

Cycle Back Through the Steps

You can get bogged down and frustrated during any segment of the Problem Solution phase. If so, you need to cycle back to Problem Discussion. Simply pick up the floor again and resume your discussion. Getting stuck can mean you haven't talked through some key issues or that one or both of you are not feeling validated in the process. It is better to slow things down than to continue to press for a solution that may not work. While you're getting used to the process, or when you're dealing with more complex and difficult issues, you might cycle through the steps several times.

Halfway Can Get You All the Way

The best solution you can reach in one problem solution session may not always be the conclusive solution to a problem. At times, you should set the agenda just to agree on the next steps needed to get to the best solution. For example, you might brainstorm about the kind of information you need to make your decision. Say you were trying to decide together if you should move to another place to live, and if you should, when. This is certainly not a decision you can resolve in one sitting. There are too many things to consider and figure out. So perhaps early on, you brainstorm how you'll get to the next step. For example, what do you need to know to make the big decision? Which of you can find out what answers, and from whom? Divide and conquer.

When There Is No Solution

There are some problems that don't have solutions with which both of you will be happy. Suppose you've worked together for some time using the structure we suggest, yet no solution is emerging from your work together. You can either let this lack of a solution damage the rest of your marriage, or you can plan for how to live with your differences. Sometimes couples allow the rest of a good marriage to be damaged by insisting there must be a resolution to a specific unresolved conflict.

If you have a problem area that seems unsolvable, you can set the agenda in Problem Solution to protect the rest of your marriage from the fallout from that one problem area. You would be literally "agreeing to disagree" constructively. This kind of solution comes about from both teamwork and tolerance. You can't always have your spouse be just the way you want him or her to be, but you can work as a team to deal with your differences. This is acceptance in action.

One couple we worked with, Barb and Zach, had both smoked for over twenty years. Zach finally decided to quit and was able to do so. As sometimes happens, Zach became rather adamant that Barb needed to quit, too. He was becoming less and less tolerant of the smell in the house. Even when they were out, it was starting to really upset him that she'd regularly need to find a place to go smoke. They'd had a great marriage for eighteen years, but this one problem started to threaten everything. Conflicts were escalating more and becoming nastier.

Finally, we said to them, "You have to make a big decision here. It doesn't look like you're going to resolve the smoking thing right away. What you can do now is problem-solve about how to protect the rest of what's been a great life together from being destroyed by this one issue." They took our advice, working out such decisions as where it would be OK with Zach for Barb to smoke at home and what to do about her need to smoke from time to time when they went out. Note that what they did was hardly rocket science. By taking this simple advice, they got themselves back on track: they were again a team with a common goal of preserving all the good things they had together.

In this chapter, we have given you a very specific model that will work well to help you preserve and enhance your teamwork in solving the problems that come your way in life. We don't expect most couples to use such a structured approach for minor problems. We do expect that most couples could benefit from this model when dealing with more important matters, especially those that can lead to unproductive conflict. This is one more way to add more structure when you need it most, to preserve the best in your relationship.

Talking Points

1. All couples have problems; the key is in how you handle them. One path to a great relationship is to handle them as a team.

2. The biggest mistake couples make when dealing with problems is to try to fix things without first talking and building mutual understanding.

3. Problems and disagreements offer great opportunities to enhance a couple's sense of identity as a team, founded on honor, respect, and acceptance.

 ## EXERCISES

There are three separate assignments for this chapter. First, we want you to practice making XYZ statements. Second, we invite you each to rate some common problem areas in your relationship. Third, we ask you to practice the problem-solving model presented in this chapter. No amount of good ideas will help you without practice!

XYZ Statements: Constructive Griping

1. Spend some time thinking about things that your partner has done or regularly does that bother you in some way. On your own paper, list your concerns as you normally might state them. Then practice putting your concerns into the XYZ format: "When you do X in situation Y, I feel Z." Remember to be specific; to talk about behaviors, not personality; and to focus on your own feelings in the situations, not on blaming your partner for problems.

2. Next, repeat the exercise, except now list things your partner does that please you. You will find that the XYZ format also works well for giving specific positive feedback. For example, "When you came home with my favorite ice cream the other night, I felt loved." Try sharing some of the positive thoughts with your spouse.

Problem Area Assessment

The following is a simple measure of common problem areas in relationships. This is a measure originally developed by Knox in 1971, and we have used it for years in our research as a simple but very relevant measure of the problem areas in couples' relationships. As we'll explain, doing this exercise will help you practice the problem-solving skills we have presented. Use separate pieces of paper so that you can each fill out your own form independently.

Consider the following list of issues that all relationships must face. Please rate how much of a problem each area currently is in your relationship; write down a number from 0 (not at all a problem) to 100 (a severe problem) next to each area. For example, if children are somewhat of a problem, you might write 25 next to Children. If children are not a problem in your relationship, you might enter a 0 next to Children. If children are a severe problem, you might write 100. Feel free to add other areas not included in our list. *Be sure to rate all areas.*

Problem Inventory

____	Money	____	Recreation
____	Jealousy	____	Communication
____	Friends	____	Careers
____	In-laws (or other relatives)	____	Alcohol and drugs
____	Sex	____	Children (or potential children)
____	Religion	____	Household chores
____	Time together	____	Other

Practice Problem Solving

For practicing this model, it is critical that you follow these instructions carefully. When dealing with real problems in your relationship, the likelihood of conflict is significant, and we want you to practice in a way that enhances your chances of solidifying these skills.

1. Set aside time to practice uninterrupted. Thirty minutes or so should be sufficient to get started with using the sequence on some of the problems you want to solve.

2. Look over your problem inventories together. Construct a list of those areas in which you each rated the problem as being less serious. These are the problem areas we want you to use to practice the model at the start. We want you to practice with very specific problems and look for very specific solutions. Doing so will boost your skills and help you gain confidence in the model.

3. We recommend that you set aside time to practice the Problem Discussion and Problem Solution sequence several times a week for a couple of weeks. If you put in this time, you'll gain skill and confidence in handling problem areas together.

4. Keep this chapter open when practicing and refer back to the specific steps as you move through them.

8

Keeping Conflict Under Control:
Ground Rules for a Great Relationship

A s we have seen in previous chapters, the choices you make
during arguments can make the difference between being
happy and connected or distant and angry. It's crucial that you manage the conflicts and differences that will arise, without damaging
your relationship. You now understand some strategies for talking
safely without fighting and for solving problems. We end the conflict management portion of our book by sharing with you our six
ground rules for nurturing a great relationship and protecting it from
the destructive effects of conflict.

We use the term *ground rules* to highlight the importance of having a mutual understanding of and commitment to how the two of
you will deal with difficult matters. For us, the term originates with
the game of baseball. Every major league baseball park has its own
ground rules—agreements that are particular to that park. Try typ-
ing "ground rules" into an Internet search engine, and you'll come
up with the rules for several major ballparks. These rules tell the
coaches, players, and umpires such things as whether or not a ball
is considered in play when it hits the top of a particular fence and
bounces back onto the field (or whether that counts as a home run
or a double). You get the idea. Essentially, these rules are designed
to minimize conflicts about what's fair and allow people instead to
focus on enjoying the game.

That's what we want for you. We want the two of you to have some rules that you agree to follow—that you have customized to minimize conflicts that occur in your "home park." Many couples tell us that these ground rules level the playing field in that the rules are clear, easy to follow, and agreed on in advance of conflicts, when things are calm between the partners. But most of all, knowing that there are rules for relationships helps people feel safe at home.

We have had the opportunity to work with all three branches of the U.S. military. During a training we were conducting for the U.S. Navy, a chaplain, who was a lieutenant commander, remarked that it was ironic that we had a Geneva Convention for rules of warfare, but none for fighting constructively in marriage. In this chapter, we will suggest a Geneva Convention of ground rules for your relationship, but it's up to you to decide which you will use and how you might modify them to suit you best. Use these rules to help you control the difficult issues in your relationship rather than allow the issues to control you.

Ground Rule 1: *When conflict is escalating, we will call a Time Out or Pause and either (1) try talking again, using the Speaker-Listener Technique, or (2) agree to talk about the issue later, at a specified time, using the Speaker-Listener Technique.*

This simple ground rule can help you counteract the danger signs—escalation, invalidation, withdrawal and avoidance, and negative interpretations. It's a way to prevent the two of you from damaging your relationship when you know that's likely to happen—or may already have started to happen. We suggest that you not only agree to this ground rule, or something like it, but also agree on the specific signal that will mean Time Out or Pause for the two of you. You could use these terms, of course, but you can also choose something that is unique to you. It is necessary that you both know what the other is trying to do when you hear the signal. Even though one of you may call Time Out more often, it's something that the two of you are doing together. That's the whole point. Otherwise, it can look as though one partner is just avoiding the other, and as we have explained, that just fuels more escalation and anger. In fact, if a withdrawer were to use Time Out in a way that began to look more like withdrawal without follow-up, the partner would probably be wise to keep pursuing issues in an assertive manner—though hopefully choosing reasonable times for doing so.

Using Signals to Detour Around Dangerous Places

Here's a secret. It's something happy couples do that all couples, happy or not, can learn to do better: use some ways to signal each other in times when you need to take your interaction a different direction. One of the things that researchers know is that many couples who do poorly over time don't have ways to exit damaging arguments. Or the ways in which they try to exit these fights (for example, by withdrawing) cause further conflict. Happier, healthier couples have ways to cue or signal each other when it's time to calm it down and rein in the negative feelings and harsh words. The clearer your cue and the firmer your agreement to use it, the better your odds of handling your most difficult issues well. You don't have to use our suggested signals (Time Out or Pause), but at least use ones you both understand.

One couple we worked with used names of food for their conflict management cues. "Hamburger" came to mean Pause for them. So if they were escalating and getting snippy, one would say, "Hey, let's grab a burger." Sometimes this would not only get them to cool it but also get them laughing—many experts do believe humor helps in just about any situation!

It is important to remember that cues are for the two of you together. When you start to give a signal to your partner, use it also to take responsibility for calming yourself down. Mutually agreed-on signals are not an excuse to control your partner but rather a way to mutually take control of your conflict.

One important hint: you can call Pause if you realize that you, your partner, or both of you are getting out of control. You don't have to keep driving down a road that has signs all over it that say "Danger Ahead!" You are calling a Time Out on the communication at that moment, not on each other. Don't simply say "Pause" and leave the room, though. Instead, say something like "This is getting hot; let's stop the action and talk later, OK?" You are working together to stop the destructive process.

Using Time Outs gives withdrawers confidence that conflict won't get out of hand. Some withdrawers are better able to tolerate conflict knowing they can stop it at any time. However, Time Outs will not work for pursuers at all if the two of you don't come back to talking about issues that you've paused. We realize that for many couples, we're addressing this last comment to men. Although we've joked that when men call for Time Outs, it's a kind of "men-o-pause," it's no joke at all to a pursuer if a withdrawer never comes back to another time to talk. You've got to make it happen, and it's probably more important, in general, for the one who called for a Time Out to be especially diligent about following up.

If you are a pursuer, this part of the ground rule addresses your concern that Time Outs mean withdrawal and avoidance. The two of you do need to discuss important issues, but in a productive manner. By agreeing to use the Speaker-Listener Technique when you come back to talking about an issue, you are agreeing to deal more effectively with the issue that got out of hand.

When you do decide to talk later, try to set the time right then. Perhaps in an hour, or maybe the next day would be a good time to talk. If things were really heated when the Pause was called, you may find that you can't talk right then even about when you'll come back to the discussion. That's OK. You can set a time after things have calmed down between the two of you.

We are often asked an important question about Time Out: "What do I do if we use Time Outs on important matters, but my partner will not come back to talking about these issues at another time?" When this happens, we have come to believe that, unless you are in a relationship that is physically dangerous, you are likely better off pursuing the issue assertively—yet without hostility. In fact, a couple of studies hint that some marriages do better in the future when women are more negative in the present. This may sound inconsistent with some of the other things we've said, but in one way it makes perfect sense. Many of us in the field believe that such findings suggest it's generally better for women to raise issues, even if it means more conflict in the short run, if not doing so means important issues are going to be ignored.

It truly is important for each of you to raise concerns that you have in your relationship. Yet we hope you are learning (or have learned already) constructive ways to do so. Constructive does not mean peace at any price. It's better to deal with matters head on than not at all. If you are prone to withdraw, even using Time Out to avoid issues, fight that tendency within yourself. Don't put your partner into the bind of having to decide whether to pursue you or not. In the long run, that'll be far harder on both of you than facing issues as a team in the here and now.

Now we'll give two examples of the use of this ground rule by couples who have come to our PREP workshops. Luke and Tara have been married for twenty years and have two teenage sons. Before learning these techniques, they would have frequent, intense arguments that ended with shouting and threats about the future of the relationship. Both came from homes where open, intense conflict was relatively common, so changing their pattern was not easy for them. As you will see, they still escalate rather easily, but now they know how to stop it when the argument gets going:

TARA: *(annoyed and showing it)* You forgot to get the trash out in time for the garbage man. The cans are already full.

LUKE: *(also annoyed, looking up from the paper)* It's no big deal. I'll just stuff it all down more.

TARA: Yeah, right. The trash will be overflowing in the garage by next week.

LUKE: *(irritated)* What do you want me to do now? I forgot. Just leave it.

TARA: *(very angry now, voice raised)* You aren't getting a lot of the things done around here that you are supposed to.

LUKE: Let's Pause, OK? This isn't getting us anywhere.

TARA: OK. When can we sit down and talk more about it? After *Home Improvement* tonight?

LUKE: OK. As soon as the show is over.

There is nothing magic here. It's really very simple, but the effect is potentially powerful for your relationship. This couple took a Time Out by calling "Pause," and that stopped an argument that was only going to damage them. Later they did sit down and talk, using the Speaker-Listener Technique, about Tara's concern that Luke was not meeting his responsibilities at home. Then, using the problem-solving techniques we presented in Chapter Seven, they were able to come up with some possible ways for the chores to get done.

In the next example, another couple used this ground rule to save an important evening from potential disaster. Jake and Alexandra had been married for six years and had no children. They wanted kids but were having trouble getting pregnant. This added plenty of strain to their marriage. They had decided to take a weekend trip to the mountains, to get away and spend a relaxing—perhaps romantic—couple of days together. They had both been looking forward to this time together for months. They had this conversation on their first evening, as they got into bed together:

ALEXANDRA: *(feeling romantic and snuggling up to Jake)* It's so nice to get away. No distractions. This feels good.

JAKE: *(likewise inclined, and beginning to caress her)* Yeah, we should've done this months ago. Maybe a relaxed setting can help you get pregnant.

ALEXANDRA: *(bristling at the thought)* "Help *you* get pregnant"? That sounds like you think it's my fault we're not getting pregnant. Why did you have to bring that up?

JAKE: *(anxious and annoyed at himself for spoiling the moment)* I don't think it's your fault. We have been through that. I just meant . . .

ALEXANDRA: *(angry)* You just meant to say that there is something wrong with me.

JAKE: Hold on. Pause. I'm sorry that I mentioned pregnancy. Do you want to talk this through now, or set a time for later?

ALEXANDRA: *(softening)* If we don't talk about it a little bit, I think the rest of the evening will be a drag.

JAKE: OK, you have the floor. *(He picks up the remote control on the nightstand and hands it to her.)*

ALEXANDRA (SPEAKER): I got all tense when you brought up pregnancy, and I felt like you were blaming me for our infertility.

JAKE (LISTENER): So mentioning that subject raised unpleasant feelings, and more so because you felt blamed.

ALEXANDRA (SPEAKER): Yes. That whole thing has been just awful for us, and I was hoping to get away from it for the weekend.

JAKE (LISTENER): It's been really hard on you, and you wanted to just forget about it this weekend.

ALEXANDRA (SPEAKER): And I wanted us to focus on rediscovering how to be a little bit romantic, like it used to be.

JAKE (LISTENER): Just you and me making love without a care.

ALEXANDRA (SPEAKER): *(feeling really listened to and cared for)* Yes. Your turn. *(She hands Jake the floor.)*

JAKE (SPEAKER): Boy, do I feel like a jerk. I didn't mean to mess up the moment, though I see how what I said affected you.

ALEXANDRA (LISTENER): You feel bad that you said anything. You did not mean to screw things up between us tonight.

JAKE (SPEAKER): You got it. And I really don't think it's your fault we aren't pregnant. Whatever isn't working right in our bodies, I don't think of it as you or me screwing up. When I said what I said about you getting pregnant, I think of *us* getting pregnant, but really, it's you that will actually be pregnant. That's all I meant.

ALEXANDRA (LISTENER): *(with a smile)* You didn't mean to be a jerk.

JAKE (SPEAKER): *(chuckling back)* That's kind of blunt, but yeah, that's what I'm saying. I think we should just avoid that whole topic for the weekend.

ALEXANDRA (LISTENER): You think we should make infertility an off-limits topic this weekend.

JAKE: Yes! *(He hands her the floor.)*

ALEXANDRA (SPEAKER): I agree. OK, where were we? *(tossing the remote on the floor)*

JAKE: *(big smile)* You were calling me a jerk.

ALEXANDRA: *(playfully)* Oh yeah. Come over here, jerk.

JAKE: *(moving closer to kiss her)* I'm all yours.

Notice how effectively they used the Pause to stop what could have turned into an awful fight. Alexandra was too hurt to just shelve the issue. She needed to talk right then, and Jake agreed. Doing so helped them diffuse the tension and come back together, and it saved their special weekend. This is a great example of what we meant in Chapter Six about not letting events drag you into arguments about issues.

SELF-REGULATION (A FANCY WAY OF SAYING "STAYING IN CONTROL")

Most of what we've been suggesting is that you work together to manage negative emotions and disagreements well. How well you can do this depends in large measure on your ability to manage your own emotions when things are going downhill. There are two keys to self-regulation: watching how you think and knowing what you can do to relax your body.

Watching How You Think

Imagine this. Your partner has just said something that you find incredibly hurtful. Whether or not he or she meant to is one thing. How you choose to think about it is everything. Most of us react more to *our interpretation* of what was actually said than to what our partner meant and did say. What we have been calling negative interpretations researchers might call maladaptive attributions. That's a technical way to say that some people tend to make consistent, negative judgments of their partner's motives.

Research, such as that by Frank Fincham at State University of New York at Buffalo and Tom Bradbury at UCLA, confirm something potent here: the judgments you tend to make about why your mate said or did something carry a lot of weight in how you will talk to one another. Some studies show this effect of thoughts on communication to be strongest for women in unhappy marriages. Of course all kinds of other men and women can do this, too.

Take Dee and Martin. They have not been doing so well lately. Married for seven years, they are entering a period when all the pressures of life are making it hard to remember why they fell in love nine years ago. It's Tuesday night, and Dee has just come home from work. Martin was there already. Their boys, Georgie and Frankie, had been told by Martin that they could play Nintendo until dinnertime. Enter Dee.

DEE: *(not sounding particularly upset yet)* We'd agreed that the boys needed to clean up their rooms before they could play Nintendo or computer games.

MARTIN: *(remembering that he'd not remembered this, but also feeling pretty tired from work)* Oh yeah. I forgot.

DEE: *(She hears what she interprets as indifference and invalidation— but what was really simple tiredness—and now feels insulted.)* I guess you think I'm just making up rules for the sake of hearing myself think out loud, eh?

MARTIN: *(Dee isn't really looking for a response to this charge, but because she's made her negative interpretation overt, Martin responds with his defense.)* You are so darned sensitive. I just forgot we said that this morning. I didn't mean anything by forgetting.

DEE: *(Here she goes, moving this event into a full-blown issue.)* You forget a lot, you know. I think that's your way of undermining my authority. *(neatly expressing another negative interpretation)*

Let's give Martin and Dee a big benefit of the doubt here. Let's say they are able to put the brakes on this escalation before any more damage is done in this moment of time. Martin suggested a Time Out, which sounded very good to Dee. Which pair of thoughts shown here gives them the best chance of getting back on track?

MARTIN: "She's always dissing me in front of the boys. She must think I'm an idiot."

DEE: "What a jerk. He must have the most pathetic memory on the planet—or else he does this just to frustrate me. Arrgggghhh!"

MARTIN: "I bet she's had a pretty tough day. Maybe I can give her some space, then look for a way to tell her I do care about what we agree to do with the boys."

DEE: "Maybe that comment about always forgetting things was a little out there. That's not very fair of me. I forget some things, too."

In their book *We Can Work It Out,* Clifford Notarius and Howard (coauthor) labeled the kind of thoughts in the first pair *hot thoughts.* You want to stay angry? They'll do the job. As Fincham and Bradbury suggest, you'll carry these thoughts and angry feelings right back into your relationship if you don't interrupt them. You have little or no chance of handling these times of escalation well if you choose to think in these ways. It's not easy to stop, though, because doing so requires you to do something difficult: put aside righteous indignation and have the humility to give the other the benefit of the doubt. Your call. Your choice. Your relationship.

Putting the Brakes on That Runaway Train (Your Body)

John Gottman and his colleagues have been making the case that part of what is important in handling conflict well is controlling the bodily reactions that come along with it. Once you are upset, it's not just your thoughts you are trying to get hold of—it's your body, too. John's research team has found that when upset couples simply read magazines for twenty minutes or so before continuing to talk, it's far more likely that the rest of the talk will go better. To use this approach in your relationship, you need to think ahead of time about the kinds of things that you can do to help you relax. These may be very different for each of you. Here are some ideas:

- Lying down, eyes closed, thinking positive thoughts

- Taking a walk

- Reading a novel (that already has you hooked)

- Playing with the kids

- Cleaning (works for some people)

- Weightlifting

If you are a couple that is particularly prone to volatile, escalating arguments, you'll find that you have to be that much more specific with one another about how you take Time Outs and what you will do during them. Remember, it's especially important that you work on calming both your thoughts and your body.

Ground Rule 2: *When we are having trouble communicating, we will "engage" the Speaker-Listener Technique.*

We can't say it enough: it is extremely important for every couple to have at least one good way to talk when it's hardest to do so. With this ground rule, you are agreeing to use more structure when you need it. The earlier example with Jake and Alexandra highlights this point. However, there are many times when you may not need a Time Out but do need to make the transition to a more effective way to talk. Remember, talking without fighting is key.

For example, suppose that you wanted to talk about a problem such as how money is being spent. You know from your history that these talks usually get difficult. You would be wise to follow this ground rule, raising the issue in this way: "Dear, I'm pretty concerned about money right now. Let's sit down and talk using the floor." Such a statement cues your partner that you are raising an important issue and that you want to talk it out carefully. This is the most common use of this ground rule.

There are other times when things have already escalated, and a Time Out might have helped, but you skip right to using the Speaker-Listener Technique. The point of this ground rule is that the two of you have made a decision to handle difficult or sensitive topics more effectively and with increased structure, rather than to use old, destructive modes of communication.

Ground Rule 3: *We will completely separate Problem Discussion from Problem Solution.*

Too often, couples rush to agree to some solution, and the solution fails. It makes no sense to hurry when doing so only moves you backward. Review the conversation between Tessie and Peter about Jeremy and preschool in Chapter Five. Notice how they had a great discussion but did not seek a specific solution. They each expressed their concerns and were ready to try problem solving on this issue. Let's pick it up from where we left off:

TESSIE: I think we're ready for problem solving; what do you think?
PETER: I agree. I'm feeling like we had a good talk and got a lot out on the table. Now working on some solutions would be great.

With these simple comments, they have made the transition from Problem Discussion to Problem Solution. They have learned the value of separating the two, and they are using terms both understand to cue each other to shift gears. Discussion and solution are different processes: whenever you start to solve an issue, stop and ask yourself, "Do I really understand my partner's perspective? Do I feel understood?" If either answer is no, you are probably not ready to move to solutions. This ground rule is a simple reminder of the need to talk first, solve second.

Ground Rule 4: *We can bring up issues at any time, but the Listener can say, "This is not a good time." If the Listener does not want to talk at* *that time, he or she takes responsibility for setting up a time to talk in the near future.*

This ground rule accomplishes one very important thing: it ensures that you will not have an important or difficult talk about an issue unless you both agree that the time is right. How often do you begin talking about a key issue in your relationship when your partner is just not ready for it? Most couples talk about their most important issues at the worst times—dinnertime, bedtime, when it's time to get the kids off for school, as soon as you walk in the door after work, when one of you is preoccupied with an important project or task—you get the picture. These are times when your spouse may be a captive audience, but you certainly don't have his or her attention. Because these tend to be stressful times in the routine of life, they aren't good times to talk things out.

This ground rule assumes two things: (1) you each are responsible for knowing when you are capable of discussing something with appropriate attention to what your partner has to say, and (2) you

IS THIS A GOOD TIME TO TALK?

RAGNAR STORAASLI

can each respect the other when he or she says, "I can't deal with this right now."

You may ask, "Isn't this just a prescription for avoidance?" That's where the second part of the ground rule comes in. The partner who doesn't want to talk takes responsibility for making the discussion (conflict talk) happen in the near future. This is critical. Your partner will have a much easier time putting off the conversation if he or she has confidence that you really will follow through. We recommend that when you use this ground rule, you agree that you'll set up a better time within twenty-four to forty-eight hours. This may not always be practical, but it works as a good rule of thumb. Here's one example.

Martina and Nick are a couple with two children, a five-year-old girl and a two-year-old boy. As is typical of many couples with young children, they have little time for talking things out in their marriage, much less sleeping. As a result, they often are alone only at bedtime, after both kids are finally bathed and asleep.

NICK: I can't believe how Mary wants to hear the same story ten times in a row. I thought she'd never get to sleep.

MARTINA: It's the same with naps. You'd think she would be bored to death with those stories.

NICK: I would. Speaking of boring things, we need to talk about those life insurance decisions. I know that agent will call back any day.

MARTINA: I know it's important, but I just can't focus right now. I think I could focus for about ten minutes on Jay Leno, and that's about it.

NICK: Pretty wiped, eh? Me, too. Well, what would be a good time to talk about this?

MARTINA: No guarantee I will be alive, but I think I might have the energy around lunchtime tomorrow. Could you come home? Maybe we'll get lucky and catch Matt on his nap.

NICK: Sounds good. Let's watch Jay and crash.

It is now Martina's responsibility to bring it up again tomorrow and make this talk happen. Because their agreement is rather specific, Nick should be able to show up at lunchtime for their talk. They may be too tired and busy for there ever to be a "perfect" time to talk this subject out, but there are some times that are better than others.

As one variation of this ground rule, you may want to come to an agreement that certain times are *never* good for bringing up important things. For example, we have worked with many couples who have agreed that neither will bring up anything significant within thirty minutes of bedtime. These couples decided that at bedtime they are just too tired and it's important to be winding down.

This ground rule respects the need to talk about issues as well as the need not to talk, and provides a balanced compromise for you to follow as you move toward feeling safer in your relationship.

Ground Rule 5: *We will have weekly couple meetings.*

Most couples do not set aside a regular time for dealing with key issues or problems. It's hard to get most of us to do this because of the fast-paced lives so many of us live. Nevertheless, the advantages of having a weekly meeting time far outweigh any negatives. First, this is a tangible way to place high priority on your marriage by carving out time for its upkeep. We know you are busy, but if you decide that this is important, you can find the time to make it work.

Second, following this ground rule ensures that even if there is no other good time to deal with issues, you at least have this one regular time. You might be surprised at how much you can get done in thirty minutes or so of concentrated attention on an issue. During this meeting, you can talk about the relationship, talk about specific problems, or plan for what's coming up.

A third advantage of this ground rule is that having a weekly meeting time takes much of the day-to-day pressure off your relationship. This is especially true if you are snared in the pursuer-withdrawer trap. If something happens that brings up a gripe for

you, it's much easier to delay bringing it up until another time if you know there *will* be another time. Pursuers can relax. You'll have your chance to raise your issue. Withdrawers can relax during the week, knowing that events will not trigger issues. We also find that withdrawers, who of course have things they want to talk about too, may actually start looking forward to meetings, because such meetings are a safe place to talk without fighting.

You can think of the meeting as a time during which you select an issue to talk about, to engage in what we have previously called conflict talk. If you haven't made this deliberate selection, your communication—like a computer's settings—should have a default mode, which is friendship talk or casual talk.

How many of our successful couples actually have meetings? We think it varies over time. Knowing they could have a meeting and talk well gives many couples the confidence that allows them to handle conflict talk. Many couples love the idea, have meetings religiously for a while, and then taper off. Things go well for a while because of their increased confidence and skills. With luck, they will realize they need the meetings to help contain and control conflict, and start them up again. Other couples are really dedicated and maintain meetings on ongoing basis, but perhaps only a couple of times a month instead of weekly. Just as with all the other skills we have offered, be flexible and customize the ground rule to fit your needs.

You may find it tempting to skip the meetings when you are getting along really well. Don't succumb to this urge. For example, Roberto and Margaret have set aside Wednesday nights at nine o'clock as a time for their couple meeting. If they are getting along really well during the week and Wednesday night rolls around, each begins to think, "We don't need to meet tonight. No use stirring things up when we are getting along so well." Then one or the other says, "Hey, Honey, let's just skip the meeting tonight, things are going so well."

What Roberto and Margaret came to realize is that things were going so well partly because they were regularly having their meetings. After they canceled a few, they noticed that more conflicts would come up during the week. They had given up their time to deal with issues and reverted to the uncertainty of dealing with things "if and when." They decided that "if and when" was not placing the proper importance on their marriage, and they got back to the meetings.

Ground Rule 6: *We will make time for the great things: fun, friendship, and sensuality. We will agree to protect these times from conflict and the need to deal with issues.*

Just as it's important to have time set aside to deal with issues in your relationship, it's critical that you protect positive times from conflicts over issues. You can't be focusing on issues all the time and have a really great marriage. You need some time when you are together relaxing—having fun, talking as friends, making love, and so forth—when conflict and problems are off-limits. This is such a key point that later in the book we'll devote whole chapters to these important ways to connect.

For now, we'll emphasize two points embodied in this ground rule. First, *make time* for these great things. After all, they're what brought you together in the first place. Second, if you're spending time together in one of these ways, don't bring up issues that you have to work on. And if an issue does come up, table it for later—when you have your couple meeting to deal with issues constructively.

The example of Alexandra and Jake presented earlier in this chapter makes this point well. They were out to have a relaxing and romantic weekend, and this wasn't the time to focus on one of their key issues. Using Pause and the Speaker-Listener Technique helped them get refocused on the real reason they had gotten away. It's better still if you consciously decide to protect your relationship by agreeing in advance to keep such issues off-limits during positive times.

One of the most destructive things that can happen to a marriage is to have the growing sense that you are walking in a minefield. You know the feeling. You begin to wonder where the next explosion will come from, and you don't feel in control of where you're going. You no longer feel free to just *be* with your partner. You don't know when you are about to "step in it," but you know right away when you have. Your marriage just doesn't have to be this way, or ever get to be this way in the first place. These ground rules will go a long way to getting you back on safe ground. They work. You can do it.

Talking Points

1. Relationships need ground rules to level the playing field and to be sure both partners are playing by the same rules.

2. Rules are not one-size-fits-all: customize these to fit the needs of your relationship.

3. Couples need to decide on cues to help them navigate among the types of talk—casual talk, conflict talk, and friendship talk—and to avoid destructive types of talk.

EXERCISE

Using the Ground Rules

Your exercise for this chapter is very straightforward: discuss these ground rules and begin to try them out. You may want to modify one or more of them in some specific manner to make them work better for you. That's fine. The key is to review these rules and give them a chance to work in your relationship.

We've listed the rules again here. You might want to write down any changes you make to them now or after the two of you have been using them awhile.

Suggested Ground Rules for Handling Issues

1. When conflict is escalating, we will call a Time Out or Pause and either (1) try talking again, using the Speaker-Listener Technique, or (2) agree to talk about the issue later, at a specified time, using the Speaker-Listener Technique.

2. When we are having trouble communicating, we will "engage" the Speaker-Listener Technique.

3. We will completely separate Problem *Discussion* from Problem *Solution*.

4. We can bring up issues at any time, but the Listener can say, "This is not a good time." If the Listener does not want to talk at that time, he or she takes responsibility for setting up a time to talk in the near future. (You need to decide how you will define "the near future.")

5. We will have weekly couple meetings. (Schedule the time now for your weekly couple meeting. There is no time like the present.)

6. We will make time for the great things: fun, friendship, and sensuality. We will agree to protect these times from conflict and the need to deal with issues.

Part III

Enjoying Each Other

9

Safe Harbor: Preserving and Protecting Friendship

In our research, we have been surprised to learn that people from all walks of life, of all ages, both men and women, say that the most important goal for their marriage is to have a friend and to be a friend. But for too many couples, this desire for lifelong intimacy reflects the triumph of hope over reality. Too many people feel isolated and lonely, unsafe and disconnected in their marriage.

Our goal in this chapter is to help you transform the deep desire for your mate to be your best friend into a reality. Like a garden, friendship needs to be nurtured in ways that many married couples fail to realize until their friendship is gone. Here is our research-based recipe for restoring, preserving, and deepening your friendship in your marriage for many years to come.

WHAT IS A FRIEND?

How would you answer that question? When we've asked people, they've said that a friend is someone who supports you, is there to talk things through with you, is a safe haven, and is a companion in life. In short, a friend is someone with whom we can relax, open up, feel safe, and feel accepted; a friend is someone we can count on. We talk and do fun things with friends. Research suggests that the support, care, and acceptance friends provide buffer us from the trials and tribulations of life. People who have at least one really good friend do better in almost every conceivable way in life—especially in terms of physical and mental health.

The most powerful aspect of friendship is the feeling of deep intimacy and connection with another. In part this means being able to share what's in your heart, without fear of judgment and reprisal. For most of us this means talking about your hopes and dreams as well as your fears and burdens. For women this kind of sharing often takes place face-to-face, whereas for men talking as friends tends to occur while they are doing something.

People who have at least one really good friend do better in almost every conceivable way in life—especially in terms of physical and mental health.

Jean-Philippe Laurenceau, at the University of Miami, has found that people feel the greatest intimacy when they are able to self-disclose to another who is responsive to them about what has been shared. Intimacy is deepened when what is shared includes feelings. This sounds a lot like what many of us would call the best of friendship—being able to let it all hang out there, and knowing you will not be hanging out there on a limb by yourself.

Although of course we hope you have friendships of this kind outside your marriage, our goal here is to help you with your friendship with your partner. Friendship in marriage means being able to hear your partner's heart in whatever ways he or she can most readily share it. Sharing at this level will mean different things to different people, so this is one of those areas where there can be a unique blending of who each of you are in the mystery of deeper connection. Whether you are quiet or quite outspoken, learn to listen carefully for what's in your partner's heart and in your partner's soul, and to share what is in yours.

The desire to find a soul mate is almost universal. We are saddened to hear of divorces in which the person who files says that the ex-spouse was not his or her soul mate. Although we can cer-

tainly understand the loneliness that erodes unhappy marriages, we know we can help couples build bridges over years of distance by making it possible for them to be better friends. As coauthor Howard wrote in an essay in the book he edited with Janice Levine, *Why Do Fools Fall in Love?* "Don't expect to be your beloved's soul mate before you've been there as your mate's soul unfolds" (p. 204).

BARRIERS TO FRIENDSHIP

If friendship encompasses so much of what people say they want in marriage, why aren't more married couples good friends? Let's look at some common barriers.

There's No Time

We all lead busy lives. What with work, the needs of the children, the upkeep of the home, working out, browsing the Internet, the PTA, and the town council, who's got time for friendship in their marriage?

Friendship, the very core of your relationship, often takes a backseat to all these competing responsibilities, activities, and interests.

For example, Evelyn and Herman are a dual-career couple who've been together about five years. Their daughter, Linda, was a two-year-old at the time we met them. Although they were happy with their marriage and life together, they were feeling that something was slipping away.

HERMAN: We used to sit around for hours just talking about things. You know, like politics or the meaning of life. We also have had some great talks in the past about the Bible. But we just don't seem to have the time for that anymore.

EVELYN: You're right. It used to be so much fun just being together, listening to how we each thought about things.

HERMAN: Those talks really brought us together. Why don't we still have them?

EVELYN: We don't take that kind of time like we used to. Now we've got Linda, the house—not to mention that we each bring too much work home.

HERMAN: It seems like we're letting something slip away.

All too often, couples fail to take the time just to talk as friends. The other needs and cares of life crowd out this time to relax and talk. Often this is a matter of priorities. When couples date before marriage, they usually find lots of time for being together. Life may or may not be less busy then, but finding the time to be together is a higher priority.

We're Not Friends, We're Married

Many people have told us that they were friends with their spouses to begin with, but not anymore; now they are "just married." It's as if once you're married, you can't be friends anymore. That's a very mistaken belief.

The strongest marriages we've seen have maintained a solid friendship over the years. Take Geena and Pierre, who've been happily married for over forty years. We asked them, "What's the secret?" Without hesitation, they answered "friendship and commitment." They started out with a great friendship and never let it go. They've maintained a deep respect for one another as friends who freely share thoughts and feelings about all sorts of things—in an atmosphere of deep acceptance and total safety. That's kept their bond strong and alive.

Don't buy into an expectation which says that because you're married—or planning to be—you can't stay friends. You can!

We Don't Talk Like Friends Anymore

If you've been married for some time, think for a moment about a friendship you enjoy with someone other than your mate. How often do you have to talk with that person about problems between the two of you? Not often, we'd bet. Friends aren't people with whom we argue a lot. In fact, one of the nicest things about friendships is that you don't usually have to work out a lot of issues. Instead you're able to focus on mutual interests in a way that's fun for both of you.

Friends talk about sports, spiritual matters, politics, philosophy of life, fun things they've done or will do, dreams about the future, and thoughts about what each is going through at this point in life. In contrast, what do couples talk about most after they've been together for years? Problems with the kids, problems with money and budgets, problems with getting the car fixed, concerns about who's got time to get some project around the home done, concerns about in-laws, problems with the neighbor's dog, concerns about each other's health. . . . We could go on and on, but we think you've got the picture.

If the two of you are not careful, most of your talks will be about problems and concerns—not points of view and points of interest. Problems and concerns are part of married life, and you must deal with them, but you'll lose that deeper sense of being friends if they're all you talk about.

Talking with Your Buddy

Studies show that women are generally more comfortable and more interested in talking about relationships. For example, our colleague Danielle Julien at the University of Quebec at Montreal has conducted a great deal of research on the differences between men and women. In one study, she asked females to bring in one of their female friends and asked males to bring in a male friend, and had them talk about concerns in their marriages. Here's what she told us about what she saw over and over again: "Having observed hundreds of conversations of wives and (some) husbands confiding marital problems to their best friends, I could say that wife-friend conversations look like happy fishes swimming in fresh water. Talking about relationships seemed so natural and enjoyable to them that we often had to interrupt them because they would not stop. Several husband-friend conversations looked uneasy, and we surely never had to interrupt them: their conversations were short."

That sounds like a real difference that matches what most of us think about men and women. Women are more inclined than men to want to talk about their relationships with both their friends and their partners. Women's higher comfort level with talking about feelings and relationships could certainly be taken as evidence that women are more inclined toward intimacy than men, but that's true only if we consider talking to be the only way to be intimate.

Walls, Moats, and Towers: The Ravages of Conflict

Ever taken a good look at a castle in Europe? They were built with conflict in mind. They were built for defense. One of the key reasons couples have trouble staying friends is that friendship is cut off by the walls of conflict. For example, when you're angry with your partner about something that's happened, you're not going to feel much like being friends right then. You may feel far more like putting up a wall. We believe that this is the chief reason that some couples talk less and less like friends over the years. They're allowing their issues to damage their friendship.

One couple, Claudia and Kevin, were having real trouble preserving friendship in their relationship. They'd been married for fifteen years, had three kids, and were rarely able to get away just to be together. They bred dogs together, but hadn't been away to a dog show since they first had children. On one occasion, they'd gotten away to a show and had left the kids with his parents. This was their first chance to be away alone in years.

They were sitting in the hot tub of the hotel, really enjoying talking together about the show and the dogs they breed, when a conflict came up that ended their enjoyable time together.

CLAUDIA: (very relaxed) This is such a nice setting for the dog show.

KEVIN: (equally relaxed, as he held Claudia's hand) Yeah. This is great. I can't believe the size of that shepherd.

CLAUDIA: Me either. I don't think I've ever seen a German shepherd that big. This reminds me. If we're going to breed Sasha again this year, we'd better fix that pen.

KEVIN: (tensing up a bit) But I told you how big a job that was. We'd have to tear out that fence along the property line, build up the side of the hill, and pour concrete for the perimeter of the fence.

CLAUDIA: (sensing his tension, and now her own) Would we really have to do all that? I know we have to get the pen fixed, but I don't think we'd have to make that big a deal out of getting it done.

KEVIN: (growing angry) There you go, coming up with things for me to do. I hate having all these projects lined up. That's a really big job if we're going to do it right.

CLAUDIA: (getting ticked off, too) You always make such a big production out of these projects. We don't have to do the job that well to make the pen usable again. We could do it on a Saturday.

KEVIN: *(turning away)* Maybe *you* could. But I don't want to do it unless we do it right, and we can't afford to fix that fence the right way right now.

CLAUDIA: *(looking right at Kevin, with growing contempt)* Heck, if you watched how you spent money for a couple of months, we could pay someone else to do the whole thing right, if that's so important to you.

KEVIN: *(angry, getting out of the tub)* You spend just as much as I do on stuff. I'm going up to the room.

Notice what happened here. There they were, relaxed, spending some time together, being friends. But their talk turned into a conflict about issues. As Claudia raised the subject of breeding their dog Sasha, they got into an argument in which many issues were triggered—projects around the home, their different styles of getting things done, and money. Perhaps some hidden issues were triggered as well. What had the potential of being a great talk as friends turned into a nasty argument as spouses. Worse, the next time they have an opportunity to talk as friends, they may be less likely to risk sharing for fear of conflict erupting again.

One of the most painful things that can happen in a marriage is that this aspect of friendship, which should be precious and pleasurable, becomes scary instead. When you start to feel that time with your partner is most often going to be a hassle or even painful, your relationship may be on the road to serious trouble.

A great many couples have told us they're nervous when they're together and even when just thinking about being together. When you sense that talking leads to fighting, you may end up just stopping talking.

We Are the Victims of Reckless Words

Couples build up one of the major barriers to friendship in marriage when things that they shared at tender and intimate moments are later used as weapons in fights. This behavior is incredibly destructive to your friendship. When we are upset, we often say nasty things that erode intimacy and friendship. Who is going to feel it's safe to share deep feelings if what he or she says can get used later in a fight? Feeling unsafe leads us to act to protect ourselves, rather than to reveal ourselves.

PROTECTING FRIENDSHIP
IN YOUR MARRIAGE

We've developed what couples find to be very powerful ideas for protecting friendship. If you have a good friendship rolling along, these principles will help prevent you from losing that wonderful connection. If you've lost that friendship feeling, these ideas can help you regain it.

Make the Time

Although it's great to be friends no matter what you're doing, we think you can benefit from setting time apart specifically for friendship. Simply put, you must make the time happen because it won't happen by itself. Most of us are way too busy to do things we don't intentionally make time for. Sad but true. We let all the busy stuff of life crowd out friendship.

We mentioned how Geena and Pierre had preserved and deepened their friendship over the forty years they've been married. One of the things they've done to keep friendship alive is plan time to be alone together. They take long walks together and talk as they walk. They go out to dinner. They'd take weekend vacations from time to time, without the kids. They've always made the time, and it's been paying off for over forty years.

If you are really serious in thinking that friendship is important, you need to plan time to be together as friends. That means giving priority to this aspect of

The problem we all face is that there is much less opportunity for quality time when there is little quantity time.

your intimacy. Making time for friendship is one of the key invest-ments you can make in your relationship. The problem we all face is that there is much less opportunity for quality time when there is little quantity time. You need to put some boundaries around all the other things you do in life to carve out time for friendship. But that's not all you need to do to protect friendship.

Protect Your Friendship from Conflict and Issues

The strategies for handling conflict that we presented in the first part of the book are powerful tools, but the two of you didn't marry each other with the goal of having a great conflict management partner. You do have to handle conflict well, though, if you want to protect the more wonderful aspects of intimacy and connection in your marriage. That means setting time aside to deal with issues as issues, taking Time Outs when conflicts are intruding on times you set aside for friendship, and forgiving one another for problems in the past so that you nurture the trust, safety, and acceptance that friendship thrives on. Acting on all the material presented earlier in this book will make it much more likely that you'll have a great friendship that can grow deeper over time.

You might be surprised how effective it can be for the two of you to agree that some times are "friend time" and are off-limits for con-flicts and issues. For example, you could decide that whenever you take a walk in your neighborhood, it's automatically friend time. Or you could go out to dinner and agree that "this is friend time, tonight, OK?" Some couples benefit from agreeing that unless they've decided otherwise, they are in friendship talk mode, not conflict talk mode. By keeping issues in their place, you allow room for the deepening of friendship between the two of you.

You Need a Friend

One of the significant changes in our work with couples since the publication of the first edition of our book has been to make friendship a high priority. All three of us have increasingly come to believe that the simple ideas in this chapter are the most powerful of all for keeping couples on the right path. If you can do what we're suggesting, and keep doing it well, you're likely to do very well in life together.

In our research, we have couples talk as friends as well as talk about areas of disagreement. One important finding to date is that couples who are happy over time are able to talk about things that friends talk about (telling funny stories about work, sharing tales about their children, and the like), whereas couples heading for problems allow relationship conflicts to intrude on their friendship talks.

Most important, we have found in our workshops and clinical work that couples love the idea of being better friends and are able to start doing so immediately. Being a friend to our spouse is not a skill we have to learn as much as it is a part of our nature we need to protect and explore. Too often we ignore or inhibit our natural friendship tendencies. You can start changing that right now!

How to Talk Like Friends

Now let's move on to discuss how you can talk like good friends. We want to highlight a couple of points about how friends talk that can help you protect and enhance your relationship.

Friends Aren't Focused on Solving Problems

Most of the time, when you are with a friend you don't have to solve a problem. You may have a limited amount of time together, but there's no pressure to get something done. When you feel pressed to solve a problem, it's easy to cut off discussions that can bring you closer together. That's why it's so important not to talk about issues when you're in friendship mode.

Listen Like a Friend

Good friends listen with little defensiveness. You don't have to worry so much about feelings getting hurt or whether your friend will be offended. That's because a friend cares about what you think and feel, and relationship issues are rarely at stake.

Our friend and colleague Bill Coffin of the U.S. Navy once noted, "A friend is someone who is glad to see you and doesn't have any immediate plans for your improvement." When you're talking as friends, you aren't trying to change one another. You can both relax and just enjoy being together. Even when you let your hair down and talk about something really serious, you don't want a friend to tell you what to do as much as you want him or her to listen to your heart. That's something you can give to each other.

Unlike so many other things you've learned in this book, friendship is a not just a skill but a natural desire that you must nurture and protect. To keep your marriage strong, you need to invest in your relationship by making friendship a major priority. We can't think of anything of greater importance for the long-term health of your marriage than for you to stay friends.

Talking Points

1. Friendship is at the core of long-lasting, happy marriages.

2. Friendship needs to be nurtured: make the time to share intimate friendship talk, and protect that time from conflict.

3. Enhancing friendship in your marriage is an investment that will pay off over time in happiness and relationship satisfaction.

EXERCISES

Plan some time for these exercises. Have fun, relax, and enjoy your friendship.

Friendship Talks

Plan a quiet, uninterrupted time to talk as friends. Take turns picking topics of interest for each of you. Ban relationship conflict issues and problem solutions. Consider some of the following topics:

- Some aspect of your family of origin that you've been thinking about.

- Personal goals, dreams, or aspirations.

- A recent book or movie. Pretend you're professional critics, if you like.

- Current events: sports, politics, and the like.

Interviews

Take turns pretending to be your favorite TV interviewers; interview your partner about his or her life story. This can be a lot of fun, and it's really in the spirit of listening as friends. The best interviewers on TV are really good at listening and drawing their guests out of themselves. Try to draw one another out in your sharing together as friends, and learn something new about each other.

Making Time for Friendship

Talk together about how you can build time for friendship into your weekly routine. If you both believe friendship should be a priority, how do you want to demonstrate that?

10

Playing Together: How to Succeed in Fun Without Really Trying

When was the last time the two of you went out on a date? For too many couples, the answer is, "way too long ago." Fun plays a vital role in the health of a marriage, yet many couples put having fun together on the back burner of their relationship. To be honest, we were guilty of this mistake in the early versions of PREP. Years ago, fun was a very small part of our emphasis. Although it may seem obvious that fun is important, until recently most relationship research and books for couples ignored the role of fun. Not anymore; not in our work.

This emphasis on fun affected us professionally as well. When we started doing PREP workshops, we made a commitment to each other that we wouldn't continue if we didn't have fun doing it. Surely there are many things we all need to do in life, whether fun or not, but in our hurried, fast-paced world, people give too little notice to fun in their lives.

We've had some funny moments, too. One time, Susan got a great laugh after Scott had said that PREP was practical, simple, and fun. Susan remarked that Scott was practical, Howie was fun, and she'd keep it simple. Howard told a quick joke (at least he thought it was a joke!), and no one laughed (except Howard). Scott then made a comment about how that always happens, and everyone laughed! As Scott has consoled Howard, if you can't make other people laugh with you, let them laugh at you. But don't wait till

coming to one of our workshops to enhance the fun in your relationship. We hope you've had fun reading some parts of this book.
We've certainly tried to keep it lively.

OK, enough of our silliness. We move from the silly to a serious point: you need to know how to have fun together. If you
already know how, and are actually having fun, you need to keep
at it. It's very important. In our poll we've mentioned several times,
people responded to more than fifty questions on all aspects of their
relationships—questions looking at satisfaction, commitment, communication, sex, and just about anything else you can think of,
including, "When is the last time you went out on a date?" (We will
share this specific surprising finding later, so be patient!)

Among all these variables, we were very surprised to find that
the amount of fun partners had together emerged as a key factor in
predicting their overall marital happiness. The message: part of having a great relationship is knowing how to have fun together.

BARRIERS TO FUN

When we interview couples planning marriage, we learn that most
of them have tons of fun early in their relationships. But for too
many, fun fizzles out as time goes on. Here are some of the most
common reasons we hear from couples for why this happens.

We're Too Busy

Couples often stop making the time for fun in their busy lives. Early
in relationships, people tend to put a high priority on going to the
movies, window shopping, walking hand in hand, going bowling,
going out dancing, having dinner out, attending the theatre, or just
hanging out at home and renting a movie.

That's the way it was for Miguel, twenty-eight, and Lucy, thirty.
They'd spend many Saturdays together at the beach swimming and
talking and lying in the sun. They would also take long walks in the
sand and talk about their future together. When they got married,

they continued to go to the beach, but less frequently. A few years later they had their first child, were investing time in her and their careers, and began to spend much less time having fun. Sure—their daughter, Amanda, was a delight for them, and they generally enjoyed their work, but it became rare for Miguel and Lucy to actually go out and have fun as they used to.

Miguel and Lucy noticed over time that life wasn't as much fun as it used to be. They were happy together, and their eight-year marriage was solid, but they had let something slip away. It's really pretty simple. Life is more fun when you do fun things. The rest of life will crowd out fun if you don't make time for fun to happen. We encourage you to find the time to keep up the fun and playfulness that can make your relationship more delightful.

As we mentioned, our poll asked people how long it had been since they'd been on a date with their partner. We divided couples into groups based on stage of relationship and whether it was the husband or wife who responded. Table 10.1 shows what we found.

On average, couples were going close to two months without having a date! Although this may seem a short time for some couples (you know who you are!), we believe it's one sign that most couples are not having enough fun together. Of course we realize and hope that couples are laughing, playing, and doing fun things at other times besides dates. But having a date is one way to make sure fun times happen.

There were two other major results. First, the couples having the least fun were those in the middle six to twenty years of marriage,

Table 10.1. How Many Weeks Has It Been Since You Had a Date with Your Partner?

	Engaged	Married Less Than 5 Years	6 to 10 Years	11 to 19 Years	20 to 31 Years	32+ Years
Men	5.2	5.6	8.0	9.0	2.8	3.9
Women	5.9	7.5	12.9	17.8	11.2	2.2

when they are busy raising children and investing in their careers. The most fun-loving couples were the engaged couples (no surprise) and those married more than thirty-two years! So maybe there's light at the end of the tunnel of love! (In your case, Howard, that might be a train coming.)

Our most intriguing result is the finding that men report going out on dates substantially more frequently than women. In some groups, women said it had been twice as long as what the men reported. Why is that? Our best guess is that men and woman have different definitions or standards for what a date is. Hmm . . . sounds like it might be related to their different definitions of intimacy, don't you think? Our workshop participants (at least the women) generally think that men are more inclined to think of things like taking a walk together or watching a game on television together as something of a date. It could also be a difference in marital memory. The key for your relationship is to use this finding to stimulate some conversation (not during a date!) about what a date means to each of you.

Play Is for Kids

Many preschool experts say that playing is the work that children need to do. Through play, children gain developmentally relevant social, emotional, and cognitive abilities. We believe that the developmental importance of play doesn't fade after childhood but continues throughout life. Fun and play allow a release of oneself from all the pressures and hassles of being an adult.

The relaxed togetherness of playful times is important in the initial development of the bond between two people. That's because when we're engaged in fun through play, we're often relaxed and more ourselves. It's under these conditions that people fall in love— when one sees in the other the relaxed self in the context of fun times together. We rarely hear someone say, "I really fell in love with him when I saw how much he loved to work, and realized that we'd never have any time together."

We mentioned how Miguel and Lucy used to go to the ocean more often earlier in their relationship. During their time there they'd splash in the water, make sand castles together, rub suntan lotion on one another, and bury each other—they'd play together like kids! During these times, they'd frequently look at one another and smile in the delight of the moment. You can't put a price tag on the value of that time which builds such basic bonds between the two of you.

Miguel and Lucy still experience that kind of bond when playing with Amanda, but they could use a lot more of this kind of time together, just the two of them. As we said earlier, the couples in really super marriages create this time to play together, which keeps refreshing the bond. So be a kid from time to time.

Conflict Gets in the Way

Just as we discussed in the chapter on friendship, mishandled conflict is a real threat to fun times together. In fact, we'll make the same point in the chapter on sensuality, too. Poorly handled conflict can spill over and damage the most enjoyable aspects of any relationship. The simple tools covered earlier in this book can go a long way to restoring or enhancing mutual enjoyment.

Noreen and Dave were a middle-aged couple we talked with who were making the time for fun. That wasn't the problem. All too often they'd be out to have a fun time, and some event would trigger an issue that would kill the playfulness of the moment.

One night, they'd arranged for a sitter for the kids and went out to take a class in couple's massage. They thought, "This will push us a bit to have some fun in a new way." Great idea! The instructor was making a point to the class about paying attention to the reactions of the partner. Dave whispered to Noreen, "That's a great point." Noreen whispered back, "I've been trying to tell you that for years." Dave was instantly offended. Feeling attacked, he pulled away from Noreen, folding his hands across his chest in disgust.

This event triggered some hot issues for Dave and Noreen. For years, Noreen had felt that Dave didn't listen well to what she said—a hidden issue of caring. She was hurt that he hadn't cared enough to remember her making the same point the instructor was making. Dave had been feeling that Noreen was being critical about nearly everything and now was attacking him when he was really getting into this massage workshop with her. He felt rejected and dejected, thinking, "Can't she even lay off when we're out to have fun?" On this evening, they didn't recover well. Dave suggested they leave the class early and go home. They did—in silence.

There will be times for all couples when conflict erupts during fun times. But if it begins to happen a lot, fun times won't be much fun anymore. The whole idea with fun is that you're doing something together that is relaxing and that brings out positive emotions you can share together. Poorly handled conflict will disrupt these times. The sense that conflict can erupt at any moment isn't compatible with relaxed playfulness.

WORKING AT PLAY

You may be thinking that you know how to have fun and don't need strategies and skills. You're right. Having fun is natural, but we all sometimes allow barriers to get in the way of our fun times. Here are some pointers that can keep you on the fun track.

Making the Time

For some couples, it's hard to have fun together without setting aside time for it to happen. Sure, you can have a moment of fun just about anywhere anytime if the mood strikes you both. Even sharing a quick joke or seeing something funny on TV can be fun. These natural moments of enjoyment are wonderful and magical. So part of making the time to have fun is looking for and allowing bits of fun as you go through your busy lives. Keep the spark going by looking for small opportunities. When we get caught up in the stress of everyday life, though, it helps to look forward to fun times ahead, so it's also important to make larger blocks of time for doing fun things together.

Most people are so busy and harried by life that it takes some time just to switch gears into the fun mode. That's why for many couples, the first day or two of a vacation can be more stressful than fun. You're making a transition. The same holds true for shorter periods of fun time. It often takes time just to wind down and get relaxed. But once you are relaxed and playing together in some way, you have the opportunity to draw closer together and feel the bond of the positive emotion.

To make the time for fun, you might actually have to pull out a schedule and arrange the time together. This may not sound all that spontaneous, but for most couples there's so much else going on that it takes deliberate acts to make the fun times happen. You may also need to arrange for a baby-sitter for the kids. If you don't have a sitter you trust, it may be time to look hard and find one. There's nothing that helps you relax more when you're out to have fun than knowing your little ones are with someone you trust.

When you're making the time for fun, try to arrange for time without the possibility of distraction. For example, if your job requires you to wear a beeper, do you have to wear it when you've carved out time to play with your spouse? It's not very relaxing to know you could get beeped at any moment. Make the time and shut out the distractions of the rest of your life. It's worth it. It might even give you something to look forward to.

Protecting Fun from Conflict

The material on handling conflict presented in the first part of this book is critical if you are going to preserve fun in your relationship. As a couple, you need to control the times and conditions under which you deal with the difficult and conflictual issues in your relationship. When you've blocked out time to have fun, don't do conflict talk. Keep the focus on friendship talk and fun.

Many couples buy into the wisdom of "date night" or some such idea to get away to enjoy each other. However, in our experience, many couples try to do too much with the time they've set aside.

They try to have fun together *and* resolve difficult issues "while we have this time together."

For example, one night Frank and Karen went out to an ice skating show. As they were seated and waiting for the show to start, Frank said, "We haven't had time to talk out that budget problem. Let's see what we can get done right now." Big mistake. Their budget was a serious conflict area between them, and it deserved far more focused time than they were going to have while waiting for an ice show to start. As you can imagine, they didn't get anywhere on the budget and only succeeded in getting on edge with each other when they were out to have fun.

Although it's understandable and expected that conflicts are sometimes going to come up during fun times, we can't see why couples would set aside the time for fun and then deliberately spend some of it to deal with issues. Dealing with issues isn't compatible with what brings the greatest benefit to your relationship during time to have fun together. That's time for laughing and playing.

There's no more powerful change couples can make quickly in their relationship than to agree to keep conflict out of time set aside to have fun.

Deal with the important issues in your relationship in meetings arranged for that purpose—not during times for fun. When issues get triggered during times you set aside for fun, table them. Call a Time Out. Come back to them later. It's not hard to do once you try it a few times. In our experience, there's no more powerful change couples can make quickly in their relationship than to agree to keep conflict out of time set aside to have fun.

When we see a couple for the first time in our therapy practices, we often tell them to not talk about issues and to just focus on fun and friendship. The results for most couples are as powerful as the intervention was simple. Raymond and Fay had been fighting like cats and dogs and were on the brink of separating. We presented PREP in a nutshell, banned fighting and conflict talk, and told them to focus only on being polite and respectful and on sharing fun and friendship. They came back for session two saying they had had the best two weeks since they had kids.

So What Can We Do for Fun?

OK, you've set aside the time for fun and have agreed to put conflicts aside to protect the time. Now what? For many couples, this is a difficult question. In many ways, coming up with fun things to do is a skill like all the other skills we're emphasizing in this book. You have to practice such skills if they're going to work for you. If you're rusty at fun or want to keep your fun skills sharp, here are some of our ideas that might help.

Brainstorming About Fun Activities

Of course there are many kinds of activities couples do for fun. What do you do? Sit down together and think about the most enjoyable, interesting, and fun things you've ever done, or things you would like to do together. Use the brainstorming technique we discussed in Chapter Seven. Make a list to which you both contribute, putting down all ideas no matter how foolish or outrageous they may seem. Have fun when you are brainstorming about fun. Allow all wacky ideas and avoid ruts.

Ideas We've Heard from Couples

To help you get started, we'd like to mention some of the great ideas we've heard from couples over the years. Maybe one of them will cause a cascade of ideas in your own minds.

Couples have suggested things like exercising, yoga, or massage together. Fun doesn't have to be something that's elaborate or costly. These are things couples can do almost anywhere if they find them fun. In contrast, skiing is a wonderfully fun activity, but it can be very expensive. If you have the time and money, though, skiing can be a great way to spend the day together.

Many couples enjoy going to the movies. That's not a very original idea, and you've probably already thought of it, but how long has it been? Or if you go regularly, how long has it been since you

made out in the back row of the theater? If you haven't held hands through a movie in a while, give it a try.

You can bake cookies together and make a big mess. You can climb a mountain or collect seashells. You can go swimming or play tag. How about renting a classic movie and cuddling on the sofa with a bowl of popcorn? How long has it been since you had a soda with two straws? Have you ever tried preparing a meal together, then feeding it to each other? How about doing it in the nude?

One couple described planning a mystery trip—including blind-folding one partner when they were getting close to the destination. How about a fancy dinner, in your fanciest clothes . . . under the shade of a tree in the backyard? Many couples here in our home state of Colorado like to drive up into the mountains, choosing somewhere new each trip, and take long walks to explore new places together.

For some couples, even chores are fun because some are things they both like to do, and, more important, they like doing them together. Gardening, grocery shopping, or washing dishes or the car—knock yourselves out. What's fun for both of you? Don't forget sex, by the way. We've heard it can be fun for some couples. Remember: that's not meant to be a chore.

Getting Going

Make a personal fun deck by taking a deck of index cards and writing down on each card one of the items from your brainstorming. We suggest maybe twenty-five to thirty ideas to start with, and they can cover a whole range of topics, effort, and expense. Once you've made the deck, set aside particular times to choose activities and do them. Don't let anything stop you.

You're going to have more fun if you are both up for the activities you choose; here's one way to make sure that happens, using your fun deck. Each of you pick three cards describing things you'd find fun to do that day. Trade cards. Then you each choose one card from the three your partner picked, and you take responsibility for making that one activity happen. That way, you're each picking something you know your partner will like, but because you get to choose among the three, you're likely to enjoy the activity too. Don't worry about which one your partner wants you to pick. If you don't get to it today, you'll have another chance tomorrow!

If you follow the key points in this chapter, you'll be qualified for a degree in relationship fun. You can do it. Early in relationships, it comes easily. Yet we firmly believe that having fun is easy at any time of life, if you make the time, protect this time, and make fun happen.

Talking Points

1. Couples can choose to protect their relationship by setting aside time to enjoy each other, renewing their sense of closeness and togetherness.

2. Having fun comes naturally to everyone in childhood, but couples may need to treat having fun as a skill to be practiced in the context of their busy, conflict-laden lifestyle.

EXERCISE

Making and Using a Fun Deck

We'd like you to go through the steps we discussed in this chapter. Here they are again:

1. Brainstorm a list of fun things. Be creative. Anything goes, so have fun coming up with ideas.

2. Write these ideas out on three-by-five cards to make your fun deck. It'll come in handy when you don't have much time to decide what to do but are ready for some fun.

3. Set aside time. Pick from the deck three things you'd enjoy doing. Hand these three cards to your partner. Each of you should take responsibility for making one of your partner's choices happen in the time you've set aside.

Go for it!

11

Sense and Sensuality: Enhancing and Protecting Your Sex Life

Many experts believe that the major problem couples will be facing in the decades to come is decreasing interest in sex! Although there are many reasons for an individual couple's not having enough sex, here we want to focus on two related themes we see over and over again: over time, couples do not distinguish between sensuality and sexuality, and couples do not make the sensuality-sexuality part of their relationship a priority.

SENSUALITY VERSUS SEXUALITY

What comes to mind when you think about the word *sexuality*? For many, the first thoughts are of sexual intercourse, orgasms, and all the pleasurable acts that may come before and after. Anything else? Now think about *sensuality*. What comes to mind? Usually, some pleasant experience that involves touching, seeing, smelling, tasting, or feeling—such as walking on the beach or being massaged with sweet-smelling oil. How about the roughness of a beard or the silkiness of hair? The smell of your partner? Chocolate? You get the idea. These are sensual experiences that are ways of connecting in the moment. They are typically neither goal oriented nor explicitly sexual. Rather, they reflect feelings you have about being in love and attracted to your partner.

Sensuality includes physical touch or other senses but is not always associated with making love. We'd include holding hands, hugging, romantic talking, affectionate cuddling, nonsexual massages—all acts that provide sensual arousal and pleasure in nonsexual ways. We are amazed at the number of married couples for whom this very important distinction between sensuality and sexuality is blurred.

In the early stages of relationships and into the early years of marriage, many couples tend to touch quite a bit. They hold hands, hug, kiss, and so forth. Over time, however, couples tend to bypass the sensual and move more exclusively to goal-oriented sexual behavior. Less time and energy is spent on the playful, intimate, sensual contacts that were once so delightful. This leads to big problems, because it's the sensual connection that keeps partners from feeling as though they are growing apart. Over time, sex itself becomes more a matter of performance than of intimacy. For some couples, the pattern progresses to the point that they become interested in sex only for sex's sake. Once sensuality drops out of the equation, couples have no way of intimately connecting unless they have sex. That starts to put a lot of pressure on the sexual relationship. How many times have you wanted to be physically close, without necessarily desiring sex?

The Art of Sensual Talking

One of the best ways to enhance your sensual relationship is the one most couples rarely use: sensual talking. We mean telling your spouse how attracted you are to her, how sexy she is, how much you love and care for her (one of the best ways to directly short-circuit a hidden caring issue). You can talk about what you'd like to do together the next time you are alone; how much you enjoy his touch; how much you love touching his legs or arms; or how you can't wait to be alone and touch under the table or have a lingering, soulful kiss during which time stops; and so forth.

There are a virtually infinite number of expressions of love and affection and caring and attraction: whispers while doing the dishes, e-mail (be careful who can read this—or create code words), voice mail (again, think about who else can hear), flowers, balloons, and so forth. Some research has found that sensual talk when no sexual interaction is possible actually tends to lead to better sexual connection later on. Ah, the joy of anticipation!

Wanda and Eugene have been married only eight years. They used to spend a lot of time just cuddling, caressing, and talking about sensual and sexual things they'd like to do with each other. As time went by, they got busier with kids, work, and home—as most of us do. After a year or two of marriage, they had settled into a pattern of having sex about twice a week. Given time pressures and other cares of life, they devoted less and less time to sensuality. At night, in bed, one or the other would initiate sex, and they'd quickly have intercourse, usually finishing in about ten minutes—four if there was something good on television. (And if you are thinking "four whole minutes," you really need to think about our advice here.)

Wanda and Eugene had become quite efficient about making love—or rather, having intercourse. They didn't have or make a lot of extra time, so they made do. In fact, they were making do rather than making love. Their focus on sexual intercourse rather than sensuality led to dissatisfaction for both. "What happened to all those times we'd lay around for hours together?" Wanda wondered. "It seems like Wanda used to be a lot more responsive when we made love," Eugene mused. We'll come back to them in a bit.

The fact is, there needs to be a place for sensual talking and touching in your relationship—both in and outside the context of making love. This idea is similar to our distinction between Problem Discussion and Problem Solution. Just as the pressures of life lead many couples to problem-solve prematurely, too many couples shortchange the sensual and prematurely focus on just sex. This leads to sex without the overall context of touching and closeness. Over time, this actually leads to less sex. Why? Because men and women need and value the sensual side of intimacy for pleasure, attachment, and arousal. Sensual experiences set the stage for better sexual experiences.

There needs to be a place for sensual talking and touching in your relationship— both in and outside the context of making love.

PROTECTING PHYSICAL INTIMACY FROM ANXIETY

Sexual arousal is natural. However, this state of pleasurable excitement can easily be short-circuited by anxiety. Numerous studies suggest that anxiety is the key inhibiting factor to arousal. There are two types of anxiety that we'd like to discuss in this context: performance anxiety and the tension from conflict in your marriage.

Performance Anxiety: Roadblock on the Path of Lovemaking

Performance anxiety is anxiety about how you're "performing" when you make love. It is often reflected in a person's asking himself or herself such questions as "How am I doing?" or "Is my partner enjoying this?" When you're keeping an eye on your performance, you create emotional distance between you and your partner. When you have performance anxiety, you become focused on how you are doing rather than on being with your partner in the moment.

Many people report feeling distant when making love, as though they're just watching what's going on instead of participating. This kind of detachment can lead to the most common sexual problems people experience—often starting with sexual boredom and then leading to premature ejaculation and problems keeping erections, for men, and difficulty lubricating or having orgasms, for women. The focus on performance interferes with arousal because you are distracted from your own sensations of pleasure and from the pleasure you're sharing. You can't be both anxious and pleasantly aroused at the same time.

Think about Eugene and Wanda again. Eugene became aware that Wanda was less and less pleased with their lovemaking. Without a focus on sensuality and touching throughout their relationship, Wanda began to feel that Eugene was just using her sexually. This feeling was intensified because he'd have an orgasm every time they made love, but her orgasms were less frequent. As unsatisfying as their lovemaking was for both of them, it seemed to Wanda that it still was better for Eugene. So her resentment grew.

Eugene became aware of her resentment and wanted to make things better. But instead of talking it out and working on the problem together, he decided he'd just do a better job of making love to Wanda. "I'll fix this," he thought. Wrong. All that happened was that he became more and more focused on performing, and his anxiety grew. Thoughts about performance became his constant companions during their lovemaking: "How's Wanda doing? Is she getting excited? Does she like this? I wonder if she thinks I'm doing this right. Man, I'd better try more of this for a while, I'm not sure she's ready."

Pretty soon he was pleasing Wanda somewhat more, but he was growing tenser and tenser about what he was doing when they made love. Sure, he was meeting some of her needs, but he wasn't feeling at all connected with her or satisfied in their lovemaking. He was performing! Wanda knew there was some change in Eugene's attention to her arousal, which did please her to some degree. But she had this growing sense that Eugene was somewhere else when they made love. She was having more orgasms, but she didn't feel they were sharing a sensual experience.

The key for Wanda and Eugene was to rediscover the sensual side of their relationship by talking about what was going on. This is a wonderful example of the need to talk about an issue when it's not in the context of an event, as we discussed in Chapter Six. Wanda and Eugene had a reservoir of love and respect for each other, so once they committed both individually and as a team to enhancing their sensuality, things quickly got better.

As we've emphasized throughout this book, you can *prevent* problems from developing in the first place if you are willing to do so and know what to do. Physical intimacy is no exception. You can do a lot to keep problems like Wanda and Eugene's from ever developing. For some of you, their story is very familiar. For others, your lovemaking hasn't deteriorated, and that's great. The goal: learn to keep things that way.

Conflict and Anxiety: Another Serious Roadblock

Mishandled conflicts can destroy your physical relationship by adding tension both in and out of the bedroom. Let's face it: when you've been arguing and angry with each other, you don't usually feel like being sensual or making love. Some couples find that their sexual relationship is temporarily enhanced when there is conflict followed by "making up," but for most, poorly handled conflict adds a layer of tension that affects everything else in the relationship.

Tension isn't compatible with enjoyable, intimate lovemaking for most people. In fact, there may be no area of intimate connection that's more vulnerable to the effects of conflict and resentment than your physical relationship. If you are experiencing destructive conflict in other areas of your relationship, it can be difficult to feel positive about sharing an intimate physical experience. Worse, these conflicts too often are triggered in the context of lovemaking.

It's critical that you agree to keep problems and disagreements off-limits when you are being sensual or making love.

Touching sensually or making love is a powerful way to connect, but destructive conflict builds roadblocks you cannot easily get beyond. If you can protect your times for physical intimacy from conflict, you can do a great deal to keep your physical relationship alive and well. You must work to handle conflict well—for example, by using the ground rules and other techniques we've been stressing. It's critical that you agree to keep problems and disagreements off-limits when you are being sensual or making love. Protect and preserve these precious times alone when you are nourishing your relationship.

WHEN YOU'RE JUST NOT INTERESTED (IN SEX)

If you ask expert sex therapists these days, they will tell you that the single most common complaint they hear from couples is that one or the other of the partners simply has no interest in sex. Studies confirm that this problem is anything but rare—especially among women. For example, Edward Laumann, Anthony Paik, and Raymond Rosen conducted a large-scale survey of sexual problems that was published in 1999 in the *Journal of the American Medical Association*. These researchers found that 43 percent of women and 31 percent of men reported some kind of significant sexual problem. Whereas only 5 percent of the men reported the problem of low sexual desire, 22 percent of the women reported this problem. Another 14 percent of women reported that they felt desire but had difficulty becoming sexually aroused.

All these statistics are rather impersonal. What about your relationship? Do either of you (or both of you) have difficulty just being interested in sex? If you both have little interest, it may be that this causes no great strain on your relationship. But if only one of you has low interest and the other has normal or high interest, you have a problem that can cause a lot of pain. It's all the more difficult for couples to cope with this if the physical relationship is one of their primary ways to feel connected.

Experts say there can be any number of reasons why so many people have low sexual desire. The list of possible suspects is long, and we will list only a number of key ones here:

- Depression

- Side effects of medications (including antidepressants)

- Excessive alcohol use

- Chronic illnesses of many kinds

- Boredom

- Hormonal problems

- Stress

- Sleep problems (nothing works well when you are not sleeping enough)

- Fatigue

Most of this list has to do with your overall health and energy. If you are tired, run-down, sick, and stressed, you're not likely to feel very interested in sex. This isn't a book on sexual problems and their treatment, but if you are a couple coping with this problem, we do have some advice.

First, and most important, if you are the one with low desire, get a thorough physical. Be candid with the doctor about your concerns so that he or she knows what to ask you and what tests to run. If you find this embarrassing, try to get over it. It's very likely your mate would deeply appreciate your doing what you can do to give your lovemaking a new lease on life. If your sexual desire is fine but your partner is the one having more trouble being interested, be supportive and patient in trying to find what may help. Hint: it's unlikely that pressure and anger will help very much at all.

Once you've either ruled out physical problems or begun dealing with them the best you can, work together on the other things that are under your control. Talk openly about the things that are most likely to bring pleasurable touching. (You could make this fun, you know.) Work on the suggestions we present throughout this chapter. If you like, try some self-help books (there will be a whole section on related subjects in large bookstores) or see a qualified sex therapist to help out. Whatever other issues you have to cope with, you can work together to give your lovemaking the best possible chance to grow and last.

COMMUNICATING DESIRES

It's critical for you to communicate about your physical relationship in ways that protect and enhance this important way of being intimate. That goes not only for handling potential conflicts around physical intimacy, but also for telling each other what you desire. We're talking about real communication, not mind reading. The problem is that people too readily assume they know what their partner wants, and when.

You Should Know What I Like!

It's a mistake to assume that your partner will like whatever you like or that you can read each other's minds. Would you go out to a restaurant and order for your partner without talking about what he or she wanted? Of course not.

It's also too easy for some people to assume that their partner won't like the things they like. Either way, you're making assumptions. And because many couples have trouble communicating about their physical relationship, it's really easy for these assumptions to take control. You don't know what your partner's expectations are until you ask—and vice versa.

Of course, because of your previous experiences together, you can often assume correctly. And things can work out fine based on

those assumptions. However, keep in mind that people change, so checking in with each other about desires and expectations is valuable for having a great sensual and sexual relationship.

We can't tell you how many couples we've talked with in which it seems one expects the other to "know" what he or she likes most when making love. It's as if people believe that "it just isn't romantic or exciting if I have to tell you what I want. You should *know!*" That's an unreasonable expectation. If you hold this fantasy, you should probably challenge it for the health of your relationship.

We recommend that you communicate clearly about what feels pleasurable to you—while you are touching or making love. Your partner doesn't know unless you say something. We're not suggesting that you have a Speaker-Listener discussion in the middle of lovemaking. (Though if it really excites you that much, let us know how it goes!) Talk together about what is sensual for each of you. What do you enjoy? Make the time for sensual experiences that don't necessarily lead to sex. Then talk about what you enjoy most in your lovemaking, and plan time to try pleasurable things.

Couples who have the best sexual relationships have ways of communicating both verbally and nonverbally about what they like. Furthermore, they usually have a genuine desire to please one another. That desire combined with talking openly leads to great lovemaking.

Taking a Risk

Unless you feel safe and take emotional risks sharing your feelings with your partner, your relationship will not be all it can be. This is especially true when it comes to talking about sex—one of the hardest topics for any couple to discuss. Couples who are having great sex are able to risk rejection and express wants, needs, desires, and fantasies. Doing this is hard, because your desires say a lot about who you are, so to express them is to risk being hurt. Let's listen to Oly and Sharon open some new doors.

OLY (SPEAKER): I've never felt I could say this before, but I've wanted to try some different things for years.

SHARON (LISTENER): So you've wanted to try some things, but hadn't felt like you could say anything.

OLY (SPEAKER): (*feeling validated and willing to go on*) Right. It's hard to talk about sexual things; I mean, my family never did, and I don't think yours did either.

SHARON (LISTENER): You think one reason it's hard to talk about sex is because our families never did.

OLY (SPEAKER): *(feeling braver and ready to venture into new territory)* Yeah. So, I've thought a lot about making love in different places in the house, like here in the family room in front of the fireplace. Or maybe trying some massage oils.

SHARON (LISTENER): So I hear you saying you've wanted to try making love in different places or try some massage oils. I'd like the floor, please. *(Oly hands Sharon the floor.)*

SHARON (SPEAKER): *(feeling very good about this talk)* It's really great to hear you bringing up this topic—I've also felt we've been missing out on something, but I didn't know how to bring it up.

OLY (LISTENER): So you're relieved I brought this up, because you didn't know how to.

SHARON (SPEAKER): Relieved is a good word. It's kind of dumb we haven't done this before.

OLY (LISTENER): Are you kind of sad we haven't talked before?

SHARON (SPEAKER): Not really sad, just feeling we've missed out on some things in our physical relationship.

OLY (LISTENER): So you regret we've missed out on some things.

SHARON (SPEAKER): Exactly. It seems like a great time to try out some more exciting or at least different things. Like, I've always wanted to try massage oil.

OLY (LISTENER): You want to try some new exciting things too, like massage oil.

We'll give them some privacy for the rest of this discussion. They moved from Problem Discussion, about fear of talking about sexual things, to Problem Solution, about things to try, without marking the shift, as we would usually recommend. However, they were so clearly in tune with each other here that it felt natural to get right down to brainstorming about the fun stuff!

Talking is just the essential first step toward improving your physical relationship. It helps to try some new ideas to break out of ruts—as Oly and Sharon were able to do. Read a book on massage or sex together. That might help you talk about these issues. Agree to surprise each other one night. Try something new, even if just once. Exploring both the sensual and sexual sides of your relationship may relieve many concerns about performance with one another and help you find even more pleasure.

Sensuality and sexuality are among the best sources of marital fun. All too often, however, the sensual and sexual area falls victim to the barriers against fun discussed in Chapter Ten. Many professionals believe that sexual chemistry inevitably decreases over time. Yet many couples are able to sustain and even improve their sex lives over time.

We don't believe that couples fall out of love as much as they fail to protect and preserve their love by investing in and nourishing their relationship on a daily basis. The major reason attraction and passion ebb is that couples neglect the very things that build and maintain attraction in the first place—friendship, fun, and sensuality and sexuality. So the best lovers are, in a sense, fun lovers!

PRIMARY PLEASURES: MAKING YOUR SENSUAL RELATIONSHIP A PRIORITY

Pam and Joel had a happy marriage but, like so many couples, were having sex rarely—once or twice a month if they were lucky (as they put it). When they had sex, they said it went pretty well, with both getting aroused, having orgasms, and feeling connected. However, they had developed some concerns that both wanted to work through. In part, they had lost any creative aspect in their love-making, tending to do the same things over and over again. Those things worked, in that both were feeling relatively connected and both were usually having orgasms. But they'd come to a point where Pam's orgasms always followed intercourse, through Joel's stimulating her. Pam felt a bit limited in this, and Joel felt that they could never have intercourse and just relax right afterwards because he always needed to focus on helping her climax. And he did, and it was good that he did. Still, they felt there could be more.

What Pam and Joel described suggested concerns other than specific sexual dysfunctions. For so many couples, if they feel that something is not quite right or that something is limited about their physical relationship, one or both partners can too easily begin to wonder if there is something more at stake: Do they really love each other? Are they still really attracted to each other? That kind of thinking makes a relatively common situation turn into a dangerous one. For Pam and Joel, the matter was really more about the development of bad habits wherein they had made their lovemaking a low priority.

Unlike couples who simply don't have the time to devote to their physical intimacy, Pam and Joel had neglected this aspect of their relationship. They decided they both wanted to increase their investment in physical intimacy. We developed a simple but powerful plan (see the box "Your Plan for Romantic Success"). Plans such as this one are highly likely to help couples move out of ruts, as long as both partners are committed and really follow through on what they've agreed to try to do differently.

Your Plan for Romantic Success

Here's a great plan for bringing a more vital romantic spirit back to your lovemaking. It's the plan that we suggested to Pam and Joel, whom we mentioned in the chapter. We suggest you take the time to customize this

list to suit your own tastes and priorities as a couple.
Have as much fun as you can!

- Focus on being romantic and sensual (send flowers,
  romantic e-mails, whisper suggestive desires during
  dinner, touch his or her leg under the table). We
  know that talking as friends and sharing fun times are
  aphrodisiacs. We hear this often from women but
  believe it's also true for men. Do not focus on orgasms
  or other outcomes. Pressure is not an aphrodisiac.

- Focus on wooing your partner, as opposed to taking
  his or her love for granted. (Men, be her knight in
  shining armor—win her love and affection on a
  daily basis.)

- Be sensitive to your partner's rhythms, needs, and
  wishes. For example, many couples say they don't

IT'S NOT THAT I'M COMPLAINING HELGA, BUT COULDN'T WE TRY SOMETHING DIFFERENT?

have sex because one is a night person and the other a morning person. If that's the case, push yourself to be sensual during your partner's times.

- Be imaginative and creative. Let your partner know you care and are attracted to her and that you want her—but do it in a variety of ways. The possibilities are endless. You might be driving to work together and passing a motel, and could say, "Let's be an hour late." Even if the rendezvous isn't possible that day, the message is that you are attracted to him and want him. You might do this some other time if not now.

- Be a great lover. When having sex, kiss and touch sensual spots that your partner enjoys—the earlobe, neck, or whatever. Remember that marital sex is the place to explore all kinds of mutually enjoyable and agreeable lovemaking.

- Take risks by initiating lovemaking at unexpected times and places. Research suggests that a couple's love life is best when both the man and the woman initiate, rather than when only one person typically initiates—flexibility is a good thing! Also, let your partner know you appreciate the unexpected expressions of love.

Another matter of priority for couples is to make time for the physical relationship. Sad but true: over the years together, most couples take less and less time for this very important kind of bonding. There's really no good reason for this. Sure, we all get busy, and there really are competing priorities (like changing diapers or going to work). But that only means it's all the more critical that the two of you make time for this special part of your relationship. If you don't, it just won't happen, or it will happen less and less often.

By the way, do you know when the average couple in America is most likely to be making love? Some research years ago discovered this most important information: 10:35 P.M. In most parts of the United States, that's just after the nightly news and at the start of the late evening comedy shows. Johnny Carson used to joke—but it was no joke—that couples all over the country were making love during his opening monologue. Maybe he really knew more than we thought.

When publicly sharing this valuable research, Howard has asked audiences to think about why this information is so appreciated by couples. He goes on to say—with an amazingly straight face, "If you need to call a friend or a coworker late at night about some project or engagement, you don't want to call between, say, 10:35 and 10:39. Give couples who are trying to make the time to make love the respect they deserve." After you finish groaning about that joke, do give a lot of thought to the serious advice behind it. Like anything else that matters to you in life, you have to make time so that you can relax and enjoy this aspect of being together.

We believe that just about every couple can have a wonderful sensual and sexual relationship. Too many people accept the common belief that once the initial sexual passion wanes, sex naturally goes to the back burner and never again comes to the front. As Scott (coauthor) notes in an essay he wrote for Janice Levine and Howard Markman's book *Why Do Fools Fall in Love?* "For most people, passion at its height resembles something like the birth of a fire on dry wood: great fury and heat, crackling flames leaping high. The start of such a fire is magnificent. My focus here is not on the great fire, but on the coals that are begun from it. It is the long burning coals and embers that sustain the promise of heat and fire to come" (pp. 87–88).

The fires of love often burn very easily; it's what couples do with the embers that counts most! To have your love and passion last a lifetime, you both have to tend the coals from which future fires spring. You have to protect sensual and sexual life, nurture it, and, above all, make it a priority. If it's going well—that's wonderful. You can continue to think and act in ways to keep it that way and maybe even make it better. If some problems have developed, the ideas we emphasize here can help you get back on track.

MAKING IT HAPPEN, KEEPING IT HAPPENING

You know, it's old 1960s slang: you can make it happen. Corny but true. If you want the distilled essence of what we're recommending here, try taking the following to heart:

- Make the time for physical intimacy. Don't rush things.

- Protect the time from conflict. Deal with issues at other times—never, if you can help it, when together to explore physical intimacy.

- Pay attention to sensuality. Communicate your desires.

- Break out of ruts. Be creative.

These strategies work, but you need to work at them. Look each other in the eye and go for it.

Talking Points

1. Couples need to protect their sensual relationships, as well as their sexual intimacy, by communicating about their needs and desires, and guarding intimate times from conflict.

2. Anxiety is a guaranteed way to stop arousal and decrease sexual pleasure.

EXERCISES

Sensate-Focus

Years ago, Masters and Johnson began studying the various ways in which sexual relationships develop problems. They created an exercise that has benefited many couples and can be great for you— whether or not you have struggled in your physical relationship. This exercise is called the Sensate-Focus. The purposes are twofold: (1) to keep you focused on sensuality and touching in your physical relationship, and (2) to help you learn to communicate more openly and naturally about what you like and don't like in your lovemaking.

This isn't the time for sexual intercourse. That would defeat the purpose of the exercise, which is for you to focus on sensuality. Don't be goal oriented, other than to share the goal of relaxing and doing this exercise in a way that you each enjoy. If you want to make love following the exercise, that's up to you. But if you've been having a lot of concerns about feeling pressured in sexuality, we'd recommend you completely separate out these practice times from having sex. In fact, you shouldn't have sex unless both of you fully and openly agree to do so. No mind reading or assumptions!

The general idea is that you each take turns giving and receiving pleasure. The first few times, you are either the Giver or the Receiver until you switch roles halfway through the exercise. When you are in the Receiver role, your job is to enjoy the touching and give feedback on what feels good and what doesn't. Your partner does not know this unless you tell him or her. You can give either verbal or hand-guided feedback. Verbal feedback means telling your partner what actions feel good, how hard to rub, or what areas you like to have touched. Hand-guided feedback consists of gently moving your partner's hand around the part of the body being massaged to provide feedback about what really feels good.

When you are the Giver, your role is to provide pleasure by touching your partner and being responsive to feedback. Ask for feedback as often as necessary. Be aware of changes in how your partner is reacting—what feels good one minute may hurt the next. You are to focus on what your partner wants, not on what you think would feel good.

Choose roles and begin with a massage of hands or feet for about ten to twenty minutes, asking for and giving feedback. (We recommend massages of such areas as hands, back, legs, feet, and so on the first few times to get the hang of the technique. Focusing on these more "neutral" areas also helps you relax if there are some issues about sexuality between you.) Then switch roles. Repeat as often as you like, but also remember to practice these roles in other aspects of your sensual and sexual relationship.

We recommend that you try the Sensate-Focus exercise several times a week, over the course of several weeks. As you work on the exercise, there are some variations of the technique to work in over time. Assuming all is going well in your exercises, begin to move to other areas for touching. Wherever you want to be touched, including sexual areas, is great.

Over time, you can drop the rigid emphasis on the Giver and Receiver roles, and work on both of you giving and receiving at the same time—while still keeping an emphasis on sensuality and communication of desires. Or you can vary the degree to which you want to stay in these roles. If you practice the Sensate-Focus over time, it will become easier for you to communicate openly about touch. It will also be easier for you to work together to keep physical intimacy vibrant and alive.

Exploring the Sensual

In addition to the Sensate-Focus exercise, set aside specific times for sensual activities together. This works for all couples, regardless of whether they are engaging in sexual activity. Be sure you will not be interrupted. (This is the time for baby-sitters or answering machines!)

When you choose to be sensual together, talk about what's sensual for each of you and what you'd like to try doing to keep sensual experiences in your relationship. Here are some ideas:

- Give a massage to your partner, using the Sensate-Focus technique described here.

- Share a fantasy you've had about your partner.

- Cuddle and hug as you talk to your partner about the positive things you love about him or her.

- Plan a sensual or sexual activity for your next encounter.

- Plan a wonderful meal together. Prepare it together and sit close together—share the meal.

- Wash your partner's hair.

- Spend some time just kissing.

12

Sacred Places:
Core Beliefs and Spiritual Intimacy

We've discussed how to enhance your relationship with a focus on friendship, fun, and your love life. Now we're going to explore core beliefs and how you can perhaps enhance your spiritual life together. Whether or not you are religious or spiritually inclined, we believe that your beliefs matter in your relationship.

First, a little personal history. We started working with the U.S. Navy many years ago now. A man with great foresight saw a need for specific, research-based strategies to help military couples build happier and more secure marriages. That man was William Coffin. Bill had heard that we were toying with the idea of developing a spiritually oriented module in PREP. Because he was planning to bring a good number of Navy chaplains out to a training the Navy would be paying for, he thought it would be a great idea if we could develop this new material in time for that training.

We're not stupid, or even all that slow. When someone has a government contract in mind and has a suggestion for you, you tend to listen carefully to the suggestion. "Sure, Bill, no sweat." We got the contract for the training. Now all we had to do was come up with what the three of us wanted to say about this aspect of life. Now, let's see how easy this would be: Scott is a conservative Christian, Howard is a relatively liberal Jew, and Susan is a Conservative Jew who's a social liberal. The words "Sure, no sweat" reverberated in our minds. What follows is what the three of us thought we could say that would be important for nearly any couple and that, to the degree possible, would be based on research.

RELIGIOUS VERSUS SPIRITUAL

Think for a moment about the difference between the words *spiritual* and *religious*. When most people think about *religious*, the words that come to mind are formal: ceremony, church, synagogue, mosque, clergy, and so on. When people think about *spiritual*, words that come to mind include sacred, personal, soulful, peaceful, and so forth. What these words have in common is a relation to the core belief systems people hold as well as the deeper ways people become connected in life.

Whether or not you are religious, there are implications from studies related to religion that can benefit you. Many religions have codified core beliefs, values, and practices that promote stability and health in relationships. Our goal here is to decode these findings and highlight key implications for all couples—religious or not.

When we say "core beliefs," we're not talking of minor beliefs about who should refill the orange juice container and the like. Rather, we mean major, life-shaping beliefs that all people hold—about the meaning or purpose of life or about the ethics or rules of behavior between people, for example—whether those beliefs are religious, spiritual, philosophical, or something else. Since many people express their core beliefs primarily through the spiritual or religious realm, we'll use it as the focus for much of what we have to say.

Whether you believe strongly in your faith or are nonreligious, we mean this chapter to be helpful in guiding you and your partner to explore together some of the most important themes in life—themes that most couples rarely discuss. So let us tell you about realms where many couples never travel—but when they do go there, their relationships can be transformed as they are strengthened.

RESEARCH ON RELIGIOUS INVOLVEMENT

Most of the research we'll now describe for you is based on "religious" beliefs and practices rather than on "spirituality," as it's easier for researchers to agree on what religious behavior is: belonging to a denomination, going to services, reading certain writings, praying, and so forth. In contrast, people have widely varying definitions of spirituality, and researchers have a harder time deciding what, exactly, to measure. We believe that the findings on religion extend to spirituality, in general, as well as to other philosophical beliefs.

The impact of religion on marriage has been studied for years. Most of this research has been conducted with those involved in traditional religious systems, particularly within the Judeo-Christian spectrum. Despite this, the findings seem to apply to most couples.

Many studies, including our national poll, show that religious involvement is, on average, beneficial to most couples in marriage. For example, couples who are more religious tend to be a bit more satisfied in their marriages and less likely to divorce, and they have lower levels of conflict and higher levels of commitment. Moreover, those who were more religious were more likely to say that divorce is wrong, especially those who identified themselves as conservative in their beliefs. Religious couples were more likely to report being satisfied in sacrificing for one another and having a stronger sense of couple identity. These findings make sense, given the values that are emphasized in traditional religious groups.

It's not that couples who are more religious have substantially better marriages. The effects we're talking about are consistent and statistically significant but are nevertheless rather small. It would be most accurate to say that something about the dynamics associated with religious involvement gives couples an edge in keeping their marriages strong.

Given the association between religious involvement and marital success, researchers have sought to better understand what kinds of religious involvement matter most when it comes to maintaining a happy and healthy marriage. A number of major studies suggest that the positive benefits of religious involvement are strongest for those partners who actively practice their faith together.

Doing It Together

Annette Mahoney, Kenny Pargament, and their colleagues at Bowling Green State University conducted one of the most impressive studies ever done in the study of religious life and marriage. Like other researchers, they found that being religious and having similar faith backgrounds benefited couples. But, far more important, they discovered that what mattered most was what couples did together in practicing their faith.

Couples who actively practiced their faith together—and who tended to view marriage as having a transcendent meaning—tended to be happier, to have less conflict, to work more as a team, and to engage in less of what we have called the danger signs. Researchers at the Center for Marriage and Family at Creighton University conducted a study that points in a similar direction. They compared couples in which partners came from the same church background, from different church backgrounds, and from different backgrounds but in which one converted to the religion of the other. This latter group of couples was the least likely to divorce. When they were asked, most of the partners in these couples said the greatest motivation for one changing was a mutual desire to worship and practice their faith together as a couple.

These findings mean you can do something very wonderful for your relationship by engaging in more faith-

based activities together, if you are open to that. If you
and your partner are not religious, the two of you may
share other deeply held beliefs and interests that you can
pursue and that will enhance your connection. We think
that by practicing together what they believe, couples
have a powerful way to be on the "same page" in life.

WHAT DO SUCH FINDINGS MEAN FOR ALL COUPLES?

We would now like to offer an analysis of why shared religious practices have a positive impact on couples, in hopes of stimulating you
to consider how to strengthen your own relationship. Because this is
a secular book, we'll focus our understanding on pretty down-to-earth
explanations, though we recognize that some of you would consider
more spiritual explanations as well. In our attempts to decode the
meaning of these studies for nearly all couples, we focus on two key
factors: the need for social support and the effect of having—or
developing—a shared worldview.

Who's Got Your Back? The Need for Social Support

Howard has made several trips to Australia, and he's picked up this
common way of saying that you've got support from another: "I've
got your back." For many people, they find a solid support system in
the context of a religious community. There's a clear benefit for
most people in being part of a social group, religious or not—as long
as they have a clear sense that they belong or "fit" into the group.
In fact, research by Ken Pargament demonstrates that those church
and synagogue members who fit well into their religious communities have higher levels of mental health than those who don't.

Conversely, studies have consistently shown that people who
are more isolated are at greater risk for emotional problems, such as

depression and suicide; health problems; and poverty. In fact, some research now shows that the health risks of isolation are as great as those of smoking. Further, many studies in the field of stress management demonstrate how much more vulnerable you are if you have significant stressors but no social support system to help you, no one on your back. It's just not healthy for most humans to be isolated. To paraphrase Donne, "No one is an island."

We believe that one way religious involvement benefits many couples is that it provides them with ready-made social structures. Religions specify codes of behavior and rituals, many of which provide natural points of connection among those involved. For example, most religious and spiritual groups meet regularly for numerous kinds of activities. Spiritual activities include worship, prayer, reading, study, discussion groups, and so forth. Social activities can include coffee hour, ice cream socials, picnics, group outings, get-together dinners, softball leagues, and about anything else you can think of. Service activities are also common, including food drives, visiting the sick or elderly, ministries of service to disadvantaged groups, community outreach, volunteer work, and support groups.

William and Sandra are a couple who got married in the same church where they met. They had been involved for years in the denomination before they decided to tie the knot. They invited the entire church as well as friends and family. The turnout was large, the outpouring of support very clear. They didn't get married just in front of friends but in front of a whole community that knew them, supported them, and would be regularly involved in their lives.

As you can imagine, such a couple has a tremendous support system. Sandra and William are involved in weekly meetings, church on Sunday, and numerous other activities based in their religious community. Their relationship is supported and encouraged in the social network and by teachings that place great value on marriage and commitment—especially dedication.

Such deep ties to a religious community may not be for you, but it's very important for all couples to have a strong support system for their relationship. Social links to a community are important for you as a couple—no matter how you obtain them. Some couples find greater connection as well as support through involvement in charitable organizations or foundations. Susan (coauthor) and her husband have found a great sense of belonging to a community through their involvement with a local program that supports families who have children with special needs from birth to age three. After their first child was born prematurely, they used the agency to receive services, therapy, and group support. Later they started leading parent support groups themselves, and now Susan sits on the board of directors. Doing these activities together not only helped them with their own concerns about having a preemie but also brought them a circle of friends who are now part of their daily lives.

Many couples have discovered a network of support groups for having great marriages, called the Association for Couples in Marriage Enrichment (ACME). ACME is an organization built around the aim of couples helping couples through life. It's not counseling, and it's not sectarian. Rather, ACME facilitates couples coming together to share, encourage one another, and enjoy sharing aspects of life. ACME chapters are not everywhere, but they are an international organization. It's one great option for couples looking for a way to connect more with others.

For one couple we knew, John and Marsha, ACME turned out to be just what they wanted. Because neither of them is religious, their involvement turned out to be a great way to meet a need for support and connection. The friends they've made and the group activities in ACME have helped them through some tough spots in their marriage. They've also had a lot of fun participating in activities with these other couples.

There are many ways that couples enhance their connection as well as the supports for their marriage—including involvement in bowling leagues, softball teams, political groups, and so forth. If you are not interested at this point in involvement with a community of faith, there are many other ways for you to pursue a stronger network for your marriage. We don't know what would be the best fit for the two of you, or what you are open to trying, but we do know you'll likely do best in life if you have strong connections with others who get to know you as a couple and who care about how you are doing.

Finding the Right Place for the Two of You

So you want to practice your faith together, and you want to be part of a religious community. Now what? Many couples struggle with finding the right place that fits both their needs. Our colleague Joel Crohn, author of *Mixed Matches* (1995) and coauthor with Howard, Susan, and Janice Levine of *Fighting* for *Your Jewish Marriage* (2000), has developed a series of steps to help couples make this choice. This process works for couples in which the partners are of the same faith but are from different denominations or perhaps observe differently, or for couples of different faiths.

First, you need to acknowledge the differences in your needs and desires. You need to talk about your life history and the connections you feel to your own religious or spiritual traditions. Second, Joel recommends "unconditional experimentation." For example, attend services at a number of places that reflect your different interests or beliefs. This is a time to really see religious involvement through your partner's eyes.

Third, you need to make choices and choose a path. The problem-solving approach you've learned in this book can help guide this part of the process. You both need to be as clear as possible about what works and what doesn't and about where you can bend and where you cannot.

The fourth step of the process is to make provisions for renegotiations. We call this follow-up. You need to try out your chosen path and then come back together to discuss the impact of your choices. Keep repeating this process until you have found a religious home that is comfortable for both of you. Even if that is not possible, your work will help you better understand each other's views.

Shared Worldviews

Within most religions, there's a common understanding and language system for thinking and talking about core beliefs. So another explanation for the benefit of shared religious involvement is that these couples have a belief system that makes it easier to develop a shared worldview. Of course, holding shared religious beliefs is not the only way couples develop or enhance shared worldviews, but it's a very common and very powerful one. Spilka, Gorsuch, and Hood, experts in the study of religion, put it this way in the first edition of their book, *The Psychology of Religion* (1985): "Since it is fairly likely that the religious feelings of spouses tend to be similar, among the more religious, who probably come from religious homes, there may be a supportive complex of perceptions leading to increased marital satisfaction" (p. 105). That is a shared worldview.

In her research, communication expert Fran Dickson of the University of Denver has found that partners who have stayed together for fifty years and also remained happy are most likely to have developed a shared vision. When there's a shared belief system—including mutual understanding of the meanings of life, death, and marriage—it's easier to develop a relationship vision, a shared vision unique to the couple. In turn, having a relationship vision supports the long-term goal of keeping the relationship alive.

Relationships are often affected by worldviews in two other ways: through core values and relationship expectations.

Core Values

One way that involvement in religious and spiritual activities helps couples is that such activities regularly emphasize the core values in life. Some key values include commitment, respect, intimacy, and forgiveness. These kinds of values are clearly associated with good relationships. When you and your partner have similar core belief systems—religious or not— it's likely you'll have a similar understanding of these values and how you can give life to them in your marriage.

When there's a shared belief system—including mutual understanding of the meanings of life, death, and marriage—it's easier to develop a relationship vision.

We hope you can see how the four core values we just mentioned—commitment, respect, intimacy, and forgiveness—are reflected in the skills and attitudes we encourage. Most belief systems, religious or not, have been emphasizing these values for thousands of years in ethics, codes of conduct, and standards for dealing with others; and research suggests that creating a shared world image using these values is a major step on the road to marital success.

Relationship and Family Expectations

Your worldview can also have a significant impact on your marriage by shaping your expectations in such areas as child rearing and discipline, intimacy, dealing with in-laws, and marital roles. Whereas the moral viewpoints we've discussed so far have more impact in the long term, this aspect of your worldview has very significant implications for your marriage in day-to-day life.

The potential for differences in expectations to spark conflict is so great that we spend an entire chapter (Chapter Thirteen) encouraging you to make such expectations clear—no matter where they come from. When two people share a perspective on key relationship expectations, they are going to have an easier time negotiating life. Shared expectations lead to shared rituals and routines that guide couples more smoothly through the transitions and trials of life.

Presumably, couples who aren't religiously involved can derive this same benefit if they share some philosophical view that makes it easier to maintain shared expectations. Whatever your backgrounds and beliefs, you shouldn't take them for granted in your relationship. You can identify and discuss similarities and differences in your viewpoints in ways that help you work together as a team.

WHEN YOUR VIEWS ARE NOT YOUR PARTNER'S VIEWS

When couples do not share their faiths or worldviews, the impact on the relationship can be devastating, because many partners believe that a great deal is at stake. In terms of how your relationship will do over time, your actual differences in worldview may not be as critical as how you handle those differences. By this we don't mean that the views themselves are irrelevant. But staying friends and showing respect do not depend on your seeing everything the same way. Even if you don't see things eye to eye, you don't have to live life fearing conflict.

Nonshared but Respected Views

Many couples do not share a number of important beliefs, but they are not at greater risk. They handle the differences with respect. The differences don't produce alienation and may, in fact, be a source of intimacy if the couple is able to enjoy the exchange of different perspectives.

For example, Jean and Randy grew up in dramatically different denominations of the Christian faith. She was raised a Baptist, he an Episcopalian. Sure, they both consider themselves "in the Christian faith," but research has shown that such differences significantly raise the risks of marital distress. The two of them talk a lot about what each believes and desires, enjoying the intimacy that comes from these talks. Although they share some important beliefs, they acknowledge that there are also many beliefs and practices that differ significantly. However, the couple doesn't let those differences divide them.

Jean and Randy work through differences as they see issues coming over the horizon. When they were expecting their first child, they started talking about their different views on baptism. It hasn't been easy work for them to deal with all the issues that come up, but they find ways to respect each other's views and work as a team.

For a couple to accomplish this, the partners need at least two things: (1) the skills needed to maintain respect in light of the differences and (2) enough personal security about their core beliefs not to be overly threatened by the absence of agreement. These conditions are all the more important when the differences in worldviews are great. For such couples, many of their beliefs and expectations aren't shared in the sense of being similar, but they can be shared in the sense that there is an open expression that doesn't trigger hidden issues of acceptance and fear of rejection.

Nonshared Views with Conflict

Some partners don't share the same perspective and don't handle the differences well, either. Some argue nastily, some grow more and more distant over time. When partners are unable to share their deeply held beliefs with respect, it's easy for events to trigger hidden issues of acceptance. The differences in core beliefs grow to become barriers to any intimacy on the deepest themes of life.

Life transitions—marriage, birth, death, and others—have a habit of bringing us more in touch with our core beliefs. In fact, most religions specify many key rituals around such events, which help families move through the transitions with meaning and support. When conflict arises around differences in worldview, couples are often unable to take advantage of the support offered by their religious system of choice.

For example, Marjorie and Simon married at twenty-three. They fell in love in college, where he majored in marketing and she majored in English. The problem was, he was Jewish and she was Catholic. His parents were alarmed that he'd date a Gentile. Hers were concerned, but she'd dated so many guys in the past, they figured Simon for a passing fancy. He wasn't.

Marjorie's parents began to get pretty worried. "How could she not marry a Catholic boy?" Simon and Marjorie both felt pressure from their families to cool it. But they really did love each other, so did religion matter that much? No. What about children? No problem. "We'll let them choose for themselves what to believe." What about their parents? No problem. "They'll learn to accept our marriage." Religious practice? No problem. Neither was particularly involved or observant at this point in life, so they figured "You do your thing, I'll do mine."

They got married after college, and despite all threats, both sets of parents showed up for the wedding, which was conducted by a judge in a lodge. Things went along fairly well for Simon and Marjorie until the fourth year of marriage, when she got pregnant.

For Marjorie, the idea of having a child was wonderful but at the same time marred by concerns: "What kind of world am I bringing this kid into?" These natural anxieties led her to a serious reevaluation of her faith. There was no other context that seemed as relevant for grappling with such questions. For Simon, his vision of himself as a daddy returned him to an interest in his faith. "What if I have a son? I can't have the doctor do the circumcision." Suddenly, each had an interest in spiritual things—for their child and themselves—that hadn't seemed important a few years before.

As it turned out, they had a son, Benjamin. They had decided to have him baptized as well as circumcised in religious ceremonies. The trouble was, in order to do the baptism the priest wanted Marjorie to commit to raising Benjamin as a Catholic. To make things more complicated, the couple couldn't find a mohel who would ritually circumcise their son, because he was born to a Gentile woman who hadn't converted to Judaism. They ended up doing neither.

The couple made compromises that worked for a few years. Both parents read Bible stories to Benjamin, and he certainly enjoyed celebrating both Hanukkah and Christmas. But the balancing act got tougher and tougher. By the time Benjamin turned four, conflicts had become more frequent and more intense. Simon and Marjorie agreed that it would be pretty confusing to expose Benjamin to different teachings, but neither was willing to give up the idea of Benjamin learning their faith.

Negative feelings intensified to the point that their conflicts about Benjamin were erupting into all sorts of other relationship events. One by one, key areas of intimacy suffered under the weight of the conflict about Benjamin. There was no longer a safe haven for Marjorie and Simon just to relax and enjoy each other's company.

Eventually Marjorie suggested they get some professional help. Simon surprised her by agreeing. After a good number of years, they finally started to talk openly and deeply about what each was expecting and feeling.

Their counselor was very warm and supportive, which helped them a lot, considering how injured each felt at this point. Further, he helped them learn ways to talk more openly and safely together using some of the strategies in this book. Most important, the counselor guided them to work toward a much more thorough understanding of who each was, where they had each come from, and what they hoped would happen now. Marjorie and Simon both started to feel some confidence again—and some closeness. It wasn't that they saw eye to eye on everything, but now they were working on these issues as a team, and that made all the difference.

Interfaith Marriages: A Special Case of Nonshared Worldviews

Because of changes in society, people are now far more likely to marry out of their faith. One reason is that religion probably has less overall impact in our culture than it used to. People are less likely to take it into account when picking a mate. Also, as our society becomes increasingly mobile, connections with religious communities become harder to maintain, and intermarriage and divorce become more likely.

Research consistently shows that mixed-faith couples are much more likely to divorce. For example, Tim Heaton at Brigham Young University has examined these kinds of factors in very large samples. He has consistently found that couples with greater similarity of religious background have an edge in happiness.

Many interfaith marriages start out just fine, with couples thinking they can beat the odds. Love will conquer all. Although love can conquer a lot—especially if translated into loving and respectful behavior—the more there is to conquer, the greater the risk of failure. If you are in an interfaith marriage (or thinking about one), you should accept that your risks in marriage may be somewhat higher than for other folks. Does that mean couples with differences in backgrounds are doomed? Of course not. But for such couples it's especially important to be able to handle differences and clarify expectations well.

In summary, you and your partner may have different perspectives, even if you think you were raised similarly. When you think about differences in core beliefs, a lot is at stake. Everyone believes something, and it's unlikely that any pair of partners lines up perfectly on these dimensions.

You need to grapple with the ways your deepest beliefs affect your relationship. The exercises for this chapter are designed to help you do just that—grapple. We want you to explore your beliefs and talk them over together. If you have similar views, you can enhance aspects of your shared views by having these talks. If you have very different beliefs and traditions, you reduce the risks these differences can cause by facing them as a team. If you do decide to take this journey into your core beliefs together (and we hope you do), you will be rewarded with a trip filled with fun, excitement, reflection, and meaning.

Talking Points

1. The positive benefits of religious involvement are strongest for those partners who actively practice their faith together.

2. There seem to be two areas of importance when considering the role of religion in relationships: social support and a shared worldview.

3. Four core values—commitment, intimacy, forgiveness, and respect—apply to all relationships regardless of couples' level of religious or spiritual involvement.

 # EXERCISES

There are three exercises for this chapter. They follow the key themes we used to explain the research findings regarding the impact of religion and spiritual values on relationships. First, we ask you to take stock of your social support system. Second, we ask you to consider what your core values are, where they come from, and how they affect your marriage. Third, we want you to explore your core belief systems and the expectations specifically related to them. You will each need a separate pad of paper to do these exercises.

Who's Got Your Back? Your Social Supports

Talk together about your social support system. Do you have a strong support system—people to rely on, to encourage you, to hold you accountable at times? Are you involved in a community that supports and nurtures your growth in your marriage? Do you want to be? What could you do as a couple to build up more support if you see the need to do that?

Honoring Your Values

We'd like you to consider what your core values are in life. What values are central for you? Where did these values come from? Spend some time thinking about this individually. Jot down some notes on it. Then share with each other what you've been thinking about.

You may have some additional ideas after you work on the next exercise. In addition to other ideas that come up for you, specifically discuss together your views of the core relationship values mentioned in this chapter: commitment, respect, intimacy, and forgiveness. What is your view of these values?

Finding Spiritual Intimacy

Now we want you to explore on your own and share with your partner issues relevant to your core belief system. For many people, their religious faith or spiritual orientation reflects or determines core philosophical, moral, and cultural beliefs and practices. If that's the case for you, it will make the most sense to answer these questions in that light. For others, these questions may seem related less to religion than to philosophy.

Whatever your orientation, it can be very important for you and your partner to understand one another's core belief system—whether it's based in spiritual or religious beliefs or other philosophies of life. This exercise will help you accomplish this goal.

The following questions are designed to get you thinking about a broad range of issues related to your beliefs. There may be other important questions that we've left out, so feel free to answer questions we don't ask as well as those we do. We would like you to write down an answer to each question as it applies to you. Doing so will help you think more clearly about the issues and will also help you when it comes time to talk with your partner about them.

As you think about and answer each question, it can be especially valuable to note what you were taught as a child as opposed to what you believe or expect now as an adult.

Questions for Reflection

1. What is your core belief system or worldview? What do you believe in?

2. How did you come to believe in this viewpoint?

3. What is the meaning or purpose of life in your core belief system?

4. What were your beliefs growing up? How were these core beliefs practiced in your family of origin? What religious observances did you practice?

5. Do you make a distinction between *spiritual* and *religious*? What is your view on these matters?

6. What is the meaning of marriage in your belief system?

7. What vows will you say, or what vows did you say? How do these tie into your belief system?

8. What is your belief about divorce? How does this fit in with your belief system?

9. How do you practice—or expect to practice—your core beliefs in your relationship? (This could mean religious involvement, spiritual practices, or something else, depending on your belief system.)

10. What do you think the day-to-day impact of your belief system should be on your relationship?

11. Are there specific views on sexuality in your belief system? What are they? How do they affect the two of you?

12. If you have children—or plan to have children—how are they or will they be raised with respect to your belief system?

13. Do you give, or expect to give, financial support to a religious institution or other effort related to your belief system? How much? How will this be determined? Do you both agree?

14. Do you see potential areas of conflict regarding your belief systems? What are they?

15. What do you believe about forgiveness in general? How does forgiveness apply in a relationship such as the one with your partner?

16. In your belief system, what is your responsibility to other humans?

17. How do you observe (or expect to observe) religious holidays?

18. In your belief system, what is the basis for respecting others?

19. How do you view final matters of life? The meaning of death? Is there an afterlife? What about organ donation and the use of living wills?

20. Are there any other questions you can think of and answer?

After you and your partner have finished the entire exercise, plan time to talk, and begin spending time together discussing these core beliefs and values. You should plan on a number of discussions. Talk about the degree to which you each felt the spiritual or religious issue you are discussing had been shared clearly in the past. Use the Speaker-Listener Technique if you would like some additional structure to deal with these difficult issues.

Talk about the degree to which you both feel your expectations about these issues are reasonable or unreasonable, and discuss what you want to do about them.

Part IV

Staying the Course

13

Why You Can't Always Get What You Want: Unraveling the Mysteries of Expectations

In this last part of the book, our goal is to help the two of you stay the course you have chosen as you continue your journey through life together. Relationships face all kinds of obstacles. Many come from the risks and pitfalls we have discussed earlier. Many come from failing to nurture the great things that attracted the two of you as you fell in love. Many come from the normal stresses of life, career, and family. But sometimes people put up their own obstacles because of what they expect. This chapter will help each of you understand and share your expectations for your relationship.

As you will see, we believe that it's very important to check if your expectations are reasonable, to be able to talk openly together about what you each expect, and to meet each other's expectations to the degree you can. Before we explore these goals further, let's look more deeply at why expectations matter so much.

HOW EXPECTATIONS AFFECT RELATIONSHIPS

Expectations affect everything. You have specific expectations about minor things, such as who will refill the orange juice container or who will balance the checkbook—the events in your life. You have expectations about common issues, such as money, housework, in-laws, and sex. You also have expectations about the deeper, often hidden, issues:

how power will be shared (or not shared), how caring will be demonstrated, or about the level of commitment in your relationship.

In general, you will be disappointed or happy in life depending on how well your perceptions of what is happening match what you expected—what you think should be happening. It's not surprising, therefore, that expectations play a crucial role in how happy your marriage will be.

Think of the high bar at a track meet. The goal is to jump the bar at the greatest height you can manage. Some partners set their "expectation bar" too low and thus do not challenge their relationship to be the best it can be. Others set their bar too high, leading to disappointment.

Meeting Your Partner's Expectations

Researchers Norm Epstein at the University of Maryland and Don Baucom at the University of North Carolina at Chapel Hill have identified three major areas in which people have expectations about the way things "should be" in their relationships:

1. *Boundaries.* Where does the line around the couple go? Who is in it, and who is out of it? How much independence is OK between the two partners?
2. *Investment.* How much time and effort does each partner feel the other should be putting into the relationship? This includes the sense of what each thinks is the "right" way to show investment.
3. *Control and power.* Who makes which decisions? Is power shared? How?

Norm Epstein told us something very important about what they have found in their work: "Discrepancies between two partners' standards are less problematic than the individuals' being dissatisfied with the ways in which their personal standards are being met within the relationship (so, two people can be different but still work out a mutually acceptable way of meeting their standards)."

What this means is that it may not be as crucial for the two of you to hold all the same expectations as it is for each of you to do your best to try to meet the important (and realistic) desires of the other. For example, many people expect that their partner will share their views on how to demonstrate love. The reality is that some people interpret gifts as signs of love, whereas others prefer hugs and kisses (to name only two ways of showing love). It isn't important that each of you may want different things from the other; what is important is to learn to give the gifts the other desires most.

Zoey and Maxwell have been married for just a year, and things have gone pretty well. However, Maxwell is upset about his wife's nights out with the girls. Like many young couples, they have different expectations about spending free time with friends, as opposed to together. This creates conflict for them, because they each hold expectations that they have not talked about.

Zoey goes out once or twice a week with her longtime girlfriends, often to go shopping and sometimes to movies. Sometimes her going out (an event) triggers major arguments, like this one:

MAXWELL: (feeling agitated) I don't see why you have to go out again tonight. You've been out a lot lately.

ZOEY: (obviously irritated, rolling her eyes) How many times do we have to argue about this? I go out once a week and that's it. I don't see any problem with that.

MAXWELL: Well I do. All your girlfriends are single, and I know
they keep their eyes open for guys.

ZOEY: So?

MAXWELL: So, they are looking for guys, and you're married.

ZOEY: (angered, feeling attacked and accused of being disloyal) We don't
go out hunting for guys. I don't like it that you don't trust me.

MAXWELL: I just don't think a married woman needs to be out so
often with her single friends. Guys notice a group of women, and
you can't tell me your friends aren't interested.

ZOEY: (turning away and walking toward the door) You sound jealous.
I have to leave now; I'll be back by ten.

Without even knowing it, Zoey and Maxwell are arguing about
differences in their expectations. He didn't expect that she'd still
go out with her girlfriends so often after they got married. Zoey
expected to cut back time with friends, but not to stop seeing them
altogether. These nights out mean a lot to her. She sees nothing
wrong, except that Maxwell isn't handling it very well.

In this example, you can't really argue that either expectation
is outrageous. What's much more important is that their expectations don't match, which fuels conflict. This example also shows
how expectations can often be linked to hidden issues. When hidden issues get triggered by events, it's often because some expectation was not met, either because the partners have different
expectations or because the expectations of one or both are unrealistic or unreasonable.

In the case of Maxwell and Zoey, Maxwell could be wondering
if she really cares to be with him, seeing as she still wants to go out
regularly with her friends. Zoey could be feeling that he's trying to
control her, a feeling that leaves her feeling angry and hurt. These
hidden issues of caring and control are lurking beneath the conflict.
For both, there is an element of an unsettled commitment issue
here—not at all uncommon early in marriages. They are still working to define "us" and how secure will they be together.

Many expectations have to do with simple but very important subjects such as what intimacy or togetherness means to the two partners. Psychologist Lillian Rubin adds an interesting twist to this issue. In her research, she describes interviewing a couple about their relationship. Each partner was interviewed separately. Dr. Rubin first talked to the wife, who said something like this: "One of the things that drives me crazy about our relationship is that he just wants to spend all his time watching television. Even if I am in the room with him, he doesn't talk. Sometimes I want to go over and pick up his softball bat and bop him over the head." When Dr. Rubin talked to the husband, he said something like this: "One of my favorite things about our marriage is that we can just sit together, watch television, sometimes to hold hands, with no pressure to talk, and at these times I feel really close to her." Unbeknownst to his wife, he valued their relationship, and especially these moments. Unbeknownst to her husband, she hated the very kind of experience he prized in the relationship. This vignette illustrates not only that men and women have different preferences for

intimacy but also that they may define the same experience entirely differently.

WHERE EXPECTATIONS COME FROM

Expectations build up over a lifetime of experiences. Although our expectations have their base in the past, they operate in the present. There are three primary sources for our expectations: our family of origin, our previous relationships, and the culture we live in.

Family of Origin

Your family experiences lay down many patterns—good or bad—that become models for how you as an adult think things are supposed to work. Expectations were transmitted both directly by what your parents (or other caretakers and parent figures) said and indirectly by what you observed. Either way, you learned what you've come to expect. No one comes to marriage with a blank slate.

For example, if you observed your parents avoiding all manner of conflict, you may have developed the expectation that couples should seek peace at any price. If there's disagreement and conflict, it may seem to you like the world is going to end.

If you observed your parents being very affectionate, you may have come to expect that in your marriage. If your parents divorced, you may have some expectation in the back of your mind that marriages don't really last. In fact, research shows that often people whose parents divorced do have somewhat less confidence in the permanence of marriages. You get the idea.

One couple we worked with, Anna and Chet, came from very different families. In Anna's family, her father made virtually all the decisions—even down to what kind of toilet paper to buy. Chet's family started out similarly, but his mother left his father because he was a tyrant, and Chet went to live with his mother. His mother taught him by her actions and words never to treat his own wife as if she were a hired hand.

As you might imagine, Anna and Chet have had some trouble making decisions. Anna deferred to Chet for many decisions, and he found this disturbing. He told us he felt the pressure from all the responsibility. From his point of view, Anna's wanting him to make all the decisions not only was the wrong thing to do but also could lead to the marriage failing—as in the case of his parents. So Chet would try to get Anna to take more responsibility, while she tried to have him take charge. He saw himself as showing respect; she saw him as weak.

Because of their mismatched expectations, hidden issues were easily triggered. They were finally able to talk this through using the Speaker-Listener Technique. This is just part of their talk, but you can see how they were able to get the issues on the table.

ANNA (SPEAKER): The key for me is that I've been expecting you to lead more, to make decisions, because that's what I grew up being used to.

CHET (LISTENER): So you've expected this from me because that's what you grew up to expect.

ANNA (SPEAKER): Exactly. I never really thought a lot about the expectation, but I can sure see that I've had it and that it's been affecting us.

CHET (LISTENER): So you're saying that even though you've had this expectation, you haven't really thought a lot about it before. Yet you can see it's affected us negatively.

ANNA (SPEAKER): Yes. That's just what I mean. (She hands Chet the floor.)

CHET (SPEAKER): I can understand better now why you've pushed me to make the decisions. I really want you to hear that it's not that I'm uncomfortable being responsible. But to me, sharing decisions is a way to show you respect.

ANNA (LISTENER): So what had looked to me like you pushing off responsibilities was really you wanting to share with me in making decisions.

CHET (SPEAKER): Yes. That's it. Because of my own background, I've thought that our marriage would be hurt if I just went ahead and took all the control. I thought it meant you didn't care about us because you didn't share in making decisions with me.

ANNA (LISTENER): So you have had an expectation that was a lot different from mine, and that led you to worry that we'd have trouble if we didn't share in making decisions.

CHET (SPEAKER): And that's really been worrying me.

ANNA (LISTENER): It's really worried you because you weren't sure I cared.

CHET (SPEAKER): Right on.

They had a much easier time dealing with decisions once they began to talk openly about their expectations. This gave them a much better shot at negotiating the expectations they wanted to share in their relationship. They were setting the bar in the same place on these issues, and they were helping each other get over it.

If we had the space, we could give literally thousands more examples. We all have so many expectations that were established during our childhood.

Previous Relationships

You also have developed expectations from all the other relationships in your life—most important, from previous dating relationships or a prior marriage. You have expectations about how much to kiss, what is romantic, how to communicate about problems, how to spend recreational time, who should make the first move to make up after a fight, and so on.

Suppose, for example, that you found in previous dating relationships that when you began to open up about painful childhood events, you would get dumped. Logically, you might have developed the expectation that such a topic is off-limits with certain people. On a deeper level, you may expect that people can't be trusted with knowing the deepest parts of who you are. If you have such an expectation, you'll pull back and withhold a level of intimacy in your present relationship. This strategy is not without consequences, though. As we mentioned earlier in the book, a key dynamic of intimacy is that you can share things you feel vulnerable about and be heard and accepted.

Studies show that people who have come to expect that others can't be trusted have more difficulties in relationships. If you look at such a person's entire life, it will usually make sense why he or she has such an expectation. Yet it can lead to trouble if the mistrust is so intense that the person can't even allow someone he or she really loves to get close.

In contrast, many expectations are about such minor things that it's hard to imagine they could become so important—but they can. It all depends on what meanings and issues are attached to the expectations. For example, one man, Phil, told us that his past girlfriend had drilled it into him that she didn't want him opening doors for her. He thought, "OK, no big deal." Now, with his wife Susan, he was finding quite the opposite. She liked men to hold doors, and she'd get upset with Phil if he forgot. He had to work hard to unlearn the expectation he'd finally learned so well.

Events of the "door-opening" variety happen pretty often in life. For Phil and Susan, they triggered conflict because she'd interpret his trouble remembering as a sign that he didn't care about what was important to her. This is another example of negative interpretations causing more damage than the actual events. His devotion challenged, he'd get angry at her. This just confirmed what she already believed: "I knew he didn't care."

Are you aware of how many expectations you have of your partner that are really based in experiences with others? It's worth thinking about: your partner isn't the same person as those you've known, dated, or been married to in the past.

To Get the Door or Not to Get the Door; That Is the Question

Through some exciting new research we've been conducting with such colleagues as Sarah Whitton and Allan Cordova, we're seeing that male dedication plays a special role in marital happiness. It raises an interesting issue that we're hesitant to talk about because it's not very politically correct to do so. Being fearless as we are, however, here goes.

For some time now, we've been hearing more and more women say they are yearning for something in their relationships with men—and to us it sounds a lot like chivalry. It's not that women are saying they want to be subservient or dependent on men. Yet in the desire to make things more equal, people lost something that some now miss, and it may have been related to an important way in which men have historically demonstrated commitment. What does chivalry 2001 look like? Your own answers to this question are more important than ours, but here are a few ideas that occur to us:

- Being polite and respectful
- Treating a woman as a lady and acting like a gentleman
- Being a knight or a hero—at the right times (and it can be very difficult for men to figure out when just the right time is)
- Choosing to give up something (sacrifice) for your relationship
- Getting the door

It's noteworthy that women and men do not tend to score very differently on measures of commitment to their partners. But that doesn't mean that men and women have similar ways of showing commitment. It's important to understand that your partner may demonstrate commitment in ways different from you, and this is something important to talk about. That's a door you can open and walk through together.

Cultural Influences

There are a variety of cultural factors that influence our expectations. Television, movies, religious teachings, our ethnic backgrounds, and what we read can all have powerful effects on our expectations.

What expectations would you have about marriage, for example, based on watching thousands of hours of TV in America? For most of us, this is not a hypothetical question. Shows like *I Love Lucy*, *The Honeymooners*, *The Brady Bunch*, *The Cosby Show*, *Roseanne*, *Home Improvement*, *Dharma and Greg*, *Mad About You*, *Survivor*, *Who Wants to Marry a Millionaire?* and *Temptation Island* all send very powerful messages about what is expected and acceptable and what isn't. Some of these shows send great messages; some send very destructive messages. Then there are the daytime soaps and talk shows—many of which we can confidently say portray beliefs about relationships that raise the bar to unreachable heights or drop it to unimaginable lows for couples. What shows have influenced you most?

Religious and cultural backgrounds are a rich field for the development of expectations about marriage and family relationships. One of the ways in which relationships have become more complicated for people comes from the increasing diversity of the communities in which most of us live.

WHAT TO DO ABOUT EXPECTATIONS

Expectations can lead either to massive disappointment and frustration or to deeper connection between the two of you. There are four guidelines for handling expectations well. Couples who do the best in life usually are doing a pretty good job on all four.

1. Being *aware* of what you expect

2. Being *reasonable* in what you expect

3. Being *clear* about what you expect

4. Being *motivated* to meet the other's expectations, even when you don't have the same expectations

Being Aware of What You Expect

Whether you are aware of them or not, unmet expectations can lead to great disappointment and frustration in your relationship. You don't have to be fully aware of the expectations to have them affect your relationship.

Clifford Sager, a pioneer in this field, noticed how people bring to marriage a host of expectations that are never made clear. In effect, these expectations form a contract for the marriage. The problem is, people are not clear what's in the contract when they get married. Sager went further to suggest that many expectations are virtually unconscious and therefore very hard to be aware of. We don't mean to say that all expectations are deeply unconscious. But many do become such a part of us that they function automatically. Like driving a car, much of what you do is so automatic, you don't even have to think about it.

In the exercises at the end of this chapter, you'll have the opportunity to increase your awareness of your expectations. A major clue to understanding your own expectations is disappointment. When you're disappointed, some expectation hasn't been met. When you're disappointed, stop and ask yourself what you expected.

Paul would get very sad when he'd ask his wife to go boating with him and she'd say, "That's OK; go ahead without me and have

a great time." She'd rather stay home and garden. He worked very hard during the week as a repairman, and boating was the greatest relaxation for him. Dawn didn't care for boating but really wanted him to feel OK about having a nice time without her.

His sadness was a clue that an important expectation was at work. In thinking about it, he realized that he'd expected that they'd share this very important interest of his. If she didn't want to, what did that mean? If nothing else, he felt torn between spending time with her and time on his boat.

Although Paul knew that his wife loved him dearly, his expectation or hope that she'd become interested in his hobby stirred sadness about deeper issues of wanting to feel cared for. Once Paul became aware of his expectation and the reasons for his sadness, he was able to express what boating with her meant to him. She'd had no idea. She didn't love boating, but she was glad to come more often once she knew it meant so much to him.

Being Reasonable in What You Expect

Your being aware of expecting something does not make that expectation reasonable. Many expectations people have just aren't reasonable or realistic. Some unreasonable expectations are very specific. For example, is it reasonable to expect that your partner will never seriously disagree with you? Of course not. Yet you'd be surprised just how many people expect this.

Acting on unreasonable expectations is likely to lead to conflict. Sara and Randy are a good example of this problem. Both had high-pressure jobs in accounting, so it was very critical that they learn how to handle conflict and "free time" well.

In counseling, they made tremendous progress with all the techniques we presented in the first section of this book. They were handling what had been significant conflicts far better than they ever had before. Unfortunately, their progress was held back by Randy's expectation that because they had these techniques under their belts, they wouldn't have any more unpleasant arguments. That's just not a reasonable expectation.

Meanwhile, Sara felt really unappreciated for all the efforts she'd made to change the relationship. Randy saw even minor conflicts as evidence that they hadn't made any progress at all. His expectation became a perceptual filter leading him to miss all the great changes that were actually occurring.

We hope couples who consistently apply our principles will have fewer, less intense negative events. But events will always happen, and sometimes issues will erupt. There's a difference between handling issues well and not having any issues. Randy's expectation for no conflict was unreasonable and actually generated a lot of conflict until we pushed him to take a hard look at it. To overcome it, he had to become aware of the unrealistic expectation and challenge it within himself. It wasn't an expectation the couple had to meet; it was one that Randy had to change—and he did.

Being Clear About What You Expect

A specific expectation may be perfectly reasonable but never clearly expressed. It's critical to express expectations, not just to be aware of them or to evaluate their reasonableness. We all tend to assume that our model of the ideal marriage is the same as our partner's.

Why should we have to tell him or her what we expect? In effect, we assume that our spouse knows what we expect, and failures to meet our expectations can therefore be interpreted as intentional.

For example, how many people make the assumption that their partner should know just what is most pleasing sexually? We see this over and over again. One or both partners are angry that the other is failing to meet a desire or expectation. But more often than not, they've never expressed their expectation. That's expecting your partner to be good at mind reading.

Martha and Jay had regular eruptions of conflict whenever they went to his parents' house. Martha had the expectation that he'd stay close by when at his parents'. She didn't like being left alone in conversations with his mother, whom she perceived as prying into the secrets of their marriage. In contrast, Jay was thinking that he should give Martha as much opportunity as possible to get to know his parents. He often sensed that Martha was distant after visiting, but didn't understand why.

You need to be aware of your expectations, willing to evaluate them, and willing to discuss them. Otherwise, expectations have the power to trigger all the biggest issues in your relationship.

Martha's expectation for Jay to stay nearer when visiting his mother was perfectly reasonable. Yet until she told him what she wanted, he was left to his own assumptions. He thought Martha would like it when he went off with one parent, leaving her with the other. Once she expressed her real expectation, he could act on it to help her have a better time.

You can't work from any kind of shared perspective if you don't share your perspective! You need to be aware of your expectations, willing to evaluate them, and willing to discuss them. Otherwise, expectations have the power to trigger all the biggest issues in your relationship. Without dealing with them openly, you also miss an opportunity to define a mutual vision of how you want your marriage to be into the future.

Being Motivated to Meet Each Other's Expectations

One of the greatest reasons most relationships go so well early on is that both partners are very motivated to please each other. You try to figure out what he or she likes, and you try to give those gifts in inventive ways. These gifts can be small or large; what is most powerful is that they show you are paying attention to each other. Unfortunately, too many people quit paying close attention to what the other likes or expects. For some reason, they just get too busy with other things or just don't see it as important any longer. You don't have to be this way. You can decide (right now would be a good moment) to focus some of your energy on meeting some of your partner's expectations, just to please him or her. Try that with something specific today.

HEALTHY GRIEVING: THE DEEPEST ACCEPTANCE

One of the most painful experiences in life is coming to the realization that you may have a very reasonable expectation that you've communicated clearly to your mate, yet it's never going to come about. In his book *The Heart of Commitment* (1988), Scott (coauthor) says that we all have a list of things we would like to have in our relationships. Some items are more important, some less. None of us will get everything we wished for.

David and Claudia Arp, our coauthors on *Fighting for Your Empty Nest Marriage* (2000), refer to this idea as accepting your mate as a package deal. Sure, work for what you really want to happen in your life together, but be realistic about who the two of you are.

When you really want something that is just not going to happen, you can either sulk, get angry, or do what Scott says every couple needs to do over the long term: grieve the losses that come with commitment. When you commit to one person, you lose the possibilities another person might bring. Simple and, at times, painful.

Some will experience this more and some less, but it would be hard to find someone in a lasting relationship who did not understand it.

People who are maturing in life can acknowledge the pain of what they do not have and grieve about it rather than act out in anger and frustration. This is part of life and love. Work together to meet expectations. Face the disappointments while also looking for the larger meanings in your life together. Couples who face the good and the bad together can reach the deepest well of acceptance.

The most amazing marriages we've seen are ones in which the partners not only can accept their disappointments but also have gotten to a point where they can do it together. In other words, they are able to join together in acknowledging things they grieve, and doing so becomes a way of being more intimate. For example, one partner might say, "I know this is one of those times when you wish I'd chosen a different career. I know this schedule is not what you wanted for us." When you see a couple who can say things like this—and feel closer as a result—you are looking at a deep and tested love.

Talking Points

1. Expectations can be filters that affect how you perceive your partner and your marriage.

2. Expectations come from our experiences in our families of origin, our past relationships, and our culture.

3. Partners' expectations can be different in terms of needs and desires, but they must be shared through discussion and understanding.

 EXERCISES

The exercises for this chapter are among the most important in this book. It takes time to do them well. Please allow a total of an hour or two, over a few days, to do them thoroughly. They also take considerable follow-up, but the return on your investment of time and energy can be great. We hope you can make the time to do the work.

Exploring Your Expectations

1. Use this exercise to explore your expectations for your relationship. Spend some time thinking carefully about each area, then spend time writing your thoughts down so you can share them with your partner. Each of you should use a separate pad of paper. The points listed are meant to stimulate your *own* thinking. There may be numerous other areas in which you have expectations. Please consider everything you can think of that seems significant to you. You won't get much out of this exercise unless you are able and willing to really put some time into it. Many couples have found such an exercise extremely beneficial to their relationship.

The goal in this exercise is to consider expectations about how you want the relationship to be or think it should be, not how it is and not how you guess it will be. Write down what you expect, regardless of whether or not you think the expectation is realistic. The expectation matters, and it will affect your relationship whether or not it's realistic. Consider each question in light of what you expect and want for the future. It's essential that you write down what you really think, not what sounds like the "correct" or least embarrassing answer.

It can be valuable to consider what you observed and learned in each of these areas as you were growing up in your family. This is probably where many of your beliefs about what you want or don't want come from.

What Do You Expect Regarding . . .

1a. *The longevity of this relationship.* Is it "Till death do us part"?

 b. *Sexual fidelity.* What does that mean to you?

 c. *Love.* Do you expect to love each other always? Would anything change that? What way do you show love best? What kinds of things tell you most clearly you are loved?

d. *Your sexual relationship.* Frequency? Practices? Taboos?

e. *Romance.* What is romantic for you?

f. *Children.* Do you want children? More children?

g. *Children from previous marriages.* If you or your partner have children from a previous marriage, where do you want them to live? How do you expect that you should share in the upbringing and discipline of these children?

h. *Work, careers, and provision of income.* Who will work in the future? Whose career or job is more important? If there are or will be children, will either partner reduce work time out of the home to take care of them?

i. *The degree of emotional dependency on the other.* Do you want to be taken care of? How? How much do you expect to rely on each other to get through the tough times?

j. *Basic approach to life.* Do you see the two of you as a team or as two independent individuals?

k. *Loyalty.* What does that mean to you?

l. *Communication about problems in the relationship.* Do you want to talk these out? If so, how?

m. *Power and control.* Who do you expect will have more power and in what kinds of decisions? For example, who will control the money? Who will discipline the kids? What happens when you disagree in a key area? Who has the power now? How do you feel about that?

n. *Household tasks.* Who do you expect will do what? How much household work will each of you do in the future? If you live together now, how does the current breakdown of tasks match up with what you ideally expect?

o. *Religious beliefs and observances.* How, when, and where do you expect to practice your faith? If there are differences in religious beliefs, cultural backgrounds, or family traditions, how might they affect the relationship?

p. *Time together.* How much time do you want to spend together (as opposed to with friends, at work, with family, and so on)? How acceptable is spending time apart?

q. *Sharing feelings.* How much of what you are each feeling do you expect should be shared? What should be kept private?

r. *Friendship with your partner.* What is a friend? What would it mean to maintain or have a friendship with your partner?

s. *The little things in life.* Where do you squeeze the toothpaste? Should the toilet seat left up or down? Who sends greeting cards? Really think about the little things that could irritate you or have irritated you (or have been going really well). What do you want or expect in each area?

t. *Forgiveness.* How important is forgiveness in your relationship? How should forgiveness affect your relationship?

u. *Other relationships.* Which ones are OK? Friendships with the members of the opposite sex? Relationships with coworkers? When you are not together, how much time spent with friends is OK with you?

2. List any other expectations that you feel are important about how you want things to be and that did not appear in the foregoing list.

3. Now, with your mind primed from all this work, consider again the hidden issues we described in Chapter Six: issues of power, caring, recognition, commitment, integrity, and acceptance. Do you see any other ways now that they influence or are influenced by expectations? What do you expect in these areas that you haven't already addressed in working on the preceding list?

Rating Your Expectations

1. Now go back to each of the areas you looked at in the preceding exercise and rate each expectation on a scale of 1 to 10 according to how reasonable you think it really is. On this scale, 10

means "Completely reasonable. I really think it is OK to expect this in this type of relationship"; 1 means "Completely unreasonable. I can honestly say that even though I expect or want this, it is just not a reasonable expectation in this type of relationship."

For example, suppose you grew up in a family where problems were not discussed, and you are aware that you honestly expect or prefer to avoid such discussions. You might now rate that expectation as not very reasonable.

2. Next place a big check mark by each expectation that you feel you have never clearly discussed with your partner.

Discussing Your Expectations

1. After you and your partner have finished the exercises so far, plan time to talk, and begin spending time together discussing these expectations. *Please don't do them all at once!* You should plan to have a number of discussions, each covering only one or two expectations. Discuss the degree to which you each felt that the expectation being discussed had been shared clearly in the past. We highly recommend that you use the Speaker-Listener Technique to keep these discussions safe and structured.

2. Talk out the degree to which you both feel the expectations are reasonable or unreasonable, and discuss what you want to agree to do about any unreasonable expectations.

3. Talk about what your overall, long-term vision is for the relationship. What expectations do you share about your future together?

14

Forgiveness: Restoring Hope

Although what you probably want most from your marriage is a safe haven, being in a relationship puts you at risk of getting hurt from time to time; paradoxically, you risk more hurt in this relationship than in less intimate ones. (The only way to reduce the risk is for you to never get deeply involved with anyone.) If you've known each other well for some time, you've likely been hurt by your partner—and don't forget, that also means you've hurt your partner.

Many things we do can cause minor or major hurts: put-downs, avoidance, negative interpretations, abusive comments, forgetting something important, making decisions without regard for the needs of our partner, affairs, addictions, impoliteness, and so on. That's quite a list, with quite a range of possible impacts. Why are some couples able to move through *and beyond* these kinds of events while others bog down in despair? We think the answer is that these couples share a desire to forgive that flows from a deep well of acceptance, and we want to show you some ways to make forgiveness a reality in your relationship.

TWO PERSPECTIVES ON FORGIVENESS

Let's look at two different couples in need of forgiveness. Both examples demonstrate the need for forgiveness, but the infractions are very different—one's minor and one's major—and they have very different implications.

Oops, I Forgot: The Domicos

Beth and Tony Domico met each other in a Parents Without Partners support group and later married. Each had been married once before. Each had primary custody of the children from their first marriages. They found they had much in common, including a desire to marry again.

There's been nothing remarkable about their marriage and blended family except that the couple has done a great job of it. They have handled the myriad stresses of bringing two sets of kids together, and they've become a family. They have their ups and downs, but they handle the problems that come up with respect and skill.

Tony, who is an engineer with a construction firm, had saved the company from financial disaster by noticing a critical design flaw in the company's plans for a high-rise office building. For this and other reasons, Tony was chosen to be honored as employee of the year at an annual luncheon for the company. He was happy about the award, and happier still to receive a substantial bonus for his "heads-up" work.

Tony asked Beth to attend the luncheon, and she said she'd be glad to come. He was proud to be honored, and wanted Beth to share this moment with him. Because the company is very family oriented, most of the employees brought their spouses and "significant others" to the function. Tony told his fellow workers and his boss that Beth would be coming. A place was kept for her at the front table, right beside Tony.

Beth, who was working against a deadline for a major client, became distracted on the big day and completely forgot about the luncheon. While she was holding closed-door meetings, Tony was at the party feeling very embarrassed. He was also a little bit worried, as it was unlike Beth to miss anything. Here were his peers, honoring him, and without explanation his wife failed to show up. So he fumed and made the best of the embarrassment, telling his coworkers that "she must have had a crisis at the office."

As soon as Tony walked in the door that evening, Beth remembered what she had forgotten:

BETH: (*distressed*) Oh no! Tony, I just remembered—
TONY: (*cutting her off*) Where were you? I have never been so embarrassed. I really wanted you there.
BETH: I know, I know. I'm so sorry. I wanted to be there with you.
TONY: So where were you? I tried calling.
BETH: I was finishing the software for the Harson project. The team wasn't taking any calls, and I completely spaced out your lunch . . . I feel terrible.
TONY: So do I. I didn't know what to tell people, so I made something up about you having a crisis at work.
BETH: You were absolutely right, but that doesn't excuse my missing the ceremony. Please forgive me, Honey.

Should Tony forgive Beth? Of course. Now consider a very different example—one in which the same question has a much more complicated answer.

Maybe the Grass Is Greener: The Swensons

Johann and Megan Swenson have been together for fourteen years. They met in college, where both majored in business. They married shortly after they graduated and then moved to the Midwest. After three years they had their first child, a delightful girl named Marjorie. Two years later they had another girl, Lisa, who was serious, very bright, and a real handful at times.

Everything sailed along just fine until about the eighth year of marriage. At that time, Megan noticed that Johann was gone more and more. His job demanded a lot, but "Does he really need to be gone that much?" she wondered. She became suspicious. Without much time or open communication together, it was hard to know what was going on.

She began to feel as if she did not know Johann anymore and suspected he was having an affair. She'd been attracted to other men, so why couldn't it happen to him? She'd make phone calls to the office when he was supposed to be working late. He rarely answered. When she asked him about this, he'd say he must've been down the hall, in the copy room or talking with a colleague. That didn't wash with Megan.

Megan got sick and tired of being suspicious. One night she told him she was going to see a friend and left. They had arranged for a baby-sitter to watch the kids so he could go in to work. Borrowing her friend's car, she followed him as he left the neighborhood. She followed him right to an apartment complex, noting the door where he went in. She sat and sat—for three hours she sat. She got up to look at the name on the mailbox: Sally something-or-other.

"Not good, this is not good," she said to herself. It felt like gravity was pulling her stomach down through her intestines. Now what? Megan's not the type of woman who likes to wait to find things out. She decided to knock on the door. After fifteen minutes, Sally came to the door, in her bathrobe.

SALLY: *(seeming quite tense)* Can I help you?
MEGAN: *(calm but falling apart on the inside)* Yes. Please tell Johann I'm out here in the car and that I'd like to talk to him.
SALLY: *(gaining composure)* Johann? Who's Johann? I'm alone. Perhaps you have the wrong address.
MEGAN: *(sarcastic)* Perhaps I could take a look.
SALLY: I don't think so. Look, you have the wrong address, whatever your problem is. Good-bye!
MEGAN: *(yelling out as Sally closes the door)* Tell Johann I'll be at home—if he remembers where that is.

Johann rolled in an hour later. He denied everything for about three days. Megan was quite sure of herself and wasn't about to back down. She told Johann to get out. "An affair is bad enough, but if you can't even admit it, there's nothing left for us to talk about."

Johann fell apart. He began drinking and disappeared for days at a time. Megan felt even more alone and betrayed. Although she still loved Johann, her rage and resentment grew. "I thought I could trust him. I can't believe he would leave me for someone else!"

As his denial crumbled, Johann's sense of shame was so great that he was afraid to deal with Megan head-on. He'd just stay away from home. "She told me to get out, anyway," he told himself. Yet he was really bothered that Megan was being so tough. He wondered, "Is it really over?" In a way, though, he found new respect for her. No begging or pleading for Megan, just toughness. He liked Sally, but didn't want to spend his life with her. It became clearer to him who he wanted to be with: Megan.

Of course Megan didn't feel tough at all. She was in agony. But she was very sure of what she had seen. There was no chance she'd go on with Johann unless he dealt with her honestly. She was not sure whether she wanted to stay or leave.

Megan came home one night to find Johann sitting at the kitchen table with a terrible look of pain on his face.

JOHANN: *(desperately)* Please forgive me, Megan. I don't know . . . I'll get help. I don't know . . . I'm not sure what happened.

MEGAN: *(cool outside, rage inside)* I'm not sure what happened either, but I think you know a lot more than I do.

JOHANN: *(looking up from the table)* I guess I do. What do you want to know?

MEGAN: *(icily, controlling her rage)* I'd like to know what's been going on, without all the B.S.

JOHANN: *(tears welling up)* I've been having an affair. I met Sally at work, we got close, and things sort of spun out of control.

MEGAN: I guess they did. How long?

JOHANN: What?

MEGAN: *(voice raised, anger coming out)* How long have you been sleeping with her?

JOHANN: Five months. Since the New Year's party. Look, I couldn't handle things here at home. There's been so much distance between us . . .

MEGAN: *(enraged)* So what! What if I couldn't handle it? I didn't go looking for someone else. I don't want you here right now. . . . Just go. *(turning away, heading into the next room)*

JOHANN: If that's what you want, I'll go.

MEGAN: *(as she walks away)* Right now, that's just what I want. Please leave me alone. Just let me know where you'll be, for the kids' sake.

JOHANN: *(despondent)* I'll go to my parents'. That's where I've been lately.

MEGAN: *(sarcastic)* Oh, thanks for telling me.

JOHANN: I'll leave. Please forgive me, Megan, please.

MEGAN: I don't know if I can. *(She goes upstairs, and Johann slips out the back door.)*

At this point, Megan had some big decisions to make. Should she forgive Johann? *Could* she forgive Johann? She'd already decided that she might never trust him again, not fully. He clearly wanted to come back, but how would she ever know he wouldn't do this again the next time they had trouble together?

What do you think? Should she forgive Johann, and what does it mean to forgive?

WHAT IS FORGIVENESS?

Forgiveness is a decision to give up your perceived or actual right to get even with, or hold in debt, someone who has wronged you. *Webster's New World Dictionary* defines *forgive* this way: "1. to give up resentment against or the desire to punish; . . . 2. to give up all claim to punish; . . . 3. to cancel or remit (a debt)." The picture of forgiveness is a canceled debt. Note that *to forgive* is a verb: it's active; it's something you must *decide* to do. When one of you fails to forgive, you can't function as a team because the unforgiven partner is kept "one down" by being indebted to the other.

One of the best illustrations of the meaning of forgiveness that we've ever heard came from a pastor at one of our conferences. He was a black man from South Africa. That he came from a country with such a painful history of division and offense might tell you he had thought a lot about what forgiveness means. His illustration had a particular African flavor, as well.

> *Forgiveness is a decision to give up your perceived or actual right to get even with, or hold in debt, someone who has wronged you.*

Historically, one of the ways people might trap a big animal would be to dig a large pit on a trail where such an animal traveled and cover it over so that it looked like there was nothing there. When all worked as intended, the animal the hunters were trying to catch would travel the path, walk on the covering of the pit, and fall in. The animal would be trapped because the pit was too deep for it to climb or jump out of on its own power.

The pastor's point was this: when one spouse has hurt the other, it's as though he or she has fallen into the pit. That spouse has done something wrong that has put him or her in the one-down position relative to the other. Forgiving means helping the partner up and out of the pit. Not forgiving means keeping the partner in the pit, such that no relationship on an equal footing is possible again. When one of you does not forgive the other, you aren't on equal ground any longer, and the one is kept indefinitely in the position of debt, with painful reminders of why he or she is now in the pit. Lack of forgiveness is expressed in such statements as these:

"I'm going to make you pay for what you did."

"You are never going to live this down."

"You owe me. I'm going to get even with you."

"I'll hold this against you for the rest of your life."

"I'll get you for this."

These statements sound harsh, but they translate into marital realities. When you fail to forgive, you are at risk for acting in ways that make these kinds of statements come true and thereby doing great damage to both yourself and your relationship.

Essentially, an unwillingness to forgive is the ultimate in score-keeping, the message being "You are way behind on my scorecard, and I don't know if you can catch up." Scorekeeping fosters resentment and anger. The real message is that "maybe you can't do enough to make this up." If such a situation persists long enough, it leads to a crisis of confidence accompanied by hopelessness and, often, depression. People often walk away from debts they see no

hope of paying off. So forgiveness is needed not only to keep partners moving ahead in life but also to preserve hope.

The Degree of Infraction Matters

Although situations requiring forgiveness may always involve some
element of keeping one in debt or in a one-down position, this does
not mean that different kinds of hurt feel similar or are similar in
terms of damage. All other things being equal, the degree of damage caused between the two of you when one hurts the other in
some way is related to the degree to which *trust* was violated. So
although forgetting an appointment may create a sense of debt, typically there would not be a very great violation of trust. An affair,
however, would cause both a sense of debt and a huge loss of trust.

What Forgiveness Isn't

Maxine, a fifty-five-year-old woman in her second marriage, had
been brought up to believe that to forgive meant to forget. She
asked us, "It seems so hard to forgive and forget; how can you really
do this?"

In defining forgiveness, we said nothing about forgetting. You
hear the phrase "forgive and forget" so often that the two get
equated when they have nothing to do with one another. This is
one of the greatest myths about forgiveness. Can you remember a
very painful wrong someone has caused in your life, for which you
feel you have forgiven that person? We bet you can. Just because
you have forgiven—and given up a desire to harm the other in
return—doesn't mean you have forgotten the event ever happened.

A related misconception is the belief that if a person still feels
pain about what happened, he or she has not really forgiven. You
can still feel pain about being hurt in some way yet have fully forgiven the one who harmed you. We call such pain *grief*, because
there may be an irreplaceable loss, but this doesn't mean that the
wronged person hasn't forgiven or cannot forgive.

Megan Swenson, who we met earlier in the chapter, may come to a point of completely forgiving Johann for having an affair. She may work through and eliminate her rage and desire to hurt him back. However, even in the best of circumstances, what happened will leave her with a wound and a need to grieve that will remain for many years. In part that's because of the degree of deception and betrayal involved in what happened to her. Such deep wounds usually do not heal easily or completely. But couples can still work through to forgiveness and reconciliation that allow them to fully experience deeper connection again.

In the Domicos' case, the way in which Beth hurt Tony, by forgetting a special event, is far less severe and has fewer lasting consequences. As it turned out, Tony did forgive her. He didn't dwell on it, and he didn't need to grieve about it. However, when he is reminded of the incident, such as at company events, he remembers. He feels a twinge of the humiliation that he felt on that day. That doesn't mean that he's holding it over Beth or trying to get even. He has forgiven. He just has a painful memory along the road of their marriage.

RESPONSIBILITY AND TRUST

About now, some of you may be raising a very legitimate question about forgiveness that goes something like this: "In forgiving, aren't you saying that the one who did wrong is not responsible for what he or she did?" This is one of the greatest misunderstandings about forgiveness. When you forgive, you are saying nothing about the responsibility of the one who did wrong. The one who committed the infraction is responsible for his or her behavior, period. Forgiving someone does not absolve that person of responsibility for his or her actions. In fact, when one partner takes clear responsibility for hurting the other partner, the other will have an easier time forgiving and moving forward.

In this light, it's important to distinguish between punishment and consequences. You can be forgiven from the standpoint that your partner is not seeking to hurt or punish you, but you can still accept the consequences of your behavior. For example, although it may not be required for forgiveness, a great way to show your desire to take responsibility is to make amends for hurting your mate. Did you forget something that was important to your partner? You could schedule something very important and special as a way to make amends. Making amends takes humility because, if genuinely done, it shows that you accept responsibility. This gives your partner the greatest reason for hope to move forward.

Let's summarize so far. If you've been wronged by your partner, it's up to you to forgive or not. Your partner can't do this for you. It's your choice. If you've wronged your partner in some way, it's your job to take responsibility for your actions. You need to apologize and mean it. In other words, apologize only for what you really agree is your responsibility, but also push yourself pretty hard to accept what you actually did. Further, if needed, take steps to see that it doesn't happen again. This assumes that the infraction is clear and that you are both humble and mature enough to take responsibility. If you want your relationship to move forward, you need to have a plan for forgiving. Even if you don't want to forgive—perhaps because of your own sense of justice—you may still need to do so for the good of your marriage.

The Domicos, whom we met earlier, followed this model in the ideal sense. Beth took complete responsibility for missing the luncheon—apologizing and asking Tony to forgive her. He readily forgave her, having no intention of holding it against her. Their relationship was actually strengthened by the way they handled this event. Tony gained respect for Beth in her total acceptance of responsibility. Beth gained respect for Tony in his loving and clear desire to forgive and move on.

Before we move on to specific steps you can take to keep forgiveness flowing, we want to discuss a crucial distinction—between forgiveness and restoration in a relationship. What do you do if one partner can't or won't take responsibility? How can you move forward then?

What If Your Partner Won't Take Responsibility?

Forgiveness and restoration usually go hand in hand in a relationship, as it did for Tony and Beth. Intimacy and openness in their relationship were quickly restored—no hanging around the pit for this couple. Each handled their own responsibility without complication. When this is the case, restoration will naturally follow. The relationship is again open to intimacy and connection.

But what do you do if you've been wronged in some way and your partner takes no responsibility? Do you allow the relationship to continue as it was? For one thing, you must be open to examining the possibility that your partner really didn't intend to do anything wrong, even though you were hurt by what happened. There can be a sincere difference in the interpretation of what happened and why, and some negative interpretations are powerful enough to put a permanent barrier in the road to restoration.

Thelma and Charles Barker, for example, had such an event. They'd been married eleven years, with things generally going well. Although they weren't handling conflict that well, their dedication remained strong. On one occasion, Charles was cleaning out the garage, and he threw out all sorts of old boxes. He thought he was doing a great job, too—the garage hadn't looked this good in years.

Thelma was away for a few days at the time. When she returned, she was very pleased, just as Charles thought she'd be. The problem was, he had thrown out a box containing mementos from her days as a track star in high school. It was an accident. He'd even noticed the box and had thought he'd put it aside to protect it. Perhaps his daughter, who was helping him, had put it with the other boxes by mistake. Anyway, it was gone—for good. Big city. Big dump. No chance.

When Thelma realized the box was gone, she went into orbit. She was enraged. She accused Charles of being "stupid, insensitive, and domineering." She felt he didn't care and that his throwing out her stuff was just another sign of his needing to control everything. She interpreted his disposal of the box as a power move on his part, to show her who was boss.

What happened was unfortunate. Thelma had every right to be upset; those things meant a lot to her. But it really was a mistake. With the control issue triggered, Thelma was being unfair in accusing Charles of intentionally hurting her. This was a very negative interpretation. In fact, he had been trying to do something he knew she'd like.

When you are harmed in this way, it's OK to expect an apology—not because your partner *intended* to hurt you but because a mistake did hurt you. Charles can apologize to Thelma. However, Thelma has a long wait ahead if she expects to hear him say, "You're right. I threw out your things because I'm a control freak and think I can do whatever I want with anything in our house. I'll get in therapy right away to work on it. Please, please give me another chance." Not likely. It would actually show a lack of integrity on Charles's part for him to say this. It's not what he thinks, and it's not what motivated him.

Whether or not you both agree on the nature of the infraction or mistake, you can still move ahead and forgive. It may be hard, but if you don't, you and the relationship will suffer added damage. In fact, there's good reason to believe that when you hang on to resentment and bitterness, you put yourself at risk for psychological and physical problems, such as depression, ulcers, high blood pressure, and rage—not to mention divorce. That's no way to live. If Charles does the best job he can in taking responsibility for not being careful enough, Thelma should forgive him, for the good of their relationship. From time to time she will grieve, such as when a high school reunion comes up and she wants to look through those lost items. But she can choose to forgive.

Now for the really difficult case. Suppose it's very clear to you that your partner did something quite wrong and isn't going to take any responsibility, as in Johann's and Megan's situation. Virtually no one is going to deny that Johann did something wrong. He must be responsible for his own behavior if the marriage is to have any chance of moving forward. Sure, they are *both* responsible for letting their marriage slip—if it had indeed slipped. Affairs don't necessarily begin because of a marital slide. Johann and Megan had grown very distant, and neither is more to blame than the other for that. However, in response to this situation, it was his decision to have the affair. Johann alone is responsible for that action, not Megan.

When Johann showed up in the kitchen, asking for forgiveness, the worst thing Megan could have done would be to go on as if everything had returned to normal. It hadn't. You can't sweep things like this under the rug. Megan could have decided then to forgive him—but that's a separate decision from whether or not she should allow a full restoration of the relationship. When he came back to the house that night, she didn't know what level of responsibility he was taking for the affair. "What if he really blames me for it? What if he thinks it's my fault for not being more affectionate?" she thought. If she thought he felt justified or was not serious about changing, why should she allow restoration of the relationship? It really would be a great risk to take him back. Still, she could forgive. Even after forgiving occurred, restoration would take time.

Here is what actually happened. For a few days, they had some very nasty talks on the phone. With so much tension in the air, it was easy to escalate. Yet Johann persistently stated his desire to rebuild the marriage. He wanted to come back.

Megan asked Johann to come to the house one night for a talk. She arranged for the kids to be with her parents for the evening. She met with him and poured out her anguish, pain, and anger. He listened. She focused on how his behavior had affected her, not on his motives and weaknesses. He took responsibility to the point of a sincere apology. He didn't blame her for the affair. Now she thought there was a chance they could get through this. Their talk concluded this way:

JOHANN: I've had a lot of time to think. I believe I made a very bad choice that hurt you deeply. It was wrong of me to begin the relationship with Sally.

MEGAN: I appreciate the apology. I needed to hear it. I love you, but I can't pick up where we left off. I need to know that you will get to the root of this problem.

JOHANN: What do you want me to do?

MEGAN: I don't want to say. I don't know. I've got so many questions that I don't know which way is up. I just know that I needed to hear you say you'd done something very wrong.

JOHANN: Megan, I did do something wrong. I know it. It's also very clear to me . . . clearer than it's been in a few years . . . that I want this marriage to work. I want you, not someone else.

MEGAN: I'd like to make it work, but I'm not sure I can learn to trust you again.

JOHANN: I know I hurt you very deeply. I wish I could undo it.

MEGAN: That's what I want. I suppose I can forgive you, but I also need some way to believe that it won't happen again.

JOHANN: Megan, I'd like to come back home.

MEGAN: That's OK with me, but I need to know we'll go and get help to get through this.

JOHANN: Like a therapist.

MEGAN: Yes, like a therapist. I'm not sure what to do next, and I don't want to screw this up. If you'll agree to that, I can handle you coming back home.

JOHANN: That makes sense.

MEGAN: Don't expect me to go on like nothing's happened. I'm very, very angry with you right now.

JOHANN: I know, and I won't pressure you to act like nothing happened.

MEGAN: OK.

As you can see, Megan really opened up, and Johann validated her pain and anger. He didn't get defensive. If he had, she was prepared to work on forgiveness but end the marriage. She gained hope from this talk. Megan knew she could forgive—she's a very forgiving person. She knew it would take some time. She's also no fool. She knew they needed help. The future looked uncertain. There was a lot to work through if they were going to restore their relationship.

Johann did the best he could under the circumstances. Next day, he began calling around to find the best therapist. He wanted a professional who knew what they needed to do to move forward. This showed Megan that he was serious about repairing their marriage—some evidence of long unseen dedication. Action speaks volumes when it comes to forgiveness and restoration.

The relationship could not be restored until they achieved forgiveness and began to work on the issues and expectations undermining their relationship. Megan remembers what Johann had done—she's not going to be able to forget—but the ache in her heart gets weaker all the time. They were able to move forward.

What About Regaining Trust?

We're often asked how you regain trust when something has so damaged it. The question is not so relevant for more minor matters of forgiveness. There is no loss of trust in the Domicos' incident. But for the Swensons, who are struggling with an affair, there's a huge loss of trust. Whatever the incident, suppose forgiveness proceeds smoothly, and you both want restoration. How do you regain trust? It's not easy. There are two key points we make about rebuilding trust.

1. *Trust builds slowly over time.* Trust builds as you gain confidence in someone being there for you. Deep trust comes only from seeing that your partner is there for you over time. Some people, for whatever reasons, have a harder time trusting others, no matter what happens in their relationships. If one or both of you have some difficulty feeling trusting and secure, it's all the more important that the two of you work carefully to build and hold on to trust in your

relationship. A great way to help your partner trust you more is to do all you can to show your dedication to him or her. That is something over which you have a lot of personal control, and we'll make some suggestions about this in the chapter on commitment.

Megan can regain her trust in Johann only slowly. The best thing that can happen is for a considerable amount of time to go by without a serious breach of trust. That takes commitment and new ways of living together. They can't afford to let the same kind of distance build up again. If Johann has another affair or lies again about the past one, it will probably be impossible for Megan to trust him again.

2. *Trust has the greatest chance to be rebuilt when each partner takes appropriate responsibility.* The most important thing Johann can do to regain Megan's trust is to take full responsibility for his actions. If she sees Johann doing all he can to bring about serious change without her prodding and demanding, her trust will grow. In seeing his effort, she gains confidence that things can get better—not perfect, but really better. It's easier to trust when you can clearly see your partner's dedication to you.

Megan can also help build Johann's trust. For one thing, he'll need to see that she doesn't plan to hold the affair over his head forever. Often it isn't only the one who was hurt who needs to see genuine desire to move ahead. Can Megan really forgive? If she reminds him about the affair, especially during arguments, he won't be able to trust that she really wants him to draw closer and move ahead.

THE POWER OF FORGIVENESS IN THE FLOW OF LIFE

We will conclude this chapter talking about how you can work toward forgiveness about specific events and issues together. Before we go there, we want to emphasize something that's so obvious it's often not stated: your relationship needs a daily dose of forgiveness. You can cause each other minor hurts often, if not daily. Tempers flare. You forget things you should have remembered. You make mistakes in completing the tasks of life. The couples who do best over time create a climate that assumes trust and the willingness to forgive. As we've said before, how you think has a direct effect on how you will act.

Our coauthors on *Fighting for Your Empty Nest Marriage*, David and Claudia Arp, emphasize the importance of a deep, abiding attitude of forgivingness that permeates a relationship. Part of the need for this attitude comes from the fact that your partner cannot be all that you hoped he or she would be in life, nor have you been perfect for your partner. Some of what you need to forgive one another for amounts to accepting the other for

Your relationship needs a daily dose of forgiveness.

who he or she is. It's easy to accept your partner for the things that go just the way you wanted them to go in life. It's a far tougher test of your ability to forgive to accept disappointments related to who you each are as a person.

For example, maybe you are in midlife and wish you'd married someone who shares your passion for art (or hunting or reading or opera or dog breeding—you get the idea). Well, as it turned out, that's just not who your partner is. You can try to punish him or her in some way for not being exactly what you wanted, but that will not help you have the best relationship possible between the two of you. Besides, when you focus on what you didn't get, it's too easy to forget all of what you did get. Which list do you want to dwell on at this point in life? We're not saying that you don't ask for changes and work to please one another. If you love romance movies and your partner doesn't, you could well ask that he or she try going to a few with you from time to time and, when doing so, to show real interest in either the movie or at least your reaction to it. More important, we are saying here that you will do best if the greater context of your life together is one that conveys deep and abiding acceptance.

Making Forgiveness Last

Your motive for forgiving one another in life may be as important as forgiveness itself. One of the most obvious reasons to forgive others is that it frees you up to move into the future. However, researchers like Michael McCollough and Everett Worthington Jr. at Virginia Commonwealth University have been studying forgiveness, and they are finding that when people forgive mostly for personal benefit, forgiveness doesn't seem to hold up so well over time. The kind of forgiveness that lasts is that which is motivated by your desire to enhance the well-being of your mate—in these researchers' words, by the desire to be a "blessing" to the other. This is a powerful kind of sacrifice that helps restore relationships.

Toddy Holeman at Asbury Seminary has been studying how forgiveness works between partners. She finds that it doesn't matter so much which partner takes the lead in the dance of forgiveness, as long as both partners are on the dance floor. Further, she found that couples who are committed to change are the ones who make change happen, and in doing so, they grow in their commitment for more change. She also found that the couples who really heal from major wounds are those who make reconciliation the "central organizing theme" of their marriage. They change whatever in their lives they need to change. They are moving forward no matter what.

STEPS TO FORGIVENESS AND RESTORATION

So far, we've focused on the meaning of forgiveness and what it takes to make it come about. We want to give you a more specific and structured approach that can serve as a road map for achieving forgiveness.

In suggesting specific steps, we don't mean to imply that forgiveness is simple or easy. But we do want you to be able to move forward with some specific steps to get you through the toughest times.

Each step has some key pointers. We'll use the example of Thelma and Charles Barker (who threw out the box with Thelma's mementos in it) to illustrate the points. Our discussion will also summarize many of the points made in this chapter.

Step One: Schedule a Couple Meeting for Discussing the Specific Issue Related to Forgiveness

If an issue is important enough to focus on in this way, do it right. Set aside a time when you will have no distractions. Prepare yourselves to deal openly, honestly, and with respect. As we said in the chapter on ground rules, setting aside specific times for dealing with issues makes it more likely that you'll actually follow through and do it well.

After the initial rush of anger, Thelma and Charles agreed to work through the box incident. They set aside time on an evening when the kids were at a school function.

Step Two: Set the Agenda to Work on the Issue in Question

Identify the problem or harmful event. You must both agree that you are ready to discuss it in this format at this time. If not, wait for a better time.

When Thelma and Charles met, the agenda was pretty clear: how to forgive and move on from the loss of her box of mementos. They agreed this was the focus of their meeting, and they agreed they were ready to handle it.

Step Three: Fully Explore the Pain and Concerns Related to This Issue for Both of You

The goal in this step is to have an open, validating talk about what has happened that harmed one or both of you. You shouldn't try this unless you as an individual are motivated to hear and show respect for your partner's viewpoint. The foundation for forgiveness is best laid through such a talk or a series of talks.

Validating discussions go a long way toward dealing with the painful issues in ways that bring you closer together. This would be a great place to use the Speaker-Listener Technique. If there's ever a time to have a safe and clear talk, this is it.

Using the Speaker-Listener Technique, Thelma and Charles talked it out for about thirty minutes. Charles really listened to her anguish about losing the things that meant a lot to her. Thelma edited out her prior belief that he'd somehow done it on purpose. She had calmed down and could see that blaming him in this way didn't make a lot of sense. She listened to how badly he felt for her and for her loss. She also validated his statements that he had specifically tried not to throw out her things. The couple felt closer than they had in quite a while.

Step Four: The Offender Asks for Forgiveness

If you have offended your partner in some way, an outward appeal for forgiveness is not only appropriate but very healing. An apology would be a powerful addition to a request for forgiveness. A sincere apology validates your partner's pain. To say, "I'm sorry. I was wrong. Please forgive me," is one of the most healing things that one person can do for another.

Apologizing and asking for forgiveness are a big part of taking responsibility for how you have hurt your partner. This doesn't mean that you sit around and beat yourself up for what you did. You have to forgive yourself, too!

But what if you don't think you have done anything wrong? You can still ask that your partner forgive you. Charles certainly didn't feel he had done anything wrong, but he could understand why Thelma was upset anyway. Remember, forgiveness is a separate issue from why the infraction or mistake occurred. So even if you don't agree you did anything wrong, your partner can choose to forgive. That's harder, but it's doable.

Listen carefully to the pain and concern of your partner. Even if you feel you have done no wrong, you may find something in what he or she says that can lead to a change on your part for the better of the relationship.

Step Five: The Offended Agrees to Forgive

Ideally, the one needing to forgive will clearly, openly acknowledge his or her intent to forgive. This may be unnecessary for minor infractions, but for anything of significance, this step is important. Making your intent explicit feels more real and more memorable and increases accountability between the two of you to find the healing you are seeking.

There are several specific implications of this step. In forgiving, you are attempting to commit the event to the past. You are agreeing that you will not bring it up in the middle of future arguments or conflicts.

You both recognize that this commitment to forgive does not mean that the offended won't feel pain or any effects from what happened. (For example, Thelma will feel hurt for a very long time over the loss of her treasured mementos.) But you're moving on. You're working to restore the relationship and repair the damage.

Step Six: If Applicable, the Offender Makes a Positive Commitment to Change Recurrent Patterns or Attitudes That Give Offense

Again, this step depends on your agreement that there is a specific problem with how one of you behaved. It also assumes that what happened is part of a pattern, not just a one-time event. For the Domicos and the Barkers, this step is not very relevant. For the Swensons, it is critical.

If you have hurt your partner, it also helps to make amends. This is not the same as committing to make important changes. When you make amends, you make a peace offering of a sort—not because you "owe" your partner but because you want to demonstrate your desire to get back on track. It's a gesture of good will. One way to make amends is to do unexpected positive acts. This shows your investment and ongoing desire to keep building your relationship.

In the Barkers' case, Charles scheduled a dinner for just the two of them at Thelma's favorite restaurant. He went out of his way to show her that she was special to him. She'd already forgiven him, but this gesture took them farther on the path of healing. Besides, it was fun. Their friendship was strengthened.

Step Seven: Expect It to Take Time

These steps are potent for getting you on track as a couple. They begin a process, but they don't sum it up. These steps can move that process along, but you may each be working on your side of the equation for some time to come. Relationships can be healed when painful events come between you. You can choose to heal.

We hope you are encouraged by the possibility of forgiveness and reconciliation in your relationship. If you've been together for only a short time, this may seem like more of an academic discussion than a set of ideas that are crucial for your relationship. If you've been together for some time, you understand the need for forgiveness. Let's hope it happens naturally in your relationship. If so, keep at it. Do the work of prevention. The rewards are great.

If you need to initiate forgiveness but barriers of resentment have built up, get started on tearing them down. You can do it. The steps we've given you here will help you get started.

Talking Points

1. An attitude of acceptance and forgiveness is crucial for a happy marriage.

2. Forgiveness is a choice: you can choose to move forward, release your partner from owing you a debt, and work to restore your relationship.

3. Taking responsibility for your own actions and working to change offensive or destructive patterns are a central part of the healing process begun by the act of forgiveness.

EXERCISE

Working on Forgiveness

There are two parts to this exercise, one to do individually and one to work on together.

Individual Work

1. Spend some time in reflection about areas where you may harbor resentment, bitterness, and unforgivingness in your relationship. Write these things down. How old are these feelings? Are there patterns of behavior that continue to offend you? Do you hold things against your partner? Do you bring up past events in arguments? Are you willing to push yourself to forgive?

2. Now spend some time reflecting on times you may have really hurt your partner. Have you taken responsibility? Did you apologize? Have you taken steps to change any recurrent patterns that give offense? Just as you may be holding on to some grudges, you may be standing in the way of reconciliation on some issues if you've never taken responsibility for your end.

Working Together

As is true of everything else we've presented, you'll need to practice to really put positive patterns in place. Therefore, we recommend that you plan to sit down at least a couple of times and work through some issues with the model presented in this chapter. To start, pick less significant events or issues, just to get the feel of things. Doing so helps you build confidence and teamwork.

If you have identified more significant hurts that the two of you have not fully dealt with, take the time to sit down and tackle these meatier issues. This will be more successful as you practice the skills and use them more effectively. Facing harder issues is risky, but if you do it well the resulting growth in your relationship and capacity for intimacy will be well worth it. Choose to grow.

15

Sticking, Stuck, or Stopped: On the Path to Commitment

A simple question says it all: Are you sticking, stuck, or stopped? In the book *The Heart of Commitment* (by coauthor Scott), these words are used to describe the various paths on which couples find themselves in life. What path do you want to be on together? Because you are reading this book, we assume you want to stick, which means to really thrive in your journey through life together. We also know that many of you feel something closer to stuck than to sticking. Many of you are in danger of stopping altogether—getting a divorce and moving on.

If you have built and maintained a strong bond together, we want to help you really stick. We want to help you *prevent* the kinds of declines that so many couples needlessly suffer. Many of the mistakes couples commonly make stem directly from the partners' failure to be mindful of their commitment every day; a marriage can't thrive if the partners see commitment just as something they promised on their wedding day.

Many of the mistakes couples commonly make stem directly from the partners' failure to be mindful of their commitment every day; a marriage can't thrive if the partners see commitment just as something they promised on their wedding day.

For those of you who relate more to being stuck, we want to help you get sticky again—even if you've become very discouraged.

There is great power in the combined will of your two hearts to turn things around.

Most married couples consider commitment the glue that holds their relationship together. The kind and depth of your commitment have a lot to do with not only your chances of staying together but also your chances of being happy over many years together. In this chapter, we present a theory and research about commitment that lead to very practical advice for building and protecting your relationship.

We are ending this new version of our book with commitment, just as we now most often end our PREP workshops. We have saved what is probably most important for last. We want you to share this cutting-edge work and inspire you as you move forward to enjoy the magical, mysterious journey your relationship can be. At our workshops, Howard gets the ball rolling by saying we have a guest speaker: "one of the world's leading experts on commitment." The band strikes up a drum roll, and Dr. Commitment, our own Scott Stanley, appears. (OK, there's no drum roll.) Scott says, "Thank you, Dr. Prevention." (We give Howard that honorary title for his two and a half decades of work on prevention of marital distress and divorce.) Dr. Commitment takes the floor.

THE COMPLEXITY OF COMMITMENT

Commitment means many things to many people. Stop and think a few moments about what it means to you. In fact, take a piece of paper and jot down the words that come to your mind. Then, as you read the rest of this chapter, see how those ideas are reflected in some of the major themes we raise here.

In recent years, there has been an explosion of theory and research on commitment. This body of work has deepened our understanding of the themes of commitment, which in turn has led us to some very specific suggestions for you about how you can enhance your relationship for the long term. To better understand commitment, we will first describe two couples in some detail. In both marriages there is commitment, but the types of commitment are very different. One couple is sticking. The other is stuck and in danger of stopping.

Rod and Mary Anderson: Stuck, Not Sticking

Rod and Mary married thirteen years ago. They have a four-year-old son and a seven-year-old daughter. Rod manages the meat section in a large grocery store, and Mary is a secretary in a doctor's office. Like most couples, Rod and Mary started out very much in love but have gone through some tough times. Raising two kids has proven more stressful than either expected. Combined with the hassle of major job changes for both, child rearing has left Rod and Mary feeling tired and distant.

Mary has considered divorce on more than a few occasions, and increasingly finds herself thinking about leaving Rod. Rod also feels unhappy with the marriage, but, like many men, he hasn't considered divorce as much of an option. He also hasn't thought of any ways to improve the marriage. He hopes for more, but hasn't told Mary this, and thinks trying to get closer just doesn't work. When he does try to do something positive, he feels shut out by Mary. He has become anxious about the thought of her leaving, but he senses that any energy put into the marriage at this point is wasted effort.

"Maybe things will get better when the kids leave home," he thinks. "I've just got to stick with it and hope for the best." We'd call this attitude *being stuck*.

Mary and Rod work around others they find attractive. Larry is a single, good-looking man at Mary's work who has made it clear he's interested in Mary. She has been seriously contemplating an affair and finds herself thinking more and more about it.

Mary is very aware of changes she's gone through over the years, and increasingly thinks that Rod will never be the kind of partner that she hoped for. Furthermore, she feels she is putting a lot more into the marriage than Rod is, with little in return for her time and effort. She resents that he doesn't seem to appreciate and accept all she's done for him. Like Rod, she is thinking it's just not worth the effort to try harder.

As Mary thinks about leaving Rod, difficult questions plague her. First, she wonders how the kids would respond to divorce. Would it hurt them? Would Rod want custody? Would it be hard to get a divorce? Would Rod try to stop her? How could they afford lawyers? She wonders how she could support herself on her income alone. Who would get the house? Could either afford to keep the house separate from the other? Would Rod pay child support? If she married again, would another man accept her children?

As Mary considers these questions, she decides that maybe the costs of getting a divorce are greater than she wants to bear, at least for now. Sure, she's in pain, but she balances this against the pain and stress a divorce could bring. A feeling of despair hangs over her. Feeling trapped, she decides that staying is better than leaving, but staying stuck isn't a great choice.

Deidre and Eric Sempleton: Sticking, Not Stuck

Deidre and Eric were married fifteen years ago. They have three children, a seven-year-old boy, an eleven-year-old boy, and a thirteen-year-old girl. Although they've had their stressful times, both Deidre and Eric have few regrets about marrying one another. They met when both were working for a large insurance company. He was working in sales, and she had worked her way up to being manager of the claims department.

Their kids present some real challenges. The middle boy has a serious learning disability and requires attention and support. Their oldest daughter is beginning to show more signs of rebellion than they had ever imagined, and this too causes concern. Despite these challenges, Deidre and Eric usually feel the other's support in facing the tasks of life.

Eric does occasionally become aware of his attraction to women he meets in his work. However, in his commitment to Deidre, he's decided not to dwell on "what if." He is happy with Deidre and doesn't want to consider being with anyone else. Everyone has regrets at times in marriage, but for Deidre and Eric these times are few. They genuinely respect and like each other, do things for each other, and talk fairly openly about what they want out of life and marriage. Very important, Deidre and Eric have regularly made time for their relationship—to play together, to talk as good friends, and to keep their passion alive. Further, because of religious convictions, each resists thinking about divorce, even when they're not getting along so well. Each is willing to help the other attain what he or she desires in life. Simply put, they feel like a team. They stick—together.

As you can see, the Andersons and the Sempletons have very different marriages. The Andersons are miserable, and the Sempletons are enjoying life. Both marriages are likely to continue for the time being—reflecting some kind of commitment. It's not just the level of happiness that separates these two marriages. The Sempletons have a much different, deeper kind of commitment. To understand the difference, we need a broad model of commitment.

WHAT IS COMMITMENT?

There are two common ways to think about commitment. The commitment of *personal dedication* refers to the desire to maintain or improve the quality of the relationship for the mutual benefit of both partners. Personal dedication is characterized by a desire (and actions) not only to continue in the relationship but also to improve it, sacrifice for it, invest in it, link it to personal goals, and seek the partner's welfare, not just one's own.

> *The commitment of* personal dedication *refers to the desire to maintain or improve the quality of the relationship for the mutual benefit of both partners.*

In contrast, *constraint commitment* refers to forces that keep individuals in relationships whether or not they're dedicated. As we discuss in the box "The Binds That Tie," constraint commitment may arise from either external or internal pressures. Constraints help keep couples together by making ending the relationship more costly—economically, socially, personally, or psychologically. If dedication is low, constraints can keep people in relationships they might otherwise want to leave.

The Binds That Tie

What constitutes the overall constraint commitment people have depends on who they are, what they value, and what their circumstances are. Here is a list of factors that are commonly part of the constraints that keep a person in his or her marriage.

- Social pressure from friends and family
- Financial considerations
- Concerns for children's welfare or fear of loss of contact
- The difficulty of the steps to leave
- Moral factors, such as a belief that divorce is generally wrong or that a person should always finish what he or she has started
- Poor quality of alternatives

You could think of constraints this way: all other things being equal, more of any of them make it more likely that a person will choose to stay in his or her marriage, even through tough times. We believe that without constraint commitment, most couples would not make it in marriage beyond a few years because of the normal ups and downs in satisfaction in life together.

Rod and Mary have a commitment characterized by constraint. Mary in particular is feeling a great deal of constraint and little dedication—the essence of feeling stuck. She feels compelled to stay in a dissatisfying marriage for a host of reasons: their kids, money, family pressure, and so on. Rod also has high constraint commitment and little dedication, though he's less dissatisfied with their day-to-day life.

Like Rod and Mary, Deidre and Eric have a good deal of constraint commitment, but they also have a strong sense of dedication to each other. Our research at the University of Denver shows that constraints are a normal part of marriage. Any marriage will generate a significant amount of constraint over time. It's normal. Happier, more dedicated couples are just as likely to have considerable constraints as less satisfied, less dedicated couples at similar points in life. In fact, today's dedication becomes tomorrow's constraint. You fall in love, so you get engaged. You stay in love, so you get married. You're still together, so you have kids and buy a house. Dedicated couples choose to have more constraints as they move through the stages of marital and family life together. Happier couples just don't think a lot about constraints, and when they do, they often draw comfort from them. When you are sticking, you don't feel stuck; you feel as though you are sailing along on the seas of love.

HOW DOES COMMITMENT DEVELOP?

Partners become more dedicated because they like being with one another. Think about the earlier days of your relationship. As your dedication to one another became more apparent, you may have noticed that you became more relaxed about the relationship. In most relationships, there's an awkward period during which the desire to be together—and your attachment—is great, but the commitment is unclear. That produces anxiety about whether or not you'll stay together. As your mutual dedication became clearer, it seemed safer to invest in the relationship. This increase in dedication is important for all couples, but especially important for couples in which one or both partners have a tendency (for whatever reasons in their past) to be insecure about their key attachments in life.

In relationships, almost all forms of commitment can be understood as symbols of security. It is only with a deep sense of security that two people can fully experience the wonder, magic, and mystery of a great relationship.

What You Can't See Can Hurt You

Perhaps the saddest thing we've seen in our work with couples is unexpressed dedication. In so many couples, one partner has withered on the vine because he or she can't see much evidence that the other is really committed. Sometimes there really has been an erosion of dedication. But many other times it's not so much that there's a lack of dedication to one another as much as that the dedication has become harder to see.

One way this happens is that partners stop doing many of the things they used to do to show how dedicated they really are. Little things—cards, a flower, a poem, an e-mail, a call in the middle of the day, a sticky note that says "I love you" on the steering wheel—can say "I'm thinking of you, I'm here for you, and I'm committed to you." Bigger things matter too, of course. A lot.

This brings us to the other way couples can get in trouble because of hidden dedication. All too often, people lose track of the things that their partner already does—and does regularly—that demonstrate a high level of dedication. Sad but true: we all tend to get accustomed to a certain standard of living and behaving in relationships, and things that may be terrific evidence of dedication appear instead to be routine and "to be expected." If you're feeling that your mate is not so dedicated these days, ask yourself first if this is a negative interpretation. Yes, this means pushing yourself hard to see all the things he or she is doing that show dedication.

How does commitment erode? If most couples have high levels of dedication early on, such as when engaged or early in marriage, what happens to kill dedication for some couples over time? For one thing, if a couple isn't handling conflict well, satisfaction with the marriage will steadily decline. Because satisfaction fuels dedication, dedication begins to erode along with satisfaction. With dedication in jeopardy, giving to one another erodes further, and satisfaction takes a bigger dive. It's a downward spiral from there. Both partners try less, both see their partner trying less, and soon their relationship is dying.

For some couples, their constraints end up being primarily related to the presence of their children, and when their children leave home, most of the glue holding these couples together crumbles away. Even if such a couple does not break up, the erosion of commitment can lead to insecurity about the future that makes it far harder to work to make the marriage all it can be. Dedication erodes further when people feel their efforts no longer make a difference.

The secret to satisfying commitment is to maintain not just constraint but also a high level of dedication. Although constraint commitment can add a positive, stabilizing dimension to your marriage, it can't give you a great relationship. It can, however, keep you from doing immensely impulsive, stupid things when you are unhappy in the short run. Are you just existing in your relationship, or are you making it what you hoped it would be? Our research shows that dedicated couples report not only more satisfaction with their relationships but also less conflict about the problems they have and greater levels of self-disclosure.

THE POWER OF DEDICATION: CHOICES, COUPLE IDENTITY, SACRIFICE, AND THE LONG-TERM VIEW

We want to reveal to you four key dynamics underlying dedication in strong relationships: choices, couple identity, sacrifice, and the long-term view. All four dynamics point to things you have some control over and therefore are all related to strategies for having a great relationship.

Making Choices

Many aspects of commitment relate to the choices you make and how you handle the alternatives you did not choose. In essence, commitment involves making the choice to give up other choices. Any commitment you make in life requires that you choose among alternatives. Some of these decisions involve setting priorities and others involve how you handle it if you are attracted to others.

Setting Priorities

When people need to make decisions involving competing time and resources, those who are more dedicated to their partners are more likely to make decisions that protect the relationship. For example, early on in the relationship, most people will move mountains to spend time with their partner. But as the cares and hassles of life take over, too many of us allow our relationship to take a backseat. A great relationship is a front-seat deal (unless you are in the backseat together, but that's another chapter).

To some degree, problems with priorities can reflect as much a problem with overinvolvement elsewhere as one of a lack of dedication at home. Unfortunately, as people get busier and busier, too many end up doing what Scott, in his book *The Heart of Commitment,* calls *no*-ing each other rather than *knowing* each other: "No, I don't have time to talk tonight." "No, I'm too tired to even think about making love tonight." "No, I promised Fred I'd come over Saturday and help him put up that new fence." To protect your relationship, you've got to be good at saying no to things that might seem important but aren't and saying yes to your partner in ways that matter to him or her.

Alternative Monitoring: Forsaking All Others?

Just because two people make a choice to give up other choices, it does not mean that all others disappeared from the planet. In our research, we talk about *alternative monitoring,* which is a technical way of referring to how much you keep an eye out for other partners in life. The more you are attracted to or attuned to other potential partners, the less your personal dedication to your partner.

Do you find yourself frequently or seriously thinking about being with people other than your spouse? Our research shows that this aspect of dedication is the most sensitive to your current level of happiness. In other words, when unhappy with their partners, most people are pretty prone to thinking about the "what ifs." What if I had married her instead? What if I was no longer married to him? You can "what if" yourself to a place of despair and resentment if you choose to do so. That's a path with a pretty certain destination.

Research by Dennis Johnson and Caryl Rusbult (the latter having done extensive research on commitment) suggests that highly dedicated people mentally devalue attractive potential partners. When tempted, do you dwell on the grass that seems greener, or do you figure that every lawn has problems, and focus on taking better care of your own? You can choose to attack such thoughts about others rather than allow them a comfortable home in your mind.

Eric Sempleton—the husband we discussed earlier whose marriage is really sticking—has been tempted a couple of times by people at work, especially a woman named Libby. Although aware of the attraction, Eric considered it a threat to his marriage and made himself focus more on Libby's negative side than on the positive. He chose to focus on why the grass *wasn't* greener on the other side of the fence. If you're planning on keeping your marriage strong, keep watering and trimming your own lawn and don't linger by the fence.

Couple Identity: The Story of Us

Couples vary in the degree to which the partners view the relationship as a team rather than as comprising two separate individuals who each mostly focus on self. In the happiest and strongest marriages, "we" transcends "me" in how the partners think. If a couple doesn't have this sense of being a team, conflict is more likely, because the spouses see problems as "me against you" instead of "us against the problem." Our research clearly shows that couples who are thriving in their marriages have a strong sense of "us."

We aren't suggesting that you should merge your identities. Rather, we're suggesting that most couples do best with a clear sense of two individuals coming together to form a team—what a difference this makes in how you view life together! There's an old joke about a wedding ceremony in which the minister gets to the point of saying "and the two shall become one," and someone in the back row leans over to her friend and says, "I wonder which one?" That's not the idea here.

One couple, Melissa and Will, had a pretty stable and harmonious life up until the time their youngest child left home to take a job in another state. As happens with many couples, some of the glue that had bound them together weakened with the departure of their children. They drifted for some time, experiencing increasing distance and conflict—developing lives that were largely independent from one another. One day, they started to turn it all around.

Who's on My Side?

A colleague of ours, Natalie Monarch, has been studying couple identity by looking at the degree to which it is
reflected in three major areas:

1. The couple's view of how they have dealt with the
   past together, especially the sense that they have
   overcome things together, as a team
2. The degree to which the couple views their relationship together as special
3. The couple's view of their future together, especially in the sense of having dreams and a vision

   Notice a word that's repeated in those three major
themes: *together.* What people seem to want most in marriage is a lifelong best friend and confidante, which is
directly related to having a sense of being together in the
flow of life. Reflecting on your relationship for a
moment, how do you view it in light of the three aspects
we've listed here?

Consider the power of a talk like this, and the humility required
of both partners. They were at the breakfast table together, reading
the paper and having coffee.

WILL: *(looking up from his paper)* Can we talk a second?

MELISSA: *(putting her paper aside)* Sure, what's up?

WILL: Well, something . . . um, something important.

MELISSA: *(nodding and listening)*

WILL: I've been thinking that we're at a big point in life here. What
we do in the next year might lay down the pattern for us for the
next thirty years. I'm not sure I like the path we're on, and I've

been thinking that maybe we should really plan for the kind of relationship we want in the future. You know, to be very intentional about where we head now.

MELISSA: *(barely suppressing a large smile)* I love that idea. I've been wondering—actually worrying a bit, too—about where we're headed. I'd like us to be really close and not just share a house in the years ahead.

WILL: Me too, but I'm thinking that if we're not careful, we'll only be roommates for the next thirty years. I want to be best friends and lovers.

MELISSA: What do you think we should do next?

WILL: How about we go away for a weekend? Maybe to that cabin. No TV, no distractions. Just us. We can talk and play and plan for our future. What do you think?

MELISSA: Sounds perfect. Let's look at the calendar.

We hope you haven't gotten bored by the repetition of this critical point, demonstrated in this dialogue between Melissa and Will: the strategies we suggest throughout this book are most powerful if you make the key decisions together. This is the essence of couple identity.

Many couples have nurtured and protected their couple identity from the start. If you have it, work at keeping it. But things always are changing, and you can take this opportunity to openly discuss and plan for how you want to express your "we" in the years ahead. If you've lost that couple feeling, work at getting it back.

Here are a few ideas for preserving and deepening couple identity:

- Do just about any of the exercises throughout this book—together. That will increase your sense of having the common goal of protecting your relationship.

- Pursue some activities together that have a lot of meaning or enjoyment for both of you. Together is as together does.

- Talk to each other about what each of you could do that would increase the sense that your relationship is special.

- Talk regularly about both short-term and longer-term goals. Having clear shared goals increases your sense that you are on the same team.

Sacrifice

Our culture encourages devotion to self. Notions of sacrifice, teamwork, and the priority of one's partner have not enjoyed much positive press lately. In fact, our society seems to glorify self and vilify whatever gets in the way. Selfishness may sell in our culture, but it doesn't buy lifelong happy marriages. Selfishness seriously undercuts couple identity. We want to be clear, though: working on yourself, making improvements, and considering what you can do to make your relationship great are not examples of being selfish. These are acts of taking personal responsibility—one of the most powerful things you can do to be the best partner you can be.

Whereas selfishness fundamentally cuts across the grain of couple identity, positive attitudes about sacrifice—and sacrificial behavior—gird up a strong relationship over time. In fact, our research has shown that people who are happiest in marriage gain some sense of satisfaction from doing things that are largely or solely for their partner's benefit. By this we aren't recommending your being a martyr, but rather finding real joy in making a genuine choice to give of yourself for your partner. In the way the term is commonly used, a martyr does things for another not out of concern for what is best for that person but because the martyr wants to put the other in debt. This is not dedication.

The Andersons (the stuck couple) have stopped giving to each other. Rod doesn't think he'll get anything back if he gives more, and Mary already feels she's given more than her share for a lifetime. Neither feels like sacrificing anything at this point. They've lost the sense of "us" that promotes giving to one another without resentment. So neither is going to give much at this point, perhaps waiting for the other to do so. That could be a very long wait.

Relationships are generally stronger when both partners are willing to make sacrifices. In the absence of this willingness to sacrifice, what do you have? You have a relationship in which at least one of you is in it mostly for what you can get, with little focus on what you can give. That's not a recipe for happiness or growth.

In a culture that reinforces self, it's hard to ask, "What can I do to make this relationship better?" It's a lot easier to ask, "What can my partner do to make me happier?" The key is to think about not only what you do for your partner but also *why* you do it. Do you do things with the attitude, "You'd better appreciate what I'm doing?" Do you often feel that your partner owes you? There's nothing wrong with doing positive things and wanting to be appreciated. There *is* something wrong with believing you are owed. In couples who are doing wonderfully well, you'll find two partners who give freely to one another and appreciate what the other gives. It's a beautiful form of teamwork.

A colleague of ours at the University of Denver, Sarah Whitton, has been studying sacrifice in relationships. Among other things, she has found that both couple identity and a long-term view of the relationship were strongly related to males' willingness to sacrifice for their female partners. This makes great sense. After all, in the absence of a shared sense of a future together, sacrificing for your partner will seem more like depositing money in a bank with a "Going out of Business" sign out front. If you're thinking about the future, investing makes sense. Sacrificing is a kind of investing. When thinking only about the present, why bother to invest?

In Whitton's research, females showed a much weaker relationship between long-term view and willingness to sacrifice for their partners; having a positive couple identity was not related to their willingness to sacrifice. This research as well as a number of other studies in our lab highlight the particular importance of male dedication levels in the life and health of relationships. Without an otherwise strong commitment, males may be particularly likely to resent giving to females—or they just don't do it. To be candid, we think that on average, women have historically given more in marriages than men. There are many exceptions, but we have come to believe that it is particularly important for males to demonstrate their dedication to their mates by giving freely of themselves in ways that are clear and consistent.

When females for years see little or no evidence of their partner's dedication, they sometimes withdraw in a big way. This is very often a result of years of pursuing a withdrawing male. Males may often withdraw because of fear of fighting, but over the long term, women really start to see withdrawal as a lack of dedication and investment. Hence, the kind of withdrawal these women exhibit is very different from what we talked about earlier in the book. It's based on exhaustion and demoralization about trying to connect. It often results in moving out, filing for separation, or seeking a divorce. Paradoxically, some long-term, hard-core withdrawing males begin to really pursue their wives when their wives have checked out this far. The men who really were committed begin to try to show it in many ways, but the sad truth is that they've often waited too long to find ways to show it. Gentlemen, you don't want to go there.

The Long-Term View

When people are more dedicated to their partners, they want and expect the relationship to last. They want to grow old together. This expectation for the relationship to continue over the long term is a core part of dedication and plays a critical role in the day-to-day quality of marriage. The long-term view is crucial for one simple reason: no relationship is consistently satisfying. What gets couples through tougher times is the long-term view that commitment brings. How? When you decide you will be together *no matter what*, you can safely deal with the curve balls life throws at you. The long-term view stretches out the time perspective for you, making it easier not to overreact to the small annoying events in life.

We're not saying everybody should devote Herculean effort to save his or her marriage, no matter how abusive or destructive. However, for the great number of couples who genuinely love each other and want to make their marriages work, a long-term perspective is essential for encouraging each partner to take risks, disclose about himself or herself, and trust that the other will be there when it really counts. In the absence of a long-term view, people tend to focus on the immediate payoff. This is only natural. If the long-term is uncertain, we concentrate on what we're getting in the present.

The long-term view makes it easier not to overreact to small annoying events.

What we have called the hidden issue of commitment (Chapter Six) is easily triggered when the future of the relationship is uncertain. When commitment is unclear, partners don't feel accepted—a core issue for everyone—and instead feel pressured to perform. The message is, "You'd better produce, or I'll look for someone who can." Most of us resent feeling we could be abandoned by someone from whom we expect to find security and acceptance. People generally do not invest in a relationship with an uncertain future and reward.

Another colleague of ours, Fran Dickson at the University of Denver, has studied lifelong married couples. Among many things, she found that the happier couples reported having talked regularly about their future over their years together. In a sense, what these couples describe is one of the ways they have nurtured a vision for their future together. Such talking does not mean locking in all the details, but rather dreaming and reminding one another that the relationship has a future as well as a history. In the exercises at the end of this chapter, this is one of the powerful things we recommend the two of you try to do together. You can be creative about the ways you dream about the future. We're convinced it's a very good strategy for preserving a lasting love, together.

Our example of a more dedicated couple, the Sempletons, do not have the perfect marriage (who does?), but they have a strong expectation of a future rooted in balanced commitment. They talk about plans for life together. For couples like them, the long-term view allows each partner to cut the other some slack, leading to greater acceptance of weaknesses and failings over time. Whereas the Andersons experience anxiety or resentment around the core issue of acceptance, the Sempletons feel the warmth of a secure commitment—each conveying the powerful message, "I'll be here for you." That's the essence of what commitment is about: believing not only that you will be there for one another in the future but also that you can count on one another through the ups and downs of life.

Threatening the Long-Term View

Sometimes commitment becomes a weapon in a fight. When such a weapon is wielded, it's like an atomic bomb that leaves devastation in its wake. Despite Rod and Mary Anderson's low level of commitment, they aren't going to get a divorce any time soon. Still, the topic comes up more and more often in bad arguments. Consider the following conversation and its effects on trust, power, and commitment:

ROD: Why does this house always look like a pigsty?

MARY: Because we have two big dogs, and I'm at work every day.

ROD: I end up having to clean up all the time, and I'm tired of it.

MARY: Oh, and like I don't clean up all the time after the kids? When you're here, you usually disappear into your shop. I'm the one cleaning up constantly—not you.

ROD: Yeah, yeah, I disappear all the time. You don't even know what really happens in this marriage. I don't even know why we stay together.

MARY: Me neither. Maybe you should move out.

ROD: Not a bad idea. I'll think about it.

By the end of the fight, each was trying to convince the other that they weren't committed. You can't get much less dedicated than emphasizing the short-term view. If you're trying to keep your marriage on track, don't bring up the topic of divorce, period. Likewise, don't threaten to have affairs. Such statements trash the long-term view. They erode trust and reinforce the perception that it's risky to invest. Pushing yourself not to say such things when very frustrated is an act of dedication. Practice self-control!

IF YOU ARE FEELING STUCK AND WANT TO STICK AGAIN

This section is only for those of you who identify with being stuck more than with sticking. Because you are reading this book, we assume you want to make your marriage work. So, what can you do if you find yourself in a marriage characterized by constraint without dedication? How do you redevelop dedication when it's gone?

First, you need to believe that this is possible. Linda Waite and Maggie Gallagher, in their book *The Case for Marriage*, note that there are a great many couples who are unhappy at one point in their marriages but who stick it out and end up much happier five years later.

We cannot predict the future of your relationship (we can only predict for large groups of couples), but we find that many (although certainly not all) couples are able to repair and strengthen the most lifeless, frustrating marriages. However, you must really want to do this, because it will take sustained work, and you will have to work against some tendencies that now exist in the relationship. That entails not only new behavior but also, most important, a willingness to see the new behavior in your spouse. If you each work to make changes to please the other and build your marriage, and neither of you sees the other's efforts, you will be just as stuck. Just as we explained in our discussion of overcoming the danger sign of negative interpretations, you need to be willing to look for the things that are harder for you to see.

If you want to breathe life into your marriage, here is one approach you can try.

1. *Sit down together and talk about the state of your marriage.* It is important that you both face up to where the marriage is right now. Rather than getting defensive or arguing, this is the time when you both should try, and try hard, to validate each other and show empathy for the pain. Acceptance starts here.

In listening carefully to each other, you begin the process of drawing closer together. Paradoxically, one of the most powerful things you may share is a similar feeling of loss and sadness about your relationship. We have observed that in the strongest marriages, the couples able to share their pain about the marriage experience this as another form of intimacy. After all, is there anything about which you feel more strongly? This would be a great time to use the Speaker-Listener Technique.

2. *Remember what you used to have together.* Spend some time reminiscing together about the good old days. What were things like when you first met? What attracted you to each other? What did you do on your first date? What kinds of things did you do for fun? Do you still do any of these things? What were some reasons you decided you wanted to marry in the first place?

This kind of reminiscing brings to mind the fact that you once had some pretty great feelings for one another. Beware of the tendency to rewrite history and see experiences that were truly positive at that time as negative now. There was a spark there, a delight in getting to know the other. In some ways, this step is an attempt to regain an appetite for the relationship.

3. *Decide to turn things around.* Although you can try to repair your marriage without your partner's active participation, making a commitment to do it together is far better. Look at it this way: Considering that you are staying together due to constraints that mean a lot to you, why not agree together to make the marriage enjoyable and not simply endurable? Doing so is simply rational. You are

deciding to stay in the boat together, so why not quit shooting holes into the bottom of it, patch the worst leaks, and learn to row together? You probably both have some deeper longing for this to occur anyway, or you'd be unlikely to care about following these steps. In time, you might even learn to sail together. This choice is fundamentally a decision of your will. We believe most people have enough control over their own lives to make a decision and stick with it if they want something badly enough.

4. *Do the things you did at first.* This point is simple, but the potential impact is profound. Early in a relationship, a couple talks more as friends (see Chapter Nine), does more fun things together (see Chapter Ten), is more forgiving (see Chapter Fourteen), is more likely to look for the good and not the bad in the other (see Chapters Four and Six), and, usually, does a better job of controlling conflict (see Chapters Five through Eight). Be committed to becoming less self-centered and more other-centered. Where you have been selfish, admit it to yourself and decide to turn the pattern around. The things you can do to restore dedication in your marriage are the same things most couples can do to prevent marital distress and divorce in the first place.

5. *Stay at it.* Keep working at these steps, especially number four. Expect progress, not an instant miracle. Expect ups and downs. Recognize that your efforts can and will pay off if you both stick to it. What does this require? A long-term view and liberally applied dedication.

The ceremony on the wedding day is not as important for the long term as the daily evidences of dedication. You could think of these as small celebrations of your commitment in life together. Consciously consider and choose ways to demonstrate your dedication to one another through the priorities you live, the evidence you show of your identity as a couple, and your awareness of a future together. There's no better time than now to do all you can to affirm your commitment to one another.

Talking Points

1. Commitment is a complex concept, involving both external constraints that hold relationships together, and personal dedication, which helps keep alive the desire to stay in a relationship.

2. Choices about how you think about your partner, how you behave together, and how high a priority you give the relationship are critical factors in commitment.

3. You need to believe in the future of your relationship in order to keep it growing and strong.

 EXERCISES

There are several exercises to help you get the most out of this chapter. You'll have the opportunity to examine your constraint and dedication commitment, consider your priorities, and think about a rededication of your devotion to one another.

Assessing Constraint Commitment

Jot down your response to these statements on a separate piece of paper, assigning a point value between 1 and 7 to indicate how true the statement seems to you. Use the following scale for your answers: 1 = strongly disagree, 4 = neither agree nor disagree, and 7 = strongly agree.

1. The steps I would need to take to end this relationship would require a great deal of time and effort.

2. A marriage is a sacred bond between two people and should not be broken.

3. I would have trouble finding a suitable partner if this relationship ended.

4. My friends or family really want this relationship to work.

5. I would lose valuable possessions if I left my partner.

6. I stay in this relationship partly because my partner would be emotionally devastated if I left.

7. I couldn't make it financially if we broke up or divorced.

8. My lifestyle would be worse in many ways if I left my partner.

9. I feel trapped in this relationship.

10. It is important to finish what you have started, no matter what.

Your answers to these few questions can tell you a lot. We can't give you an average score on these items because we don't use them in quite that way in our research. But it is obvious that the higher the score, the greater the level of constraint. In any case, we want you to use your responses for reflection. What constraints are you aware of? How powerful are these constraints? What kind of constraint seems most powerful?

Most important, do you feel trapped or stuck? Just about everyone does from time to time, which is normal. Having a good deal of constraint but not feeling trapped is normal in a healthy couple relationship. The best relationships are those in which both partners are dedicated to each other and feel comfortable with the stability implied by constraint.

Assessing Dedication Commitment

These next items will help you gauge your level of dedication. Use the same 7-point rating scale you used to examine constraint commitment: 1 = strongly disagree, 4 = neither agree nor disagree, and 7 = strongly agree. Again, jot down your responses on a separate piece of paper.

1. My relationship with my partner is more important to me than almost anything else in my life.

2. I want this relationship to stay strong no matter what rough times we may encounter.

3. It makes me feel good to sacrifice for my partner.

4. I like to think of myself and my partner more in terms of "us" and "we" than "me" and "him [or her]."

5. I am not seriously attracted to anyone other than my partner.

6. My relationship with my partner is clearly part of my future life plans.

7. When push comes to shove, my relationship with my partner comes first.

8. I tend to think about how things affect us as a couple more than how things affect me as an individual.

9. I don't often find myself thinking about what it would be like to be in a relationship with someone else.

10. I want to grow old with my partner.

We can give you an idea of what your score means on these dedication items. To calculate your score, simply add up your ratings for each item. In our research—with a sample of people who were mostly happy and dedicated in their relationships (including some who had been married for over thirty years)—the average person scored about 58 on the items in this scale. If you scored at or above 58, we'd bet you're pretty highly dedicated. However, your dedication may be quite low if you scored below 45. Whatever your score, think about what it may mean for the future of your marriage.

Considering Priorities

An important way to look at dedication is to consider your priorities. How do you actually live your life? What does this say about your commitment?

Take a piece of paper you can divide into three columns. In the first column, list what you consider your top five priorities in life, with number one being the most important. Possible priority areas might include work and career, your partner, adult children, religion, house and home, sports, future goals, education, possessions, hobbies, pets, friends, relatives, coworkers, television, car. Feel free to list whatever is important to you. Be as specific as you can.

Now, in the second column, list what you think your partner would say are your top five priorities. For example, if you think your partner would say work is your top priority, list that as number one. In the third column, list what you believe are your partner's top five priorities.

When both of you have completed your lists, compare them. Don't be defensive. Consider how the answers each of you have given affect your couple relationship. Use the Speaker-Listener Technique if necessary. If you see a need to make your relationship a higher priority, talk together about specific steps you can take to make this happen. You might find it helpful to use the problem-solving process you learned in Chapter Seven. The chapters on enhancing your relationship have provided additional suggestions of ways to make your relationship a higher priority.

Nurturing the Long-Term View

As we noted earlier, one of the most powerful things you can do to keep your relationship on a great path is to talk from time to time in various ways about your future together. Doing this stretches your perspective out beyond just the here and now. That does not mean you have to try to lock in your path in any way, but it does mean having a clear sense of a future together. Where would you like to be in thirty years? What would you like to do when you retire? Where would you like to travel someday? How do you feel about becoming a grandparent one day, or about having reached that stage already? You'll have to decide how best to nurture your long-term view as a couple, but there are many ways to do this. You could take dream walks together during which you talk about your future. You could try to sprinkle your regular time together as friends with thoughts about a future. Be creative.

16

What to Do Now

Bill Coffin, a colleague and prevention specialist who works for the U.S. Navy, suggests that couples think about relationship fitness as they might think about physical fitness. Just as you should work out three or four times a week for twenty to thirty minutes, you and your partner should devote at least that much time to working on your relationship. This doesn't just mean having couple meetings; it also means planning fun times together, having friendship talks, making love, giving back rubs, just hanging out together reading a book in the same room, listening to music, or playing with the children. Make the time for your relationship to be regularly renewed in these ways.

MAKING FIGHTING FOR YOUR MARRIAGE A REALITY

If you're serious about making some of these key ideas part of your life, here are some important points to keep in mind.

Review

To get the most out of what we've presented in this book, be sure to review the material. We all learn better when we go over key concepts again and again. Perhaps you've highlighted key sections in this book as you've read them. Go back and read those sections again. For example, it would be a great time to go back to Chapter Eight and review the ground rules. Are you using them? Have you kept at it?

It would be especially valuable to review the rules for the Speaker-Listener Technique and for problem solving, and the principles of forgiveness. None of these rules or ideas are all that complicated, but you want to master them to yield the greatest benefit to your marriage. Better yet, after some time has passed, read through the whole book again, together.

Practice

Part of the PREP approach is a very specific, skills-oriented model for building solid relationships. The key to such an approach is to practice the skills and ways of thinking we've recommended. It's not enough just to review the ideas—you need to practice the techniques and strategies to make them a part of your life.

A colleague of ours, Bob Weiss at the University of Oregon, notes the difference between being under *rule control* rather than *stimulus control*. To be under stimulus control means you're constantly *reacting* to the things happening around you—the stimuli of your life. If you don't want to live that way—and it's so easy to live that way—you need to practice the strategies that give you more control over how, when, and where you deal with issues in your life. No idea we have presented can help you unless you put that idea into action.

Engage the Skills

As you consolidate your skills through practice and the development of positive rituals, the most important goal is for you to be able to engage the skills when you need them. Knowing how to use the Speaker-Listener Technique or the problem-solving model is great, but the real benefit comes from using these skills when you need them most. Unfortunately, the times you need the most skill are the same times that it's hardest to use them, so being able to make the shift to engage more skill is critical. That's where practice and good habits really pay off.

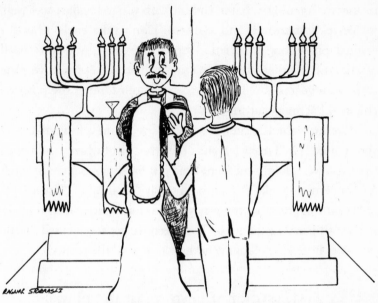

...AND DO YOU PROMISE TO USE THE SPEAKER/LISTENER TECHNIQUE...?

It's hardest to engage the skills the first few times. For example, as you work on ground rule 1—the Time Out ground rule—it'll be harder at the start than it'll be after using it a few times. It can seem like avoidance when you start using Time Outs, but the habit gets stronger as you see that the skills work. Your relationship benefits from the increased control over how and when you'll deal with difficult issues.

Reinforce, Reinforce, Reinforce

When we train other professionals and paraprofessionals to work with couples, we emphasize over and over the need to be active in reinforcing the positive steps couples make when learning the skills we teach. It's very important to reinforce new skills as well as to reinforce the positive changes that are already happening.

We make the same suggestion to you. As you work on learning new patterns and ways of thinking, reinforce each other. Praise your partner for listening well, for working with you to handle issues well, for being committed, and so forth. Don't take each other for granted. Show your appreciation for positive effort. And don't dwell on the past. In other words, don't say "Why couldn't you have done this seven years ago?" Instead, focus on reinforcing the positive changes that are occurring now.

When was the last time you said, "Gee, Honey, I sure like how you do that"? Or "I really felt great the other night when you dropped what you were doing and spent time just listening to me talk about my concerns at work." It's not hard to say "Thanks" or "Great job!" or "I really appreciated the way you did that." The effects on your relationship can be dramatic. Too often we get too focused on the negative. Instead, try looking for how to reward the positive.

CONFIDENCE FOR THE FUTURE

We've become increasingly interested in studying how confidence develops and what it does for couples. Confidence is very important in marriage because confidence promotes persistence based on hope. When you are confident, you boldly move into the future together, believing that the two of you can handle what comes your way.

As we devote more attention to confidence, we've been looking at what factors in marriages are related to having it. In some ways, it's easier to express what we've found in terms of what *kills* confidence. As part of a keynote address to the fourth annual Smart Marriages conference, Scott and Howard put our initial findings in the format of a top ten list. We'll use that list to summarize the path we've traveled together here:

Top Ten Things You Can Do to Destroy Confidence

10. Think only of yourself.

9. Push, shove, or slap one another, or throw things when upset.

8. Refuse to accept your differences.

7. Ignore signs that you are growing distant.

6. Avoid dealing with key issues.

5. Put one another down and escalate often.

4. Leave no time to talk as friends.

3. Emphasize "me" versus "you."

2. Stop doing fun things together.

1. Regularly threaten the long-term view.

These are confidence killers. Mark Twain said, "All you need in this life is ignorance and confidence; then success is sure." We're sure his point was tongue-in-cheek. In reality it's a recipe for deep disappointment. We want you to have confidence based on knowledge, wisdom, ability, and mutual commitment. Now that you've read the book, you know what to do.

Remember, keep investing *no matter what*.

Some Thoughts on Domestic Violence

Because PREP and this book deal with communication and conflict between partners, questions about domestic violence arise at times. Domestic violence is a very complex topic, and is not the subject of this book. Nevertheless, we have a few key points we would like to stress on the matter:

- PREP is not a treatment program for domestic violence, nor is this book.
- There are some couples who can reduce their chances of becoming physically aggressive by learning techniques such as those taught in this book. Those would be couples who are at risk for things becoming physical as a result of difficulty handling conflict well together—rather than couples in which there is a controlling person who uses aggression to dominate or control the partner.
- Domestic violence of any sort is unacceptable and wrong and dangerous.
- There is an alarming level of domestic violence (at various levels) taking place in families in our society.
- No matter what the nature of the violence, when males strike females, as opposed to the reverse, there is every reason to believe that females are both in greater danger and will likely suffer more long-lasting and negative aftereffects. Of course, many females strike males, too, and that is just as unacceptable.

• *When there is the presence of any kind of domestic violence, the preeminent concern should be safety.* That means you should seek whatever level of services are necessary to ensure that neither partner is in danger. That could mean seeking counsel from a therapist or clergyperson *who has experience in this area* or going to a community shelter for battered women in cases where the woman is fearful and in significant danger.

• We recommend that those who work with couples be aware of the complex issues around domestic violence and also be fully aware of local resources for help in dealing with domestic violence in ways that can increase safety (for example, law enforcement access, shelters).

For more reading about the controversies surrounding domestic violence, we recommend the following publications:

Gelles, R., & Loseke, D. (1993). *Current controversies on family violence*. Thousand Oaks, CA: Sage.

Holtzworth-Munroe, A., Smutzler, N., Bates, L., & Sandin, E. (1997). Husband violence: Basic facts and clinical implications. In K. Halford & H. J. Markman (Eds.), *Clinical Handbook of Marriage and Couples Intervention* (pp. 121–159). New York: Wiley and Sons.

Johnson, M. P. (1995). Patriarchal terrorism and common couple violence: Two forms of violence against women. *Journal of Marriage and the Family, 57*(2), 283–294.

Resources and Training

We have a variety of resources available. Further, we conduct workshops both for couples and for those who work with couples. We have included the following section for those of you who may wish to go further, either as a partner in a couple or as someone who works toward helping couples make great marriages.

THE PREP APPROACH

Books

In addition to the book you are holding, there are several titles in this series. Each represents the same basic approach for helping couples build their marriages, but each is adapted and developed for a special purpose. All are published by Jossey-Bass and can be ordered from PREP at the address on the next page or by calling (800) 366-0166, from Jossey-Bass by calling (415) 433-1740, or from any bookstore.

A Lasting Promise: A Christian Guide to Fighting for Your Marriage (1998), by Stanley, Trathen, McCain, and Bryan.

Becoming Parents: How to Strengthen Your Marriage as Your Family Grows (1999), by Jordan, Stanley, and Markman.

Fighting for Your Jewish Marriage (2000), by Crohn, Markman, Blumberg, and Levine.

Fighting for *Your Empty Nest Marriage* (2000), by Arp, Arp, Stanley, Markman, and Blumberg.

Audiocassettes and Videos

Fighting for *Your Marriage* audiocassettes and videos are available from PREP Educational Products, Inc. To order, please call (800) 366-0166 or write to us at the address below. Tapes can also be ordered from Jossey-Bass.

Workshops

We conduct workshops for mental health counselors, clergy, lay leaders, and other marriage educators who desire to be more fully exposed to the PREP approach. For information about these "instructor" workshops, please call (303) 759-9931 or write to us at the address below. We will be glad to give you information about seminars or products to help you in your own relationship or in your work to help other couples.

We also have a list of people who have been trained in this approach and who do either workshops or counseling using aspects of this model. To obtain that list, you can visit our website.

You can contact us at:

PREP
P.O. Box 102530
Denver, CO 80250-2530
E-mail: PREPinc@aol.com
Website: www.PREPinc.com

Selected Research and References

Amato, P. R., & Rogers, S. J. (1999). Do attitudes toward divorce affect marital quality? *Journal of Family Issues, 20*(1), 69–86.

Arp, D., & Arp, C. (1997). *Ten great dates to energize your marriage*. Grand Rapids, MI: Zondervan.

Arp, D., & Arp, C. (1998). *Love life for parents*. Grand Rapids, MI: Zondervan.

Arp, D., Arp, C., Stanley, S. M., Markman, H. J., & Blumberg, S. L. (2000). *Fighting for your empty nest marriage: Reinventing your relationship when the kids leave home*. San Francisco: Jossey-Bass.

Baucom, D., & Epstein, N. (1990). *Cognitive behavioral marital therapy*. New York: Brunner/Mazel.

Beach, S. R., & O'Leary, K. D. (1993). Marital discord and dysphoria: For whom does the marital relationship predict depressive symptomatology? *Journal of Social and Personal Relationships, 10*, 405–420.

Behrens, B., & Halford, K. (1994, August). *Advances in the prevention and treatment of marital distress*. Paper presented at the Helping Families Change conference, University of Queensland, Brisbane, Australia.

Birchler, G., Weiss, R., & Vincent, J. (1975). Multimethod analysis of social reinforcement exchange between maritally distressed and nondistressed spouse and stranger dyads. *Journal of Personality and Social Psychology, 31*, 349–360.

Bradbury, T. N., Beach, S.R.H., Fincham, F. D., & Nelson, G. M. (1996). Attributions and behavior in functional and dysfunctional marriages. *Journal of Consulting and Clinical Psychology, 64*, 569–576.

Call, V. R., & Heaton, T. B. (1997). Religious influence on marital stability. *Journal for the Scientific Study of Religion, 36*, 382–392.

Center for Marriage and Family. (1995). *Marriage preparation in the Catholic Church: Getting it right*. Omaha, NE: Creighton University.

Cherlin, A. J., & Furstenberg, F. F., Jr. (1994). Step families in the United States: A reconsideration. *Annual Review of Sociology, 20,* 359–381.

Christensen, A., & Heavey, C. L. (1990). Gender and social structure in the demand/withdraw pattern of marital conflict. *Journal of Personality and Social Psychology, 59,* 73–82.

Clements, M., & Markman, H. J. (1996). The transition to parenthood: Is having children hazardous to marriage? In N. Vanzetti & S. Duck (Eds.), *A lifetime of relationships* (pp. 290–310). Pacific Grove, CA: Brooks/Cole.

Clements, M., Stanley, S. M., & Markman, H. J. (1997). *Predicting divorce.* University of Denver.

Cowan, C. P., & Cowan, P. A. (1992). *When partners become parents: The big life change for couples.* New York: HarperCollins.

Crohn, J., Markman, H. J., Blumberg, S. L., & Levine, J. R. (2000). *Fighting for your Jewish marriage: Preserving a lasting promise.* San Francisco: Jossey-Bass.

Cummings, E. M., & Davies, P. (1994). *Children and marital conflict.* New York: Guilford Press.

Eidelson, R., & Epstein, N. (1982). Cognitions and relationship maladjustment: Development of a measure of dysfunctional relationship beliefs. *Journal of Consulting and Clinical Psychology, 50,* 715–720.

Fincham, F. D., Beach, S. R., Harold, G. T., & Osborne, L. N. (1997). Marital satisfaction and depression: Different causal relationships for men and women? *Psychological Science, 8,* 351–357.

Fincham, F. D., Garnier, P. C., Gano-Phillips, S., & Osborne, L. N. (1995). Pre-interaction expectations, marital satisfaction and accessibility: A new look at sentiment override. *Journal of Family Psychology, 9,* 3–14.

Fincham, F., Grych, J., & Osborne, L. (1993, March). *Interparental conflict and child adjustment: A longitudinal analysis.* Paper presented at the biennial meeting of the Society for Research in Child Development, New Orleans, LA.

Floyd, F., Markman, H. J., Kelly, S., Blumberg, S. L., & Stanley, S. M. (1995). Prevention: Conceptual, research, and clinical issues. In N. Jacobson & A. Gurman (Eds.), *Handbook of marital therapy* (2nd ed.). New York: Guilford Press.

Forthofer, M. S., Markman, H. J., Cox, M., Stanley, S. M., & Kessler, R. C. (1996). Associations between marital distress and work loss in a national sample. *Journal of Marriage and the Family, 58,* 597–605.

Fowers, B. J. (2000). *Beyond the myth of marital happiness: How embracing the virtues of loyalty, generosity, justice, and courage can strengthen your relationship.* San Francisco: Jossey-Bass.

Fraenkel, P., Markman, H. J., & Stanley, S. M. (1997). The prevention approach to relationship problems. *Sexual and Marital Therapy, 12,* 249–258.

Giblin, P., Sprenkle, D. H., & Sheehan, R. (1985). Enrichment outcome research: A meta-analysis of premarital, marital, and family interventions. *Journal of Marital and Family Therapy, 11*, 257–271.

Glenn, N. D. (1998). The course of marital success and failure in five American ten-year marriage cohorts. *Journal of Marriage and the Family, 60*, 569–576.

Gottman, J. M. (1993). A theory of marital dissolution and stability. *Journal of Family Psychology, 7*, 57–75.

Gottman, J. M., Notarius, C., Gonso J., & Markman, H. J. (1976). *A couple's guide to communication.* Champaign, IL: Research Press.

Grych, J., & Fincham, F. (1990). Marital conflict and children's adjustment. *Psychological Bulletin, 108*, 267–290.

Guerney, B. G., Jr. (1977). *Relationship enhancement: Skill-training programs for therapy, problem prevention, and enrichment.* San Francisco: Jossey-Bass.

Hahlweg, K., & Markman, H. J. (1988). The effectiveness of behavioral marital therapy: Empirical status of behavioral techniques in preventing and alleviating marital distress. *Journal of Consulting and Clinical Psychology, 56*, 440–447.

Hahlweg, K., Markman, H. J., Thurmaier, F., Engl, J., & Eckert, V. (1998). Prevention of marital distress: Results of a German prospective longitudinal study. *Journal of Family Psychology, 12*, 543–556.

Halford, K., & Bouma, R. (1997). Individual psychopathology and marital distress. In K. Halford & H. J. Markman (Eds.), *Clinical handbook of marriage and couples intervention* (pp. 291–321). New York: Wiley.

Halford, K., & Markman, H. J. (Eds.). (1997). *Clinical handbook of marriage and marital interaction.* London, England: Wiley.

Heaton, T. B. (1984). Religious homogamy and marital satisfaction reconsidered. *Journal of Marriage and the Family, 46*, 729–733.

Holtzworth-Munroe, A., Markman, H. J., O'Leary, D. K., Neidig, P., Leber, D., Heyman, R. E., Hulbert, D., & Smutzler, N. (1995). The need for marital violence prevention efforts: A behavioral-cognitive secondary prevention program for engaged and newly-marriage couples. *Applied and Preventive Psychology, 4*, 77–88.

Jacobson, N. S., & Christensen, A. (1998). *Acceptance and change in couple therapy: A therapist's guide to transforming relationships.* New York: Norton.

Johnson, M. P. (1995). Patriarchal terrorism and common couple violence: Two forms of violence against women. *Journal of Marriage and the Family, 57*, 283–294.

Johnson, M. P., Caughlin, J. P., & Huston, T. L. (1999). The tripartite nature of marital commitment: Personal, moral, and structural reasons to stay married. *Journal of Marriage and the Family, 61*, 160–177.

Jones, W., & Adams, J. (1999). *Handbook of interpersonal commitment and relationship stability.* New York: Plenum.

Jordan, P., Stanley, S. M., & Markman, H. J. (1999). *Becoming parents: How to strengthen your marriage as your family grows.* San Francisco: Jossey-Bass.

Karney, B. R., & Bradbury, T. N. (1995). The longitudinal course of marital quality and stability: A review of theory, method, and research. *Psychological Bulletin, 118,* 3–34.

Kiecolt-Glaser, J. K., Malarkey, W. B., Chee, M., Newton, T., Cacioppo, J. T., Mao, H. Y., & Glaser, R. (1993). Negative behavior during marital conflict is associated with immunological down-regulation. *Psychosomatic Medicine, 55,* 395–409.

Knox, D. (1971). *Marriage happiness.* Champaign, IL: Research Press.

Kurdek, L. A. (1993). Predicting marital dissolution: A 5-year prospective longitudinal study of newlywed couples. *Journal of Personality and Social Psychology, 64,* 221–242.

Larsen, A. S., & Olson, D. H. (1989). Predicting marital satisfaction using PREPARE: A replication study. *Journal of Marital and Family Therapy, 15,* 311–322.

Laumann, E. O., Paik, A., & Rosen, R. C. (1999). Sexual dysfunction in the United States. *Journal of the American Medical Association, 281,* 537–544.

Lehrer, E. L., & Chiswick, C. (1993). Religion as a determinant of marital stability. *Demography, 30,* 385–404.

Levenson, R. W., & Gottman, J. M. (1985). Physiological and affective predictors of change in relationship satisfaction. *Journal of Personality and Social Psychology, 49*(1), 85–94.

Levinger, G. (1980). Toward the analysis of close relationships. *Journal of Experimental Social Psychology, 16,* 510–544.

Lindahl, K., & Markman, H. J. (1990). Communication and negative affect regulation in the family. In E. Blechman (Ed.), *Emotions and families* (pp. 99–115). New York: Plenum Press.

Mahoney, A., Pargament, K. I., Jewell, T., Swank, A. B., Scott, E., Emery, E., & Rye, M. (1999). Marriage and the spiritual realm: The role of proximal and distal religious constructs in marital functioning. *Journal of Family Psychology, 13,* 321–338.

Margolin, G., John, R., & Gleberman, L. (1988). Affective responses to conflictual discussions in violent and nonviolent couples. *Journal of Consulting and Clinical Psychology, 56,* 24–33.

Markey, B., Micheletto, M., & Becker, A. (1985). *Facilitating Open Couple Communication, Understanding, and Study (FOCCUS).* Omaha: Archdiocese of Omaha.

Markman, H. J. (1981). The prediction of marital distress: A five year follow-up. *Journal of Consulting and Clinical Psychology, 49,* 760–762.

Markman, H. J., Floyd, F., Stanley, S. M., & Jamieson, K. (1984). A cognitive-behavioral program for the prevention of marital and family distress: Issues in program development and delivery. In K. Hahlweg & N. Jacobson (Eds.), *Marital interaction.* New York: Guilford Press.

Markman, H. J., Floyd, F., Stanley, S. M., & Storaasli, R. (1988). The prevention of marital distress: A longitudinal investigation. *Journal of Consulting and Clinical Psychology, 56,* 210–217.

Markman, H. J., & Hahlweg, K. (1993). The prediction and prevention of marital distress: An international perspective. *Clinical Psychology Review, 13,* 29–43.

Markman, H. J., & Kraft, S. A. (1989). Men and women in marriage: Dealing with gender differences in marital therapy. *Behavior Therapist, 12,* 51–56.

Markman, H. J., Renick, M. J., Floyd, F., Stanley, S. M., & Clements, M. (1993). Preventing marital distress through communication and conflict management training: A four and five year follow-up. *Journal of Consulting and Clinical Psychology, 62,* 1–8.

Matthews, L. S., Wickrama, K.A.S., & Conger, R. D. (1996). Predicting marital instability from spouse and observer reports of marital interaction. *Journal of Marriage and the Family, 58,* 641–655.

McCollough, M. E., Worthington, E. L., Jr., & Rachal, K. C. (1997). Interpersonal forgiving in close relationships. *Journal of Personality and Social Psychology, 73,* 321–336.

McManus, M. (1993). *Marriage savers.* Grand Rapids, MI: Zondervan.

Miller, S., Wackman, D. B., & Nunnally, E. W. (1976). A communication training program for couples. *Social Casework, 57*(1), 9–18.

Noller, P. (1996). What is this thing called love? Defining the love that supports marriage and family. *Personal Relationships, 3,* 97–115.

Notarius, C., & Markman, H. J. (1993). *We can work it out: Making sense of marital conflict.* New York: Putnam.

Ooms, T. (1998). *Toward more perfect unions: Putting marriage on the public agenda.* Washington, DC: Family Impact Seminar.

Parrott, L., & Parrott, L. (1995). *Saving your marriage before it starts: Seven questions to ask before (and after) you marry.* Grand Rapids, MI: Zondervan.

Pasch, L. A., & Bradbury, T. N. (1998). Social support, conflict, and the development of marital dysfunction. *Journal of Consulting and Clinical Psychology, 66,* 219–230.

Pistole, C. (1989). Attachment in adult romantic relationships: Style of conflict resolution and relationship satisfaction. *Journal of Social and Personal Relationships, 6*, 505–510.

Prado, L. M., & Markman, H. J. (1999). Unearthing the seeds of marital distress: What we have learned from married and remarried couples. In M. Cox & J. Brooks-Gunn (Eds.), *Conflict and cohesion in families. Causes and consequences.* Mahwah, NJ: Erlbaum.

Renick, M. J., Blumberg, S. L., & Markman, H. J. (1992). The Prevention and Relationship Enhancement Program (PREP): An empirically-based preventive intervention program for couples. *Family Relations, 41*, 141–147.

Rusbult, C. E. (1983). A longitudinal test of the investment model: The development (and deterioration) of satisfaction and commitment in heterosexual involvements. *Journal of Personality and Social Psychology, 45*, 101–117.

Rusbult, C. E., Zembrodt, I. M., & Gunn, L. K. (1982). Exit, voice, loyalty, and neglect: Responses to dissatisfaction in romantic involvement. *Journal of Personality and Social Psychology, 43*, 1230–1242.

Sanders, M. R., Halford, W. K., & Behrens, B. C. (1999). Parental divorce and premarital couple communication. *Journal of Family Psychology, 13*, 60–74.

Silliman, B., & Schumm, W. R. (1989). Topics of interest in premarital counseling: Clients' views. *Journal of Sex and Marital Therapy, 15*(3), 199–204.

Silliman, B., Schumm, W. R., & Jurich, A. P. (1992). Young adults' preferences for premarital preparation program designs. *Contemporary Family Therapy, 14*, 89–100.

Silliman, B., Stanley, S. M., Coffin, W., Markman, H. J., & Jordan, P. L. (in press). Preventive interventions for couples. In H. Liddle, D. Santisteban, R. Levant, & J. Bray (Eds.), *Family psychology intervention science.* Washington, DC: American Psychological Association.

Smalley, G. (1996). *Making love last forever.* Dallas: Word.

Spilka, B., Hood, R., & Gorsuch, R. (1985). *The psychology of religion: An empirical approach.* Upper Saddle River, NJ: Prentice Hall.

Stahmann, R. F., & Hiebert, W. J. (1997). *Premarital and remarital counseling: The professional's handbook.* San Francisco: Jossey-Bass.

Stanley, S. M. (1997). What's important in premarital counseling? *Marriage and Family: A Christian Journal, 1*, 51–60.

Stanley, S. M. (1998). *The heart of commitment: Compelling research that reveals the secrets of a lifelong, intimate marriage.* Nashville, TN: Nelson.

Stanley, S. M. (in press). Making the case for premarital training. *Family Relations.*

Stanley, S. M., Blumberg, S. L., & Markman, H. J. (1999). Helping couples fight for their marriages: The PREP approach. In R. Berger & M. Hannah

(Eds.), *Handbook of preventive approaches in couple therapy* (pp. 279–303). New York: Brunner/Mazel.

Stanley, S. M., Bradbury, T. N., & Markman, H. J. (2000). Structural flaws in the bridge from basic research on marriage to interventions for couples: Illustrations from Gottman, Coan, Carrere, and Swanson (1998). *Journal of Marriage and the Family, 62,* 256–264.

Stanley, S. M., Lobitz, W. C., & Dickson, F. (1999). Using what we know: Commitment and cognitions in marital therapy. In W. Jones & J. Adams (Eds.), *Handbook of interpersonal commitment and relationship stability* (pp. 411–424). New York: Plenum.

Stanley, S. M., & Markman, H. J. (1992). Assessing commitment in personal relationships. *Journal of Marriage and the Family, 54,* 595–608.

Stanley, S. M., & Markman, H. J. (1997). *Marriage in the 90s: A nationwide random phone survey.* Denver, CO: PREP.

Stanley, S. M., & Markman, H. J. (1998). Acting on what we know: The hope of prevention. In T. Ooms, *Strategies to strengthen marriage: What we know, what we need to know.* Washington DC: The Family Impact Seminar.

Stanley, S. M., Markman, H. J., Prado, L. M., Olmos-Gallo, P. A., Tonelli, L., St. Peters, M., Leber, B. D., Bobulinski, M., Cordova, A. D., & Whitton, S. (2001). Community based premarital prevention: Clergy and lay leaders on the front lines. *Family Relations, 50,* 67–76.

Stanley, S. M., Markman, H. J., St. Peters, M., & Leber, D. (1995). Strengthening marriages and preventing divorce: New directions in prevention research. *Family Relations, 44,* 392–401.

Stanley, S. M., & Trathen, D. (1994). Christian PREP: An empirically based model for marital and premarital intervention. *Journal of Psychology and Christianity, 13,* 158–165.

Stanley, S. M., Trathen, D., McCain, S., & Bryan, M. (1998). *A lasting promise: A Christian guide to fighting for your marriage.* San Francisco: Jossey-Bass.

Stanton, G. (1997). *Why marriage matters.* Colorado Springs, CO: Pinon Press.

Storaasli, R. D., & Markman, H. J. (1990). Relationship problems in the early stages of marriage: A longitudinal investigation. *Journal of Family Psychology, 4,* 80–98.

Sullivan, K. T., & Bradbury, T. N. (1997). Are premarital prevention programs reaching couples at risk for marital dysfunction? *Journal of Consulting and Clinical Psychology, 65,* 24–30.

Sullivan, K. T., & Goldschmidt, D. (2000). Implementation of empirically validated interventions in managed-care settings: The Prevention and

Relationship Enhancement Program. *Professional Psychology: Research and Practice, 31,* 216–220.

Thurmaier, F., Engl, J., Eckert, V., & Hahlweg, K. (1993). *Ehevorbereitung—ein partnerschaftliches lernprogramm EPL.* Munich, Germany: Ehrenwirth.

Thurmaier, F., Engl, J., & Hahlweg, K. (1999). Eheglück auf Dauer? Methodik, Inhalte und Effektivität eines präventiven Paarkommunikationstrainings—Ergebnisse nach fünf Jahren. Zeitschrift für *Klinische Psychologie, 28,* 54–62.

U. S. Bureau of the Census. (1992). *Marriage, divorce, and remarriage in the 1990s* (Current Population Reports, P23-180). Washington, DC: U.S. Government Printing Office.

Van Lange, P.A.M., Rusbult, C. E., Drigotas, S. M., Arriaga, X. B., Witcher, B. S., & Cox, C. L. (1997). Willingness to sacrifice in close relationships. *Journal of Personality and Social Psychology, 72,* 1373–1395.

Van Widenfelt, B., Hosman, C., Schaap, C., & van der Staak, C. (1996). The prevention of relationship distress for couples at risk: A controlled evaluation with nine-month and two-year follow-ups. *Family Relations, 45,* 156–165.

Weiss, R. L. (1980). Strategic behavioral marital therapy: Toward a model for assessment and intervention. In J. P. Vincent (Ed.), *Advances in family intervention, assessment and theory* (Vol. 1., pp. 229–271). Greenwich, CT: JAI Press.

Weiss, R. L., & Dehle, C. (1994). Cognitive behavioral perspectives on marital conflict. In D. D. Cahn (Ed.), *Conflict in intimate relationships* (pp. 95–115). Mahwah, NJ: Erlbaum.

Whitehead, B. D. (1997). *The divorce culture.* New York: Knopf.

Whitton, S. W., Stanley, S. M., & Markman, H. J. (in press). Sacrifice in romantic relationships: An exploration of relevant research and theory. In H. T. Reiss, M. A. Fitzpatrick, A. L. Vangelisti (Eds.), *Stability and change in relationship behavior across the lifespan.* Cambridge: Cambridge University Press.

Worthington, E. L. (1990). *Counseling before marriage.* Resources for Christian Counseling series, Vol. 23, G. R. Collins (Ed.). Dallas: Word.

About the Authors

Howard J. Markman, Ph.D., is one of the world's leading experts in the couples research and intervention fields. He is a professor of psychology at the University of Denver and president of PREP Inc. He frequently appears in the national media (including *The Oprah Winfrey Show, The Today Show, 20/20,* and *Nightline*) and is invited to give talks on relationships around the United States, Europe, and Australia. He is coauthor of the *Fighting for Your Marriage* series and *Why Do Fools Fall in Love?* from Jossey-Bass and coauthor of *The Clinical Handbook of Marriage and Couples Intervention*. He is the codeveloper of the Prevention and Relationship Enhancement Program (PREP) and the author of over one hundred scientific articles and chapters.

Scott M. Stanley, Ph.D., is codirector of the Center for Marital and Family Studies at the University of Denver, an adjunct professor of psychology, and president of PREP Educational Products, Inc. He has published widely both research reports as well as writings for couples. He is internationally known for his work on the PREP approach for reducing the risks of marital distress and divorce, as well as research and theory on marital commitment. Dr. Stanley has coauthored the best-selling book, videos, and audios titled *Fighting for Your Marriage*. He is also the coauthor of *A Lasting*

Promise and *Becoming Parents* from Jossey-Bass, and author of *The Heart of Commitment*. He contributes extensively to both print and broadcast media as an expert on marriage.

Susan L. Blumberg, Ph.D., is a licensed clinical psychologist in private practice in Denver, Colorado, working with children, families, and couples. She presents regularly on topics related to communication and conflict management skills to both professional and public audiences. She leads PREP workshops for couples and works with families and businesses interested in improving communication skills. Dr. Blumberg has coauthored the best-selling book, videos, and audios titled *Fighting for Your Marriage* and is a coauthor of *Fighting for Your Empty Nest Marriage* and *Fighting for Your Jewish Marriage*.

Index